AF263249

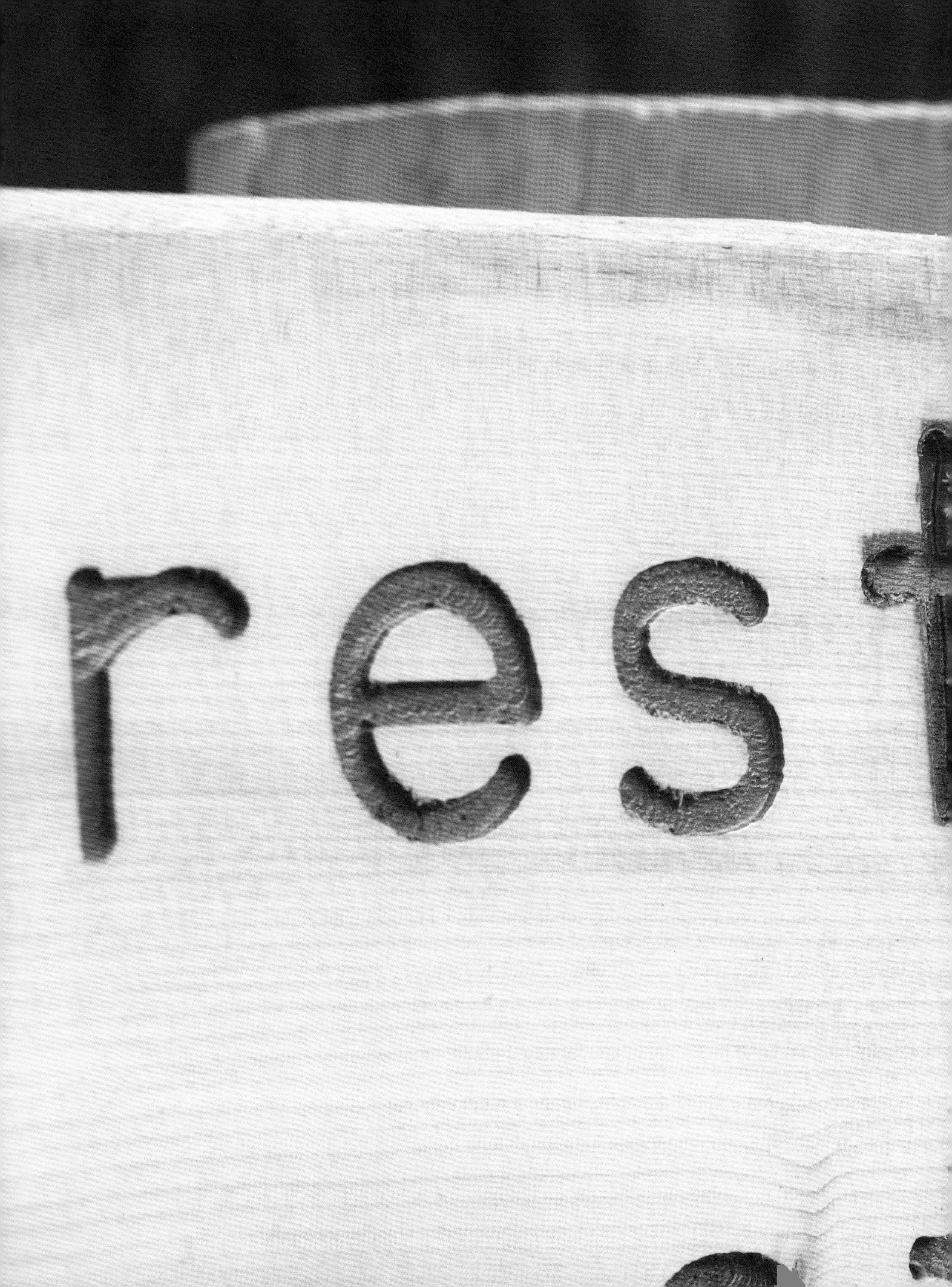

rest

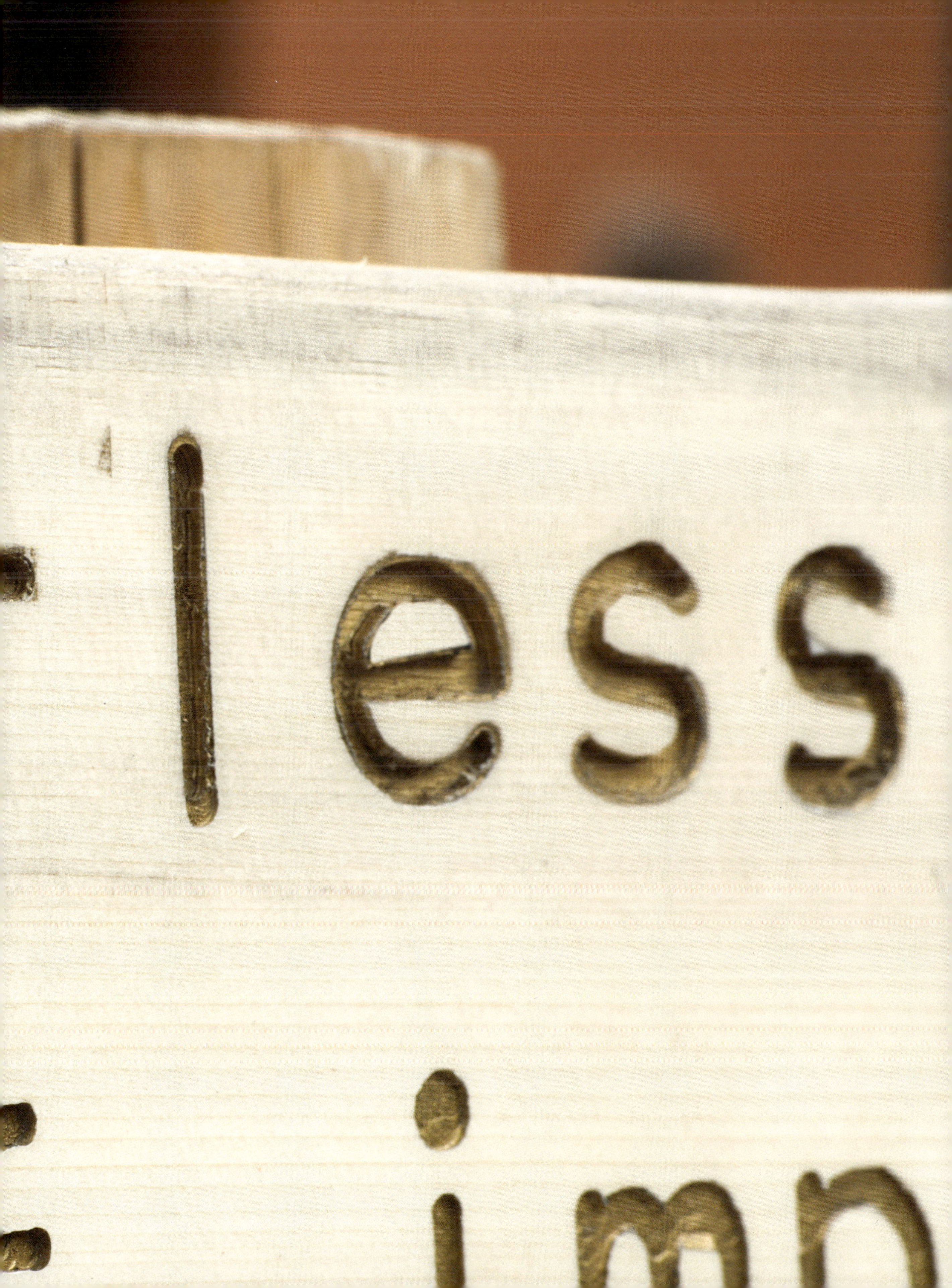

Restless Empathy

Aspen Art Museum

May 20 – July 18, 2010

Table of Contents

Restless Empathy began as an invitation. While at a regular curatorial meeting, we decided to start with an experiment: we each brought a list of artists whom we felt compelled to work with, but had not yet had a significant opportunity. We shared our short lists with each other, and upon reflection discovered that, though variegated and wide-ranging, there was a coherence to the artists' practices that was strongly felt, even if it was initially hard to articulate. We honed in on the generosity and moments of intimate surprise that each of these artists create for the viewer. In the discussions that followed, we realized that a rich, energetic empathy pervaded their work. And so we invited eight artists—Allora & Calzadilla, Pawel Althamer, Marc Bijl, Lara Favaretto, Geof Oppenheimer, Lars Ø. Ramberg, Frances Stark, and Mark Wallinger—to create new projects or rethink existing bodies of work and locate them throughout the museum and the city of Aspen.

The Aspen Art Museum's commitment to presenting art in unexpected places and removing barriers to accessing art finds a powerful expression in this exhibition. The show also sets a dramatic precedent for placing art around Aspen in large-scale exhibitions as part of an ongoing program. *Restless Empathy* challenges expectations of permanence and monumentality in art placed in public, and it broadly explores relationships between aesthetics, space, locality, and modes of address. We hope that the viewers of the exhibition will share our pleasant vertigo in engaging something unexpected, something strange, or something wonderful, and seeking to find our place therein.

As lenders to the exhibition, and for their belief in our exhibition program and willingness to support our efforts, we would like to thank Nancy and Bob Magoon, Anthony Reynolds, Martin Klosterfelde, Nicholas Logsdail, Marc Foxx, and Tim Neuger and Burkhard Riemschneider.

The time and efforts of the following individuals were invaluable in the organization of the exhibition: Alfons Klosterfelde of Klosterfelde, Berlin; Elena Crippa at Lisson Gallery, London; Maria Stathi at Anthony Reynolds Gallery, London; Maria Elisa Marchini at Neugerriemschneider, Berlin; Glenn McMillan at CRG Gallery, New York; and Rodney Hill at Marc Foxx, Los Angeles.

Photographic images for this publication were secured with the assistance of Bosko Boshkovic at the Felix Gonzalez-Torres Foundation; Pamela Caserta at the Walker Art Center; Cay Sophie Rabinowitz at Hauser and Wirth, New York; Renee Reyes at Andrea Rosen Gallery, New York; Dianne Vanderlip at Gagosian Gallery, Beverly Hills; Jenny Borland at Gavin Brown's Enterprise; Maureen Sarro at Friedrich Petzel Gallery, New York; Mieke Marple at 1301PE; Nieck de Bruijn at Upstream Gallery, Amsterdam; Ilka Tödt; Chris Svensson; and Jens Haaning.

For *Restless Empathy*, the Aspen Art Museum partnered on an unprecedented scale with other local institutions, and we would like to acknowledge the following individuals and organizations that have made these collaborations easier and more fruitful than we could have imagined.

Acknowledgements

Amy Margerum and Lisa Yorker of the Aspen Institute, and Jane Kelly and Paula Johnson of the Aspen Center for Physics, were enthusiastically receptive and helpful in arranging a complex installation, for which we are grateful.

Ed Hudson's excitement about our project, insightful counsel, and advocacy on our behalf proved invaluable.

Mike Kaplan, David Corbin, and Peter King of the Aspen Skiing Company continue to impress us with their openness and commitment to new ideas and new possibilities for collaboration, and their embrace of our proposals—past, present, and future—has been extraordinary.

Alan Fletcher and Matthew Loden of the Aspen Music Festival and School were exceedingly helpful in facilitating an unprecedented collaborative performance, and we are tremendously thankful for their generosity.

We would like to give warm thanks to Anita Thompson for her open-mindedness and thoughtful engagement with the exhibition.

Any commissioning of new artwork depends on a network of collaborators, and we are indebted to the following individuals for their invaluable work and consultation: Aaron Reed and Tricia Aragon in the City Department of Engineering, Brian Flynn in City Parks and Recreation, Chris Bendon in City Planning, Aspen City Attorney John Worcester, Brad Reed Nelson at Board By Design, Brian Howard, and Daniel Bayer.

For his intelligent and insightful engagement with the exhibition's concept in the new text he has contributed to this publication, we would especially like to thank Christian Rattemeyer.

Richard Slovak again thoroughly edited all of the texts. Jared Rippy, Aspen Art Museum Graphic Designer, thoughtfully designed this catalogue and all related exhibition graphics.

We wish to thank our colleagues at the Aspen Art Museum: Public Relations and Marketing Assistant Lee Azarcon, Visitor Services Assistant Michael Barlow, Visitor Services Coordinator Sherry Black, Education Curator Scott Boberg, Visitor Services Assistant Kasey Bullerman, Project Manager Rich Cieciuch, Membership Assistant Ellie Closuit, Education Outreach Coordinator Genna Collins, Acting Finance and Administration Director Stefan Davidson, Executive Assistant to the Director Margaret Gribbell, Visitor Services Assistant John Hansen, Assistant Development Director Christy Mahon, Public Relations and Marketing Director Jeff Murcko, Special Events Coordinator Devon Myers, Campaign Coordinator Grace Nims, Web and Graphic Design Associate Rachel Rippy, Assistant Director for External Affairs John-Paul Schaefer, and Staff Photographer Karl Wolfgang. We are indebted to each and every one of you for your hard work, open-mindedness, and participation.

We would like to single out Chief Preparator and Facilities Manager Jonathan Hagman, Curatorial Associate Nicole Kinsler, and Registrar and Manager of Exhibitions Luis Yllanes, for their work during the organization of the exhibition. This exhibition could not have been realized without their tireless effort, commitment, innovation, and humor.

We are incredibly thankful for the financial assistance of our National Council. One hundred percent of its contributions go to support our exhibitions. Major support for this exhibition is provided by Stefan Edlis and Gael Neeson, tremendous advocates of our exhibition program and unwavering supporters of our institution. We would also like to express our sincere gratitude to Toby Devan Lewis for generously supporting this publication, and for her steadfast commitment to the Aspen Art Museum and in particular to our publications program. General support for this exhibition is provided by The Andy Warhol Foundation for the Visual Arts. The public programs for the exhibition are presented as part of the Questrom Lecture Series.

It is from our deep enthusiasm for working with artists that this exhibition evolved, and we would like to express our sincere appreciation to the eight in this exhibition for their creative genius, as well for the wonder they inspire in us.

And finally to you, our readers and viewers, we appreciate in advance your openness to new ideas and empathetic interaction.

Heidi Zuckerman Jacobson
Director and Chief Curator

Matthew Thompson
Associate Curator

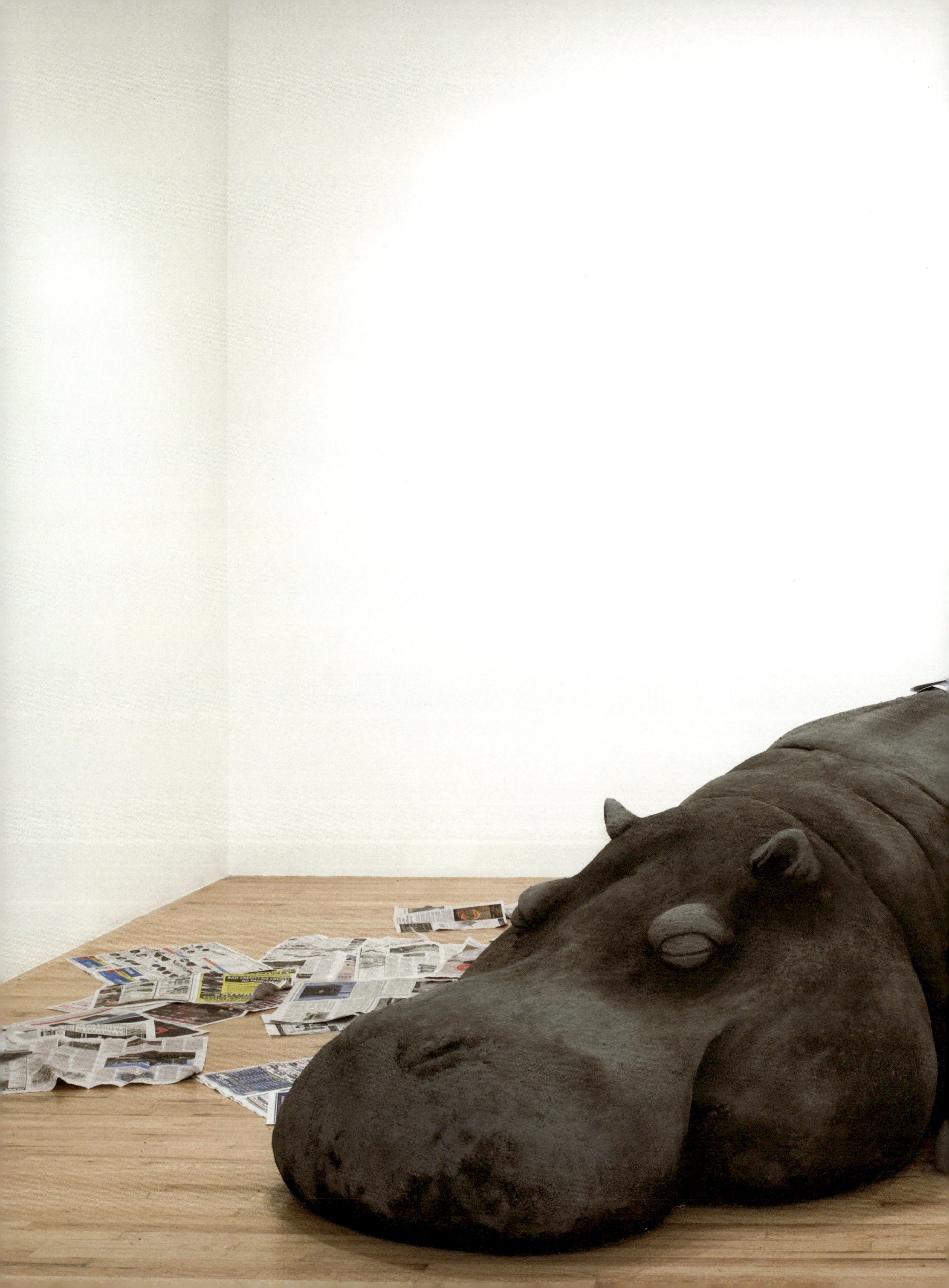

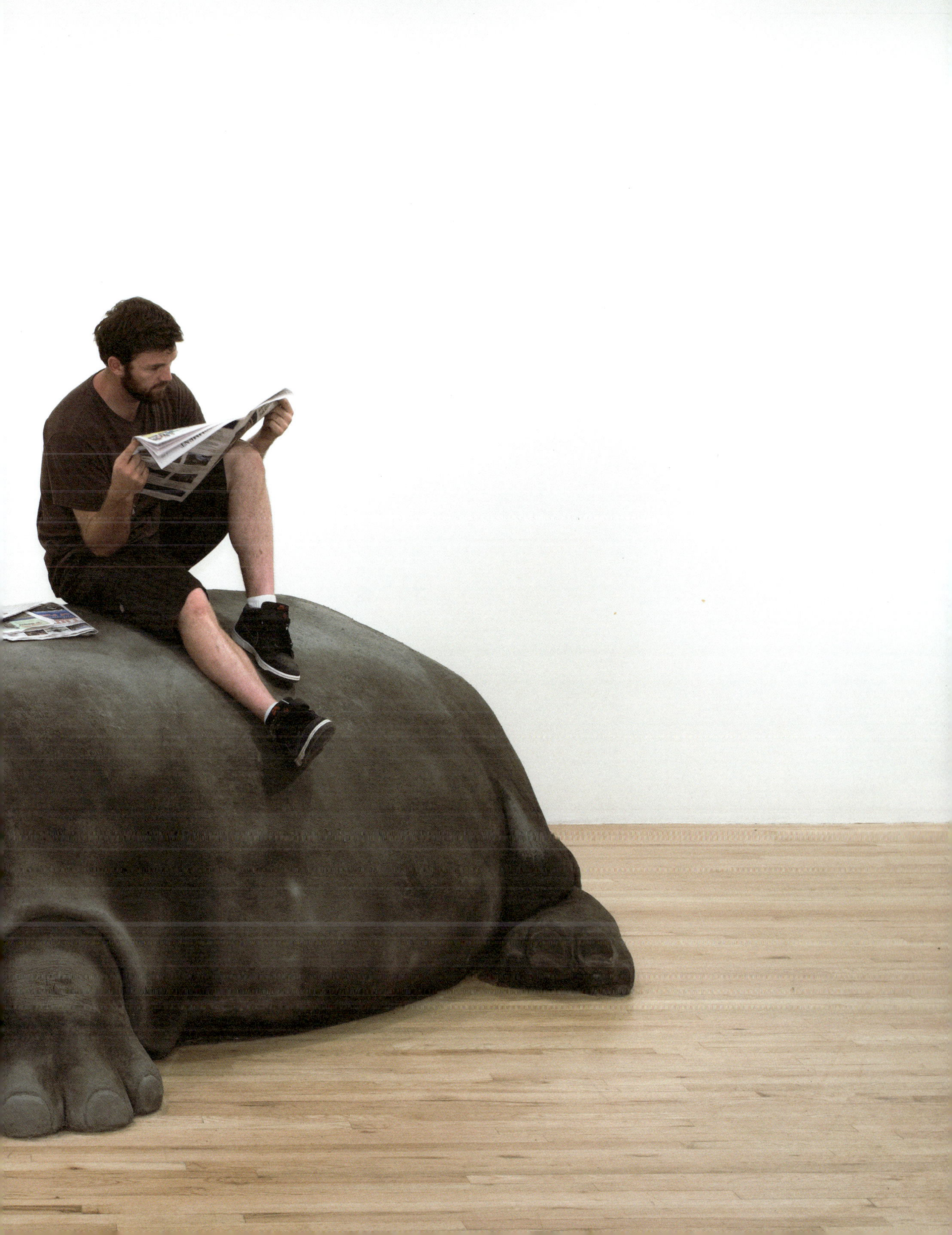

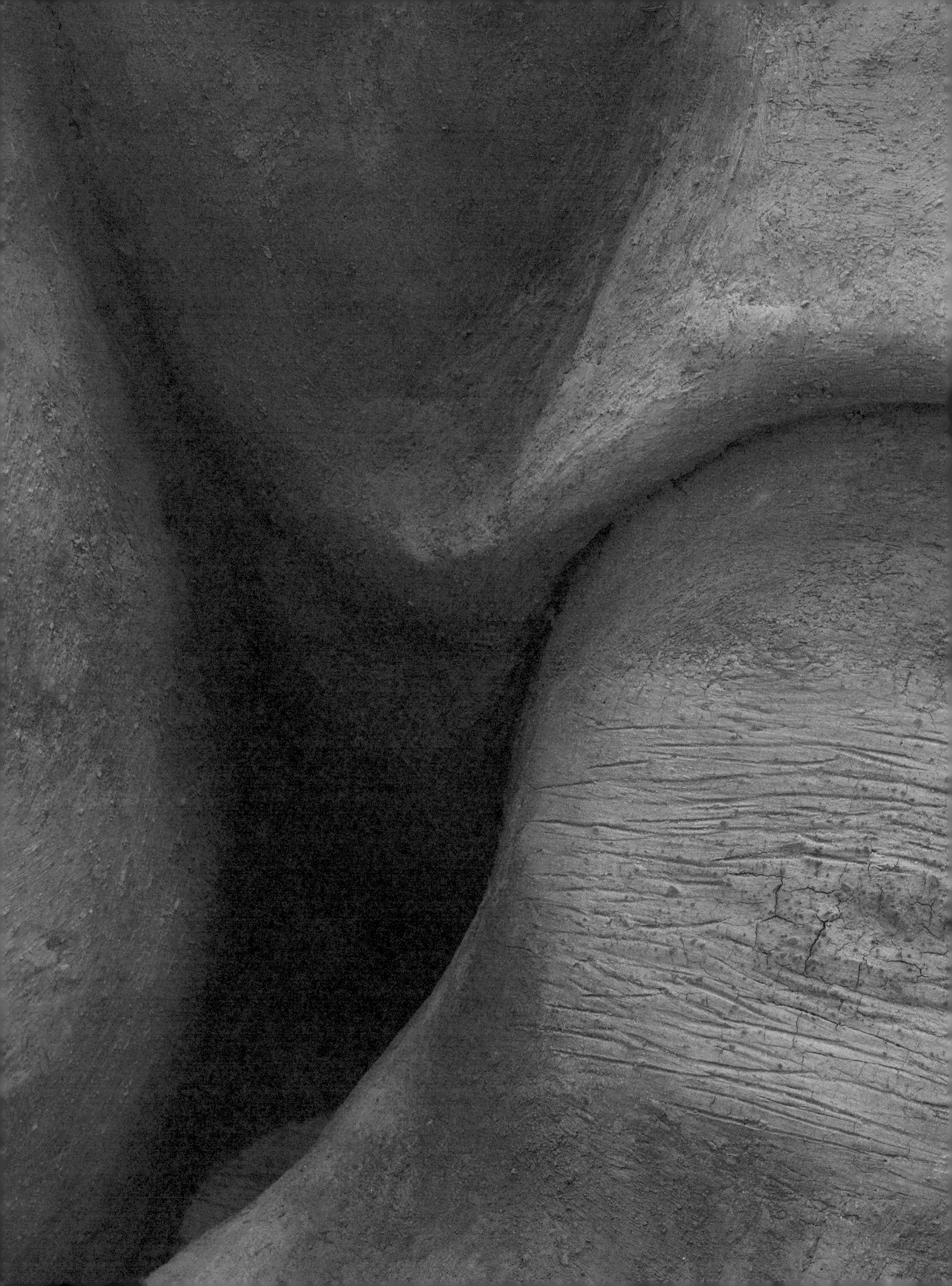

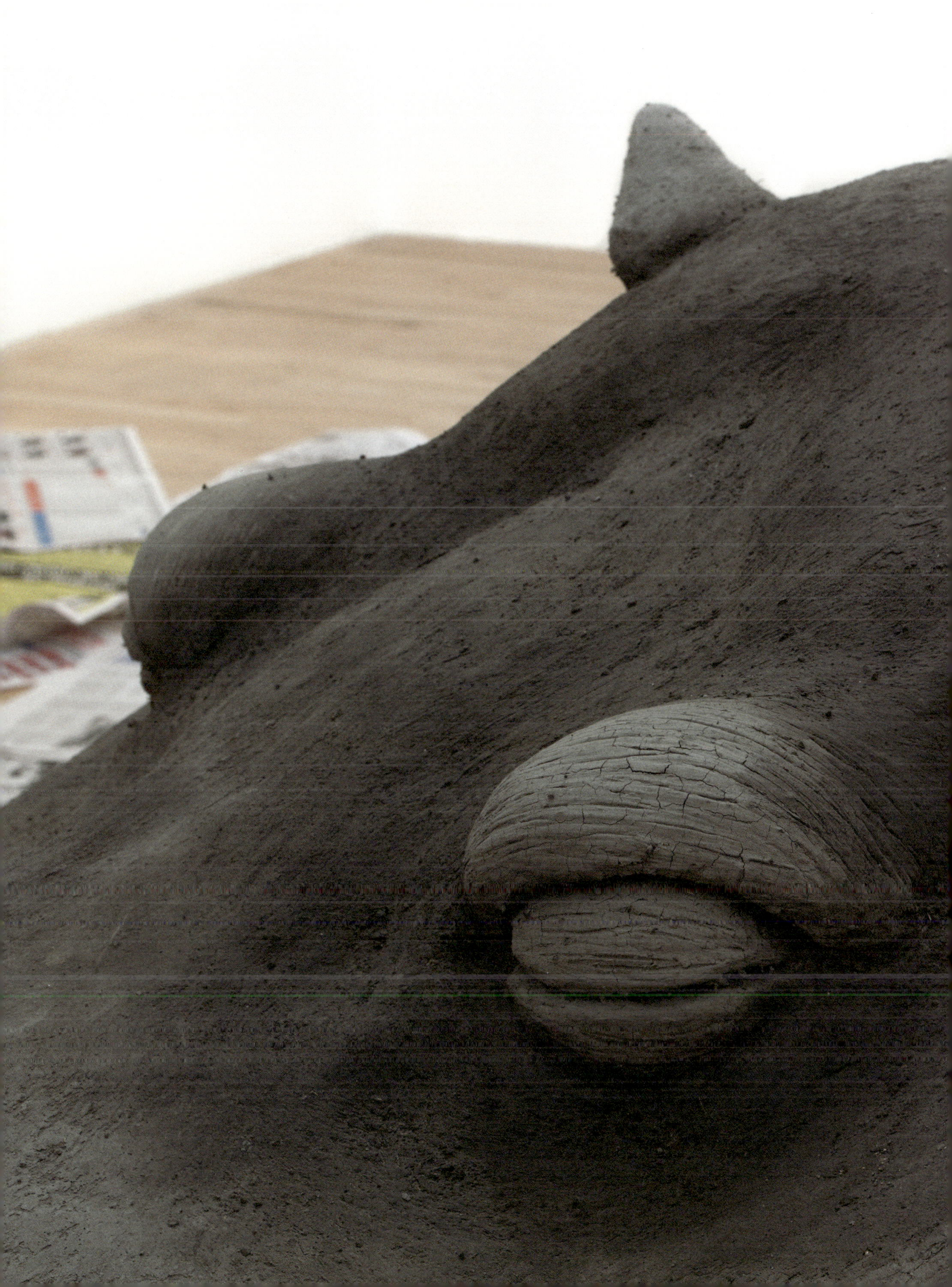

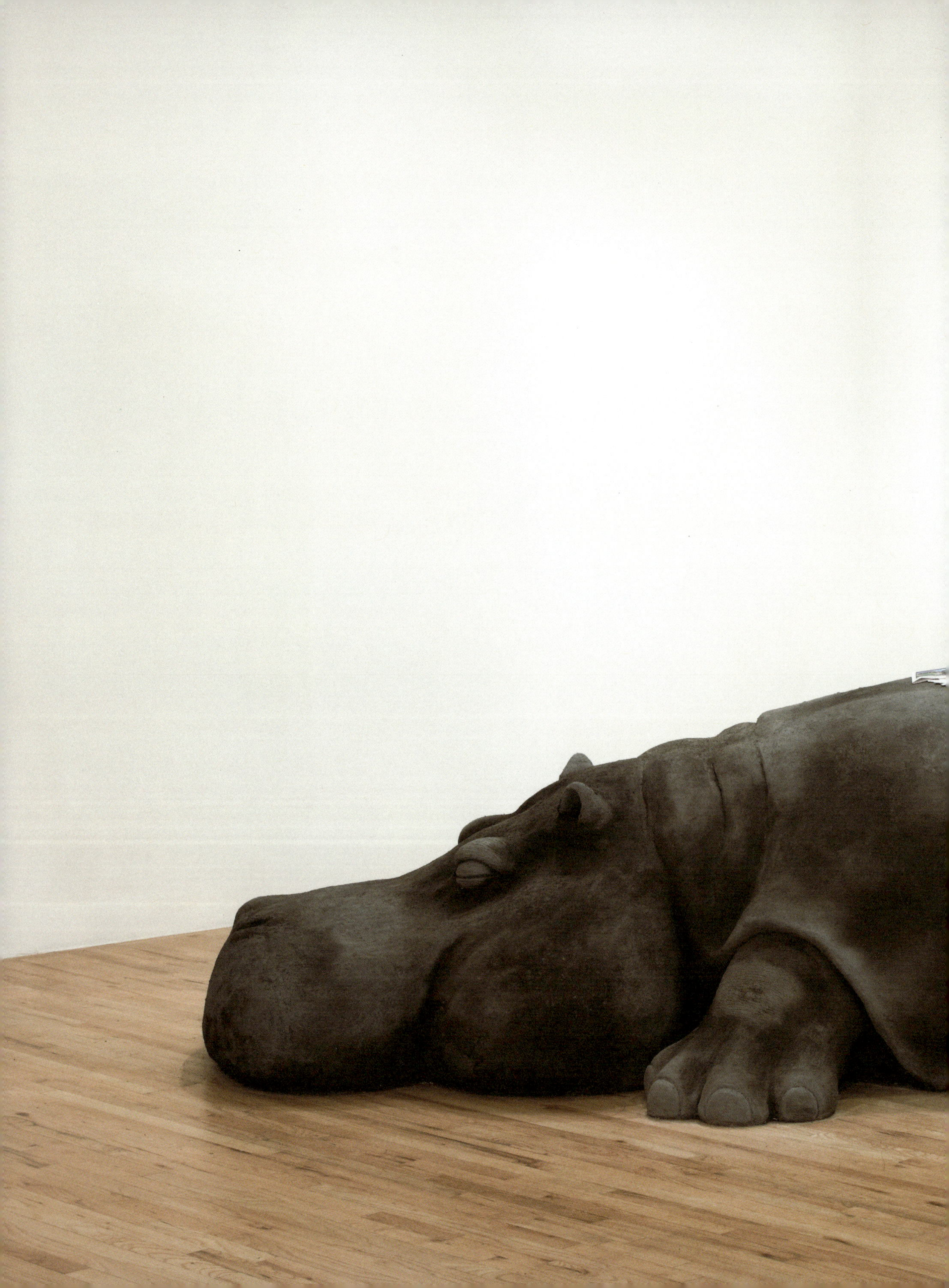

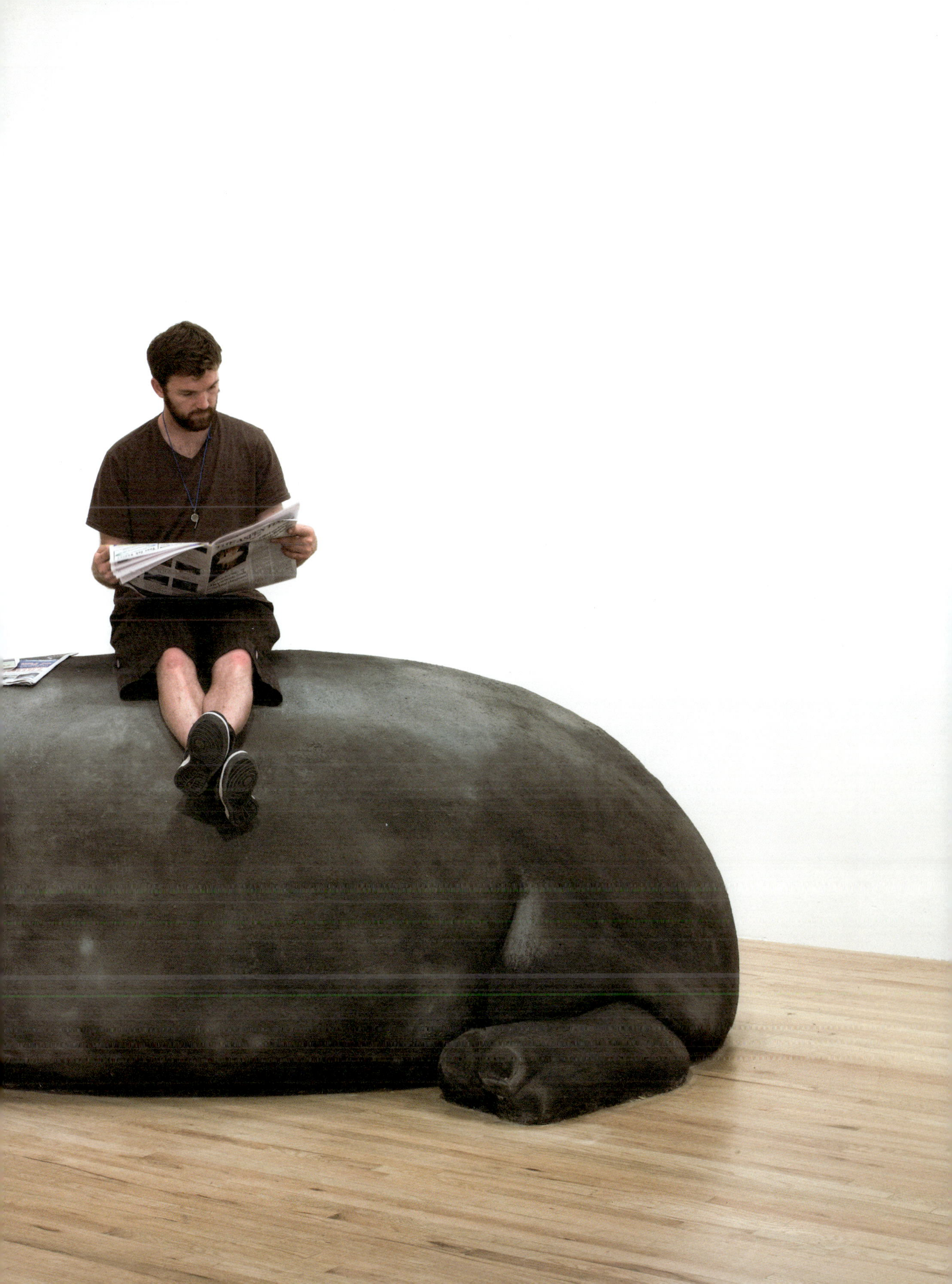

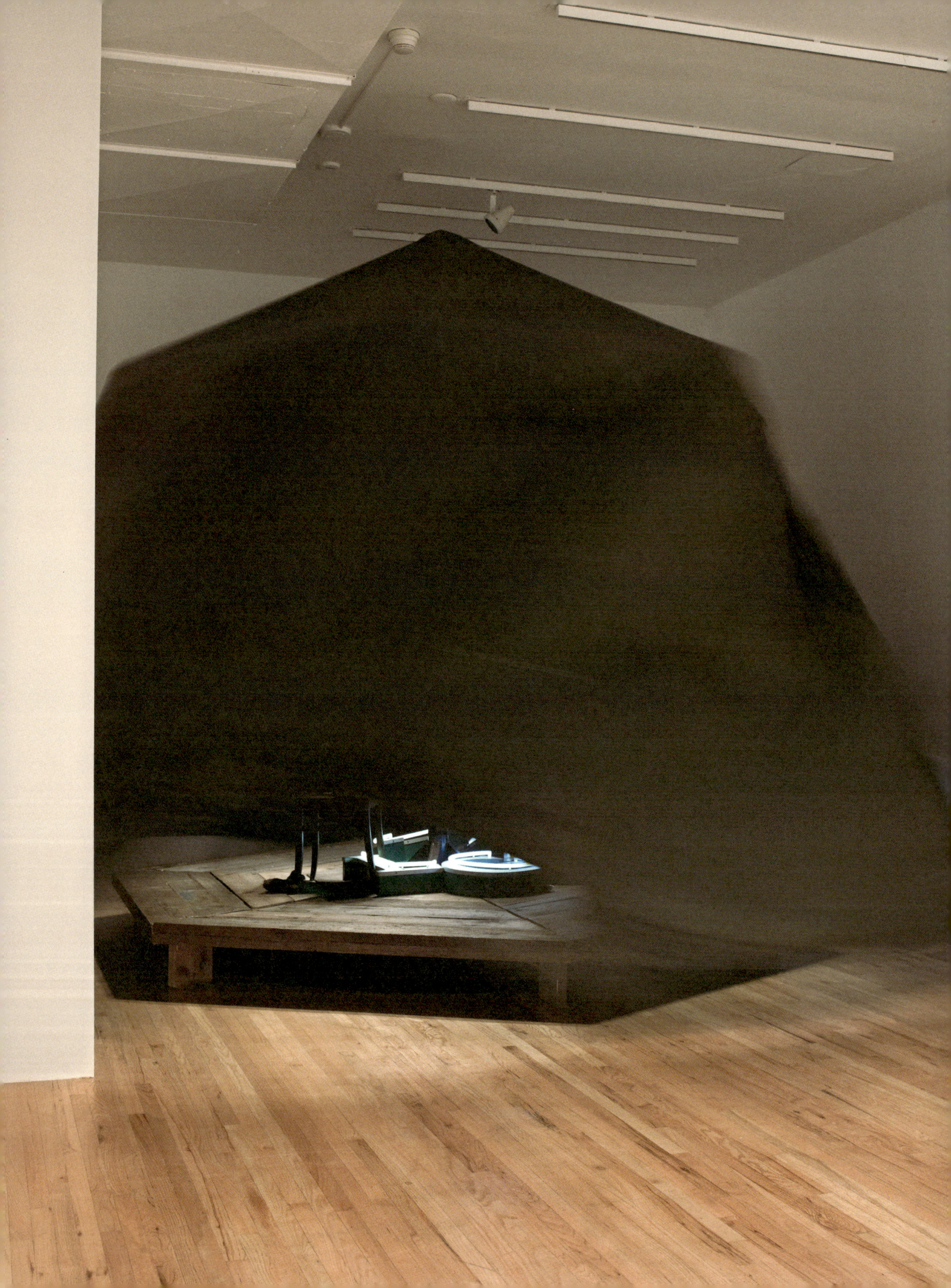

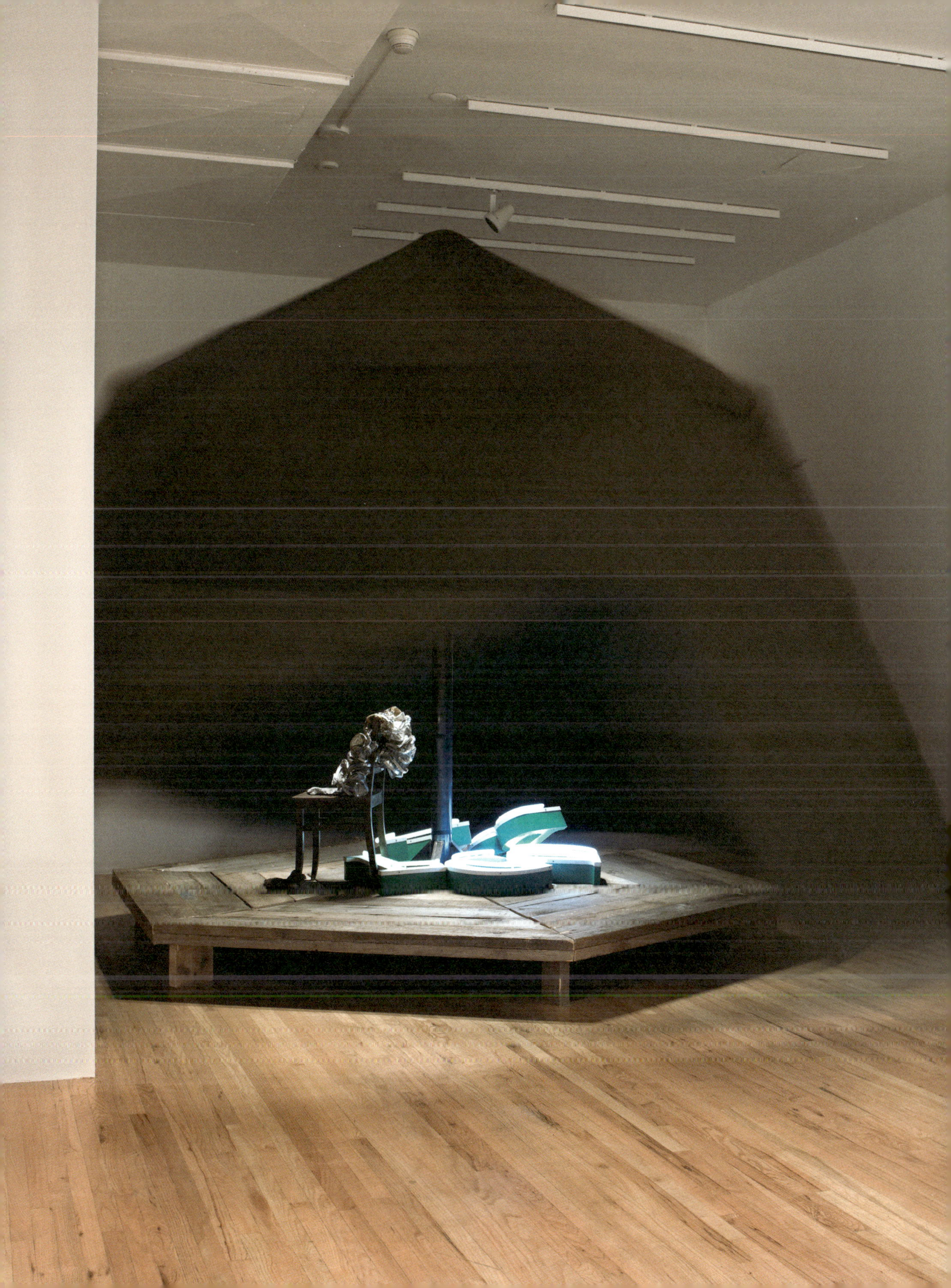

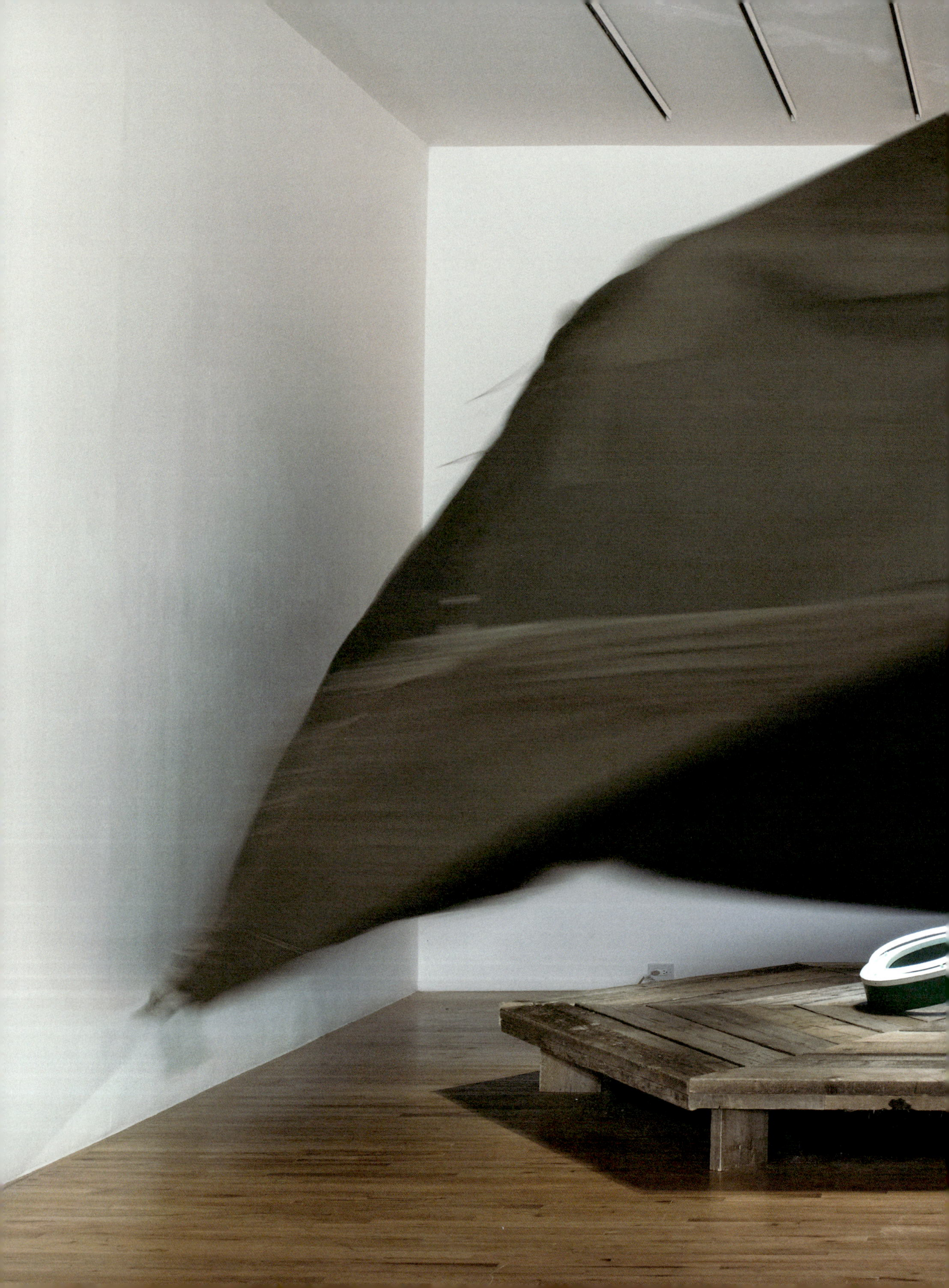

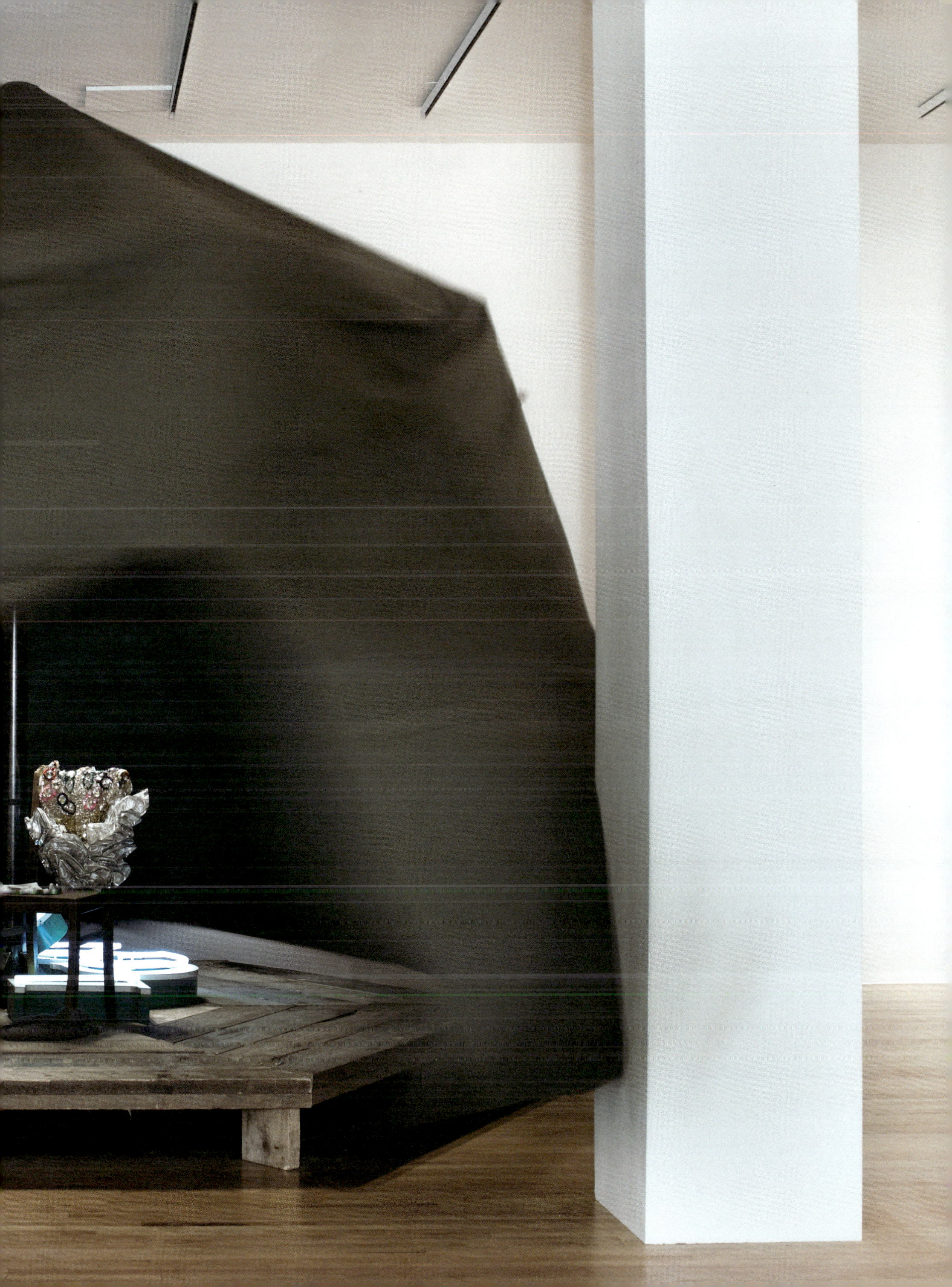

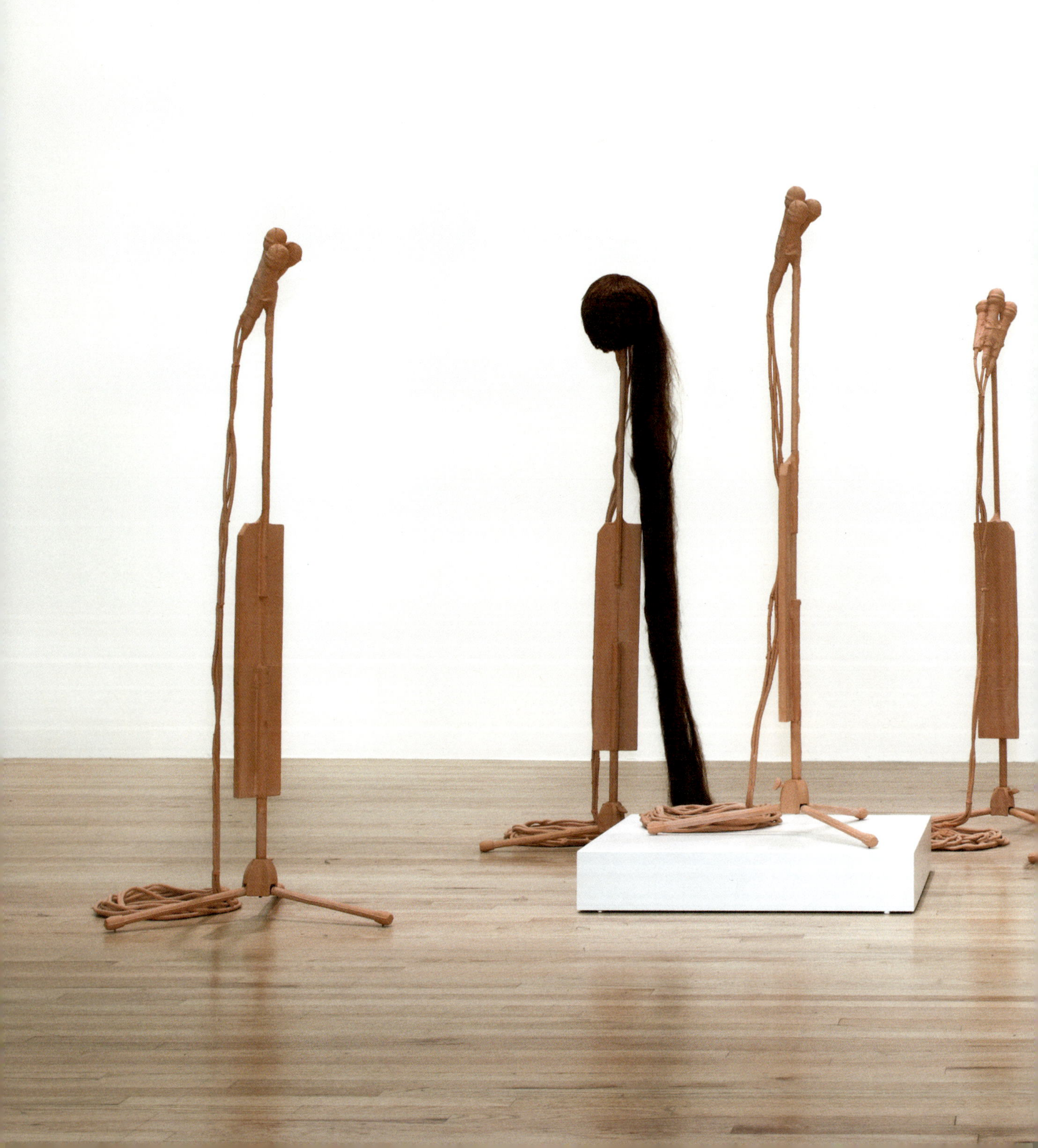

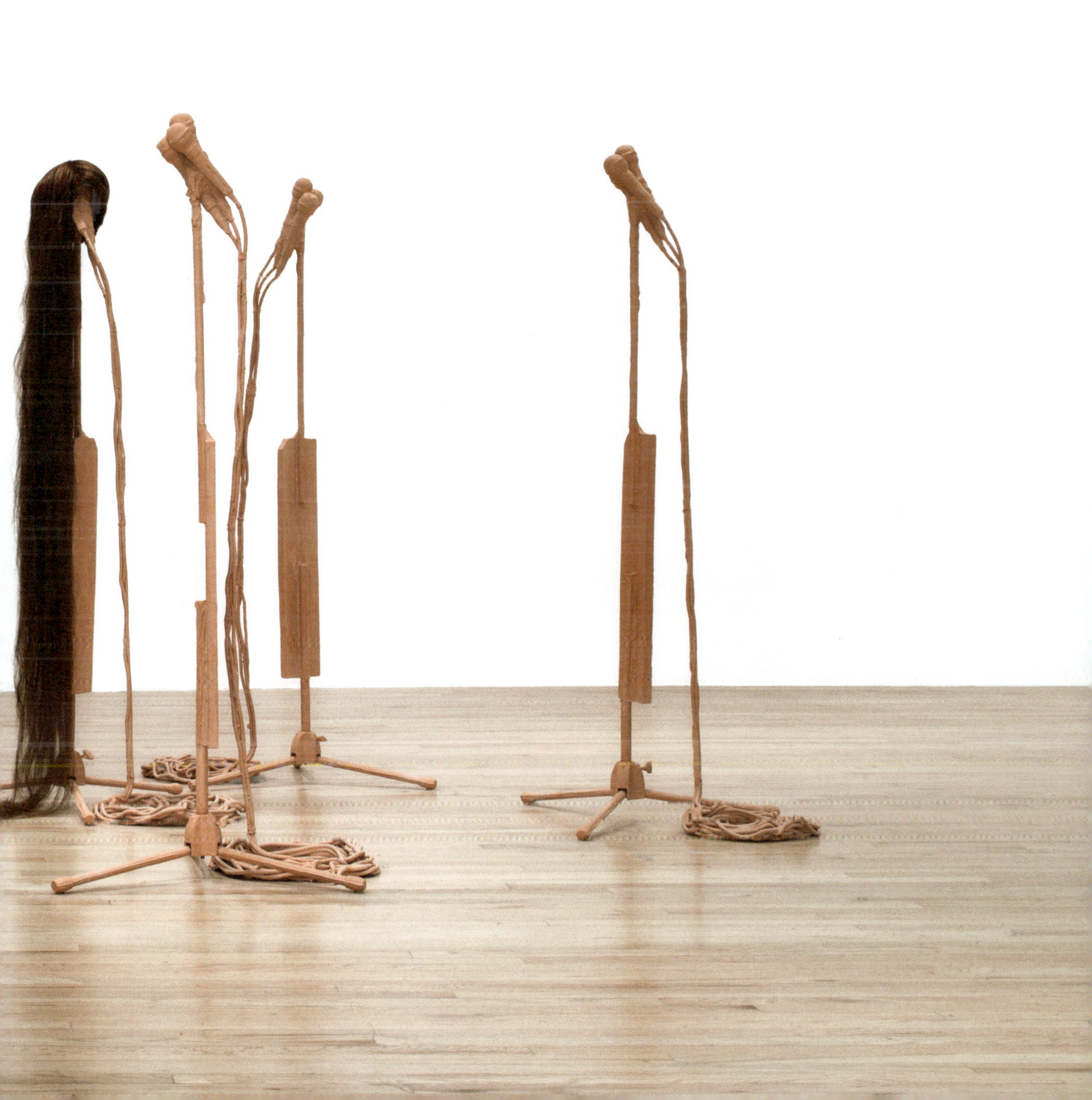

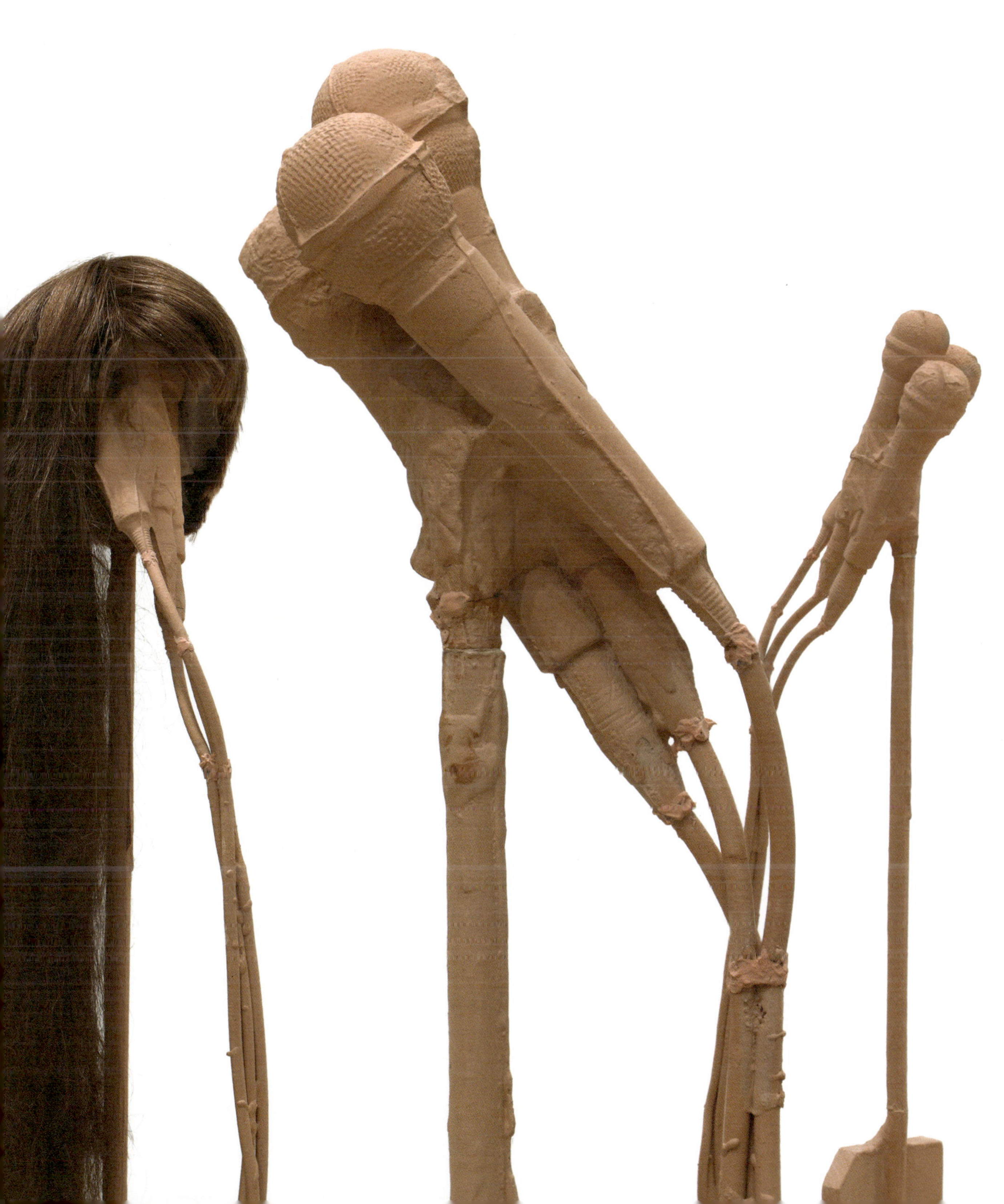

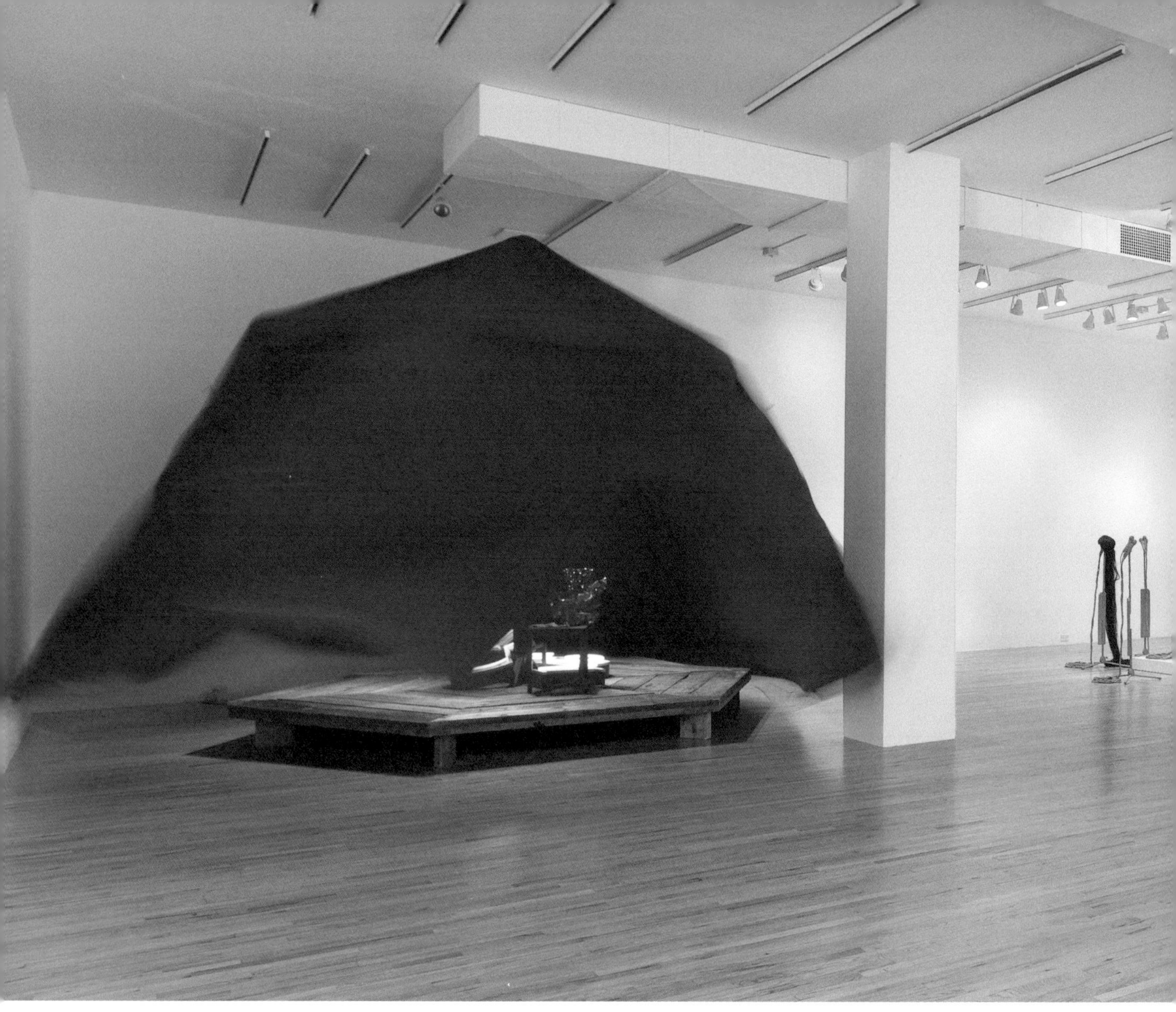

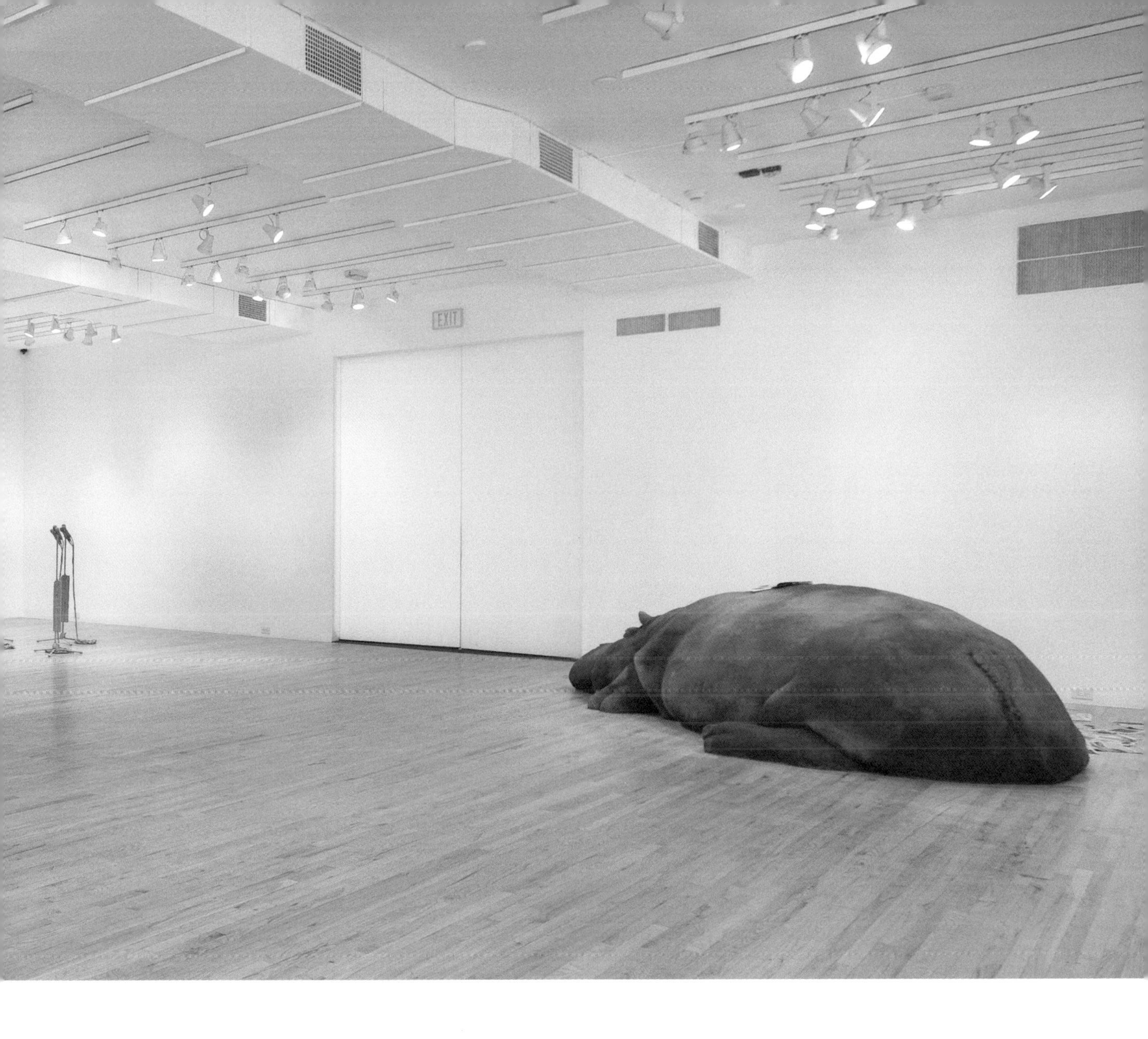

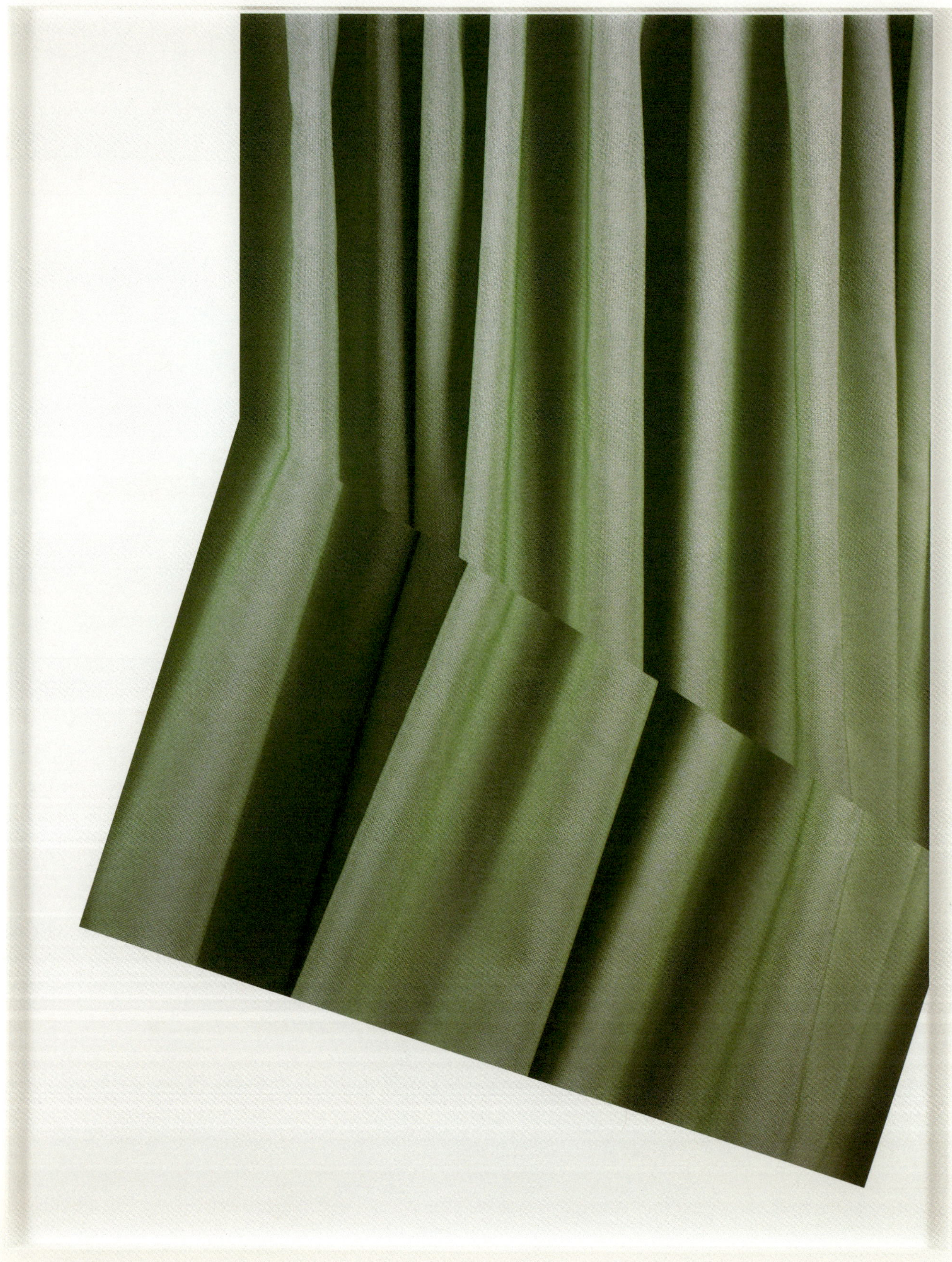

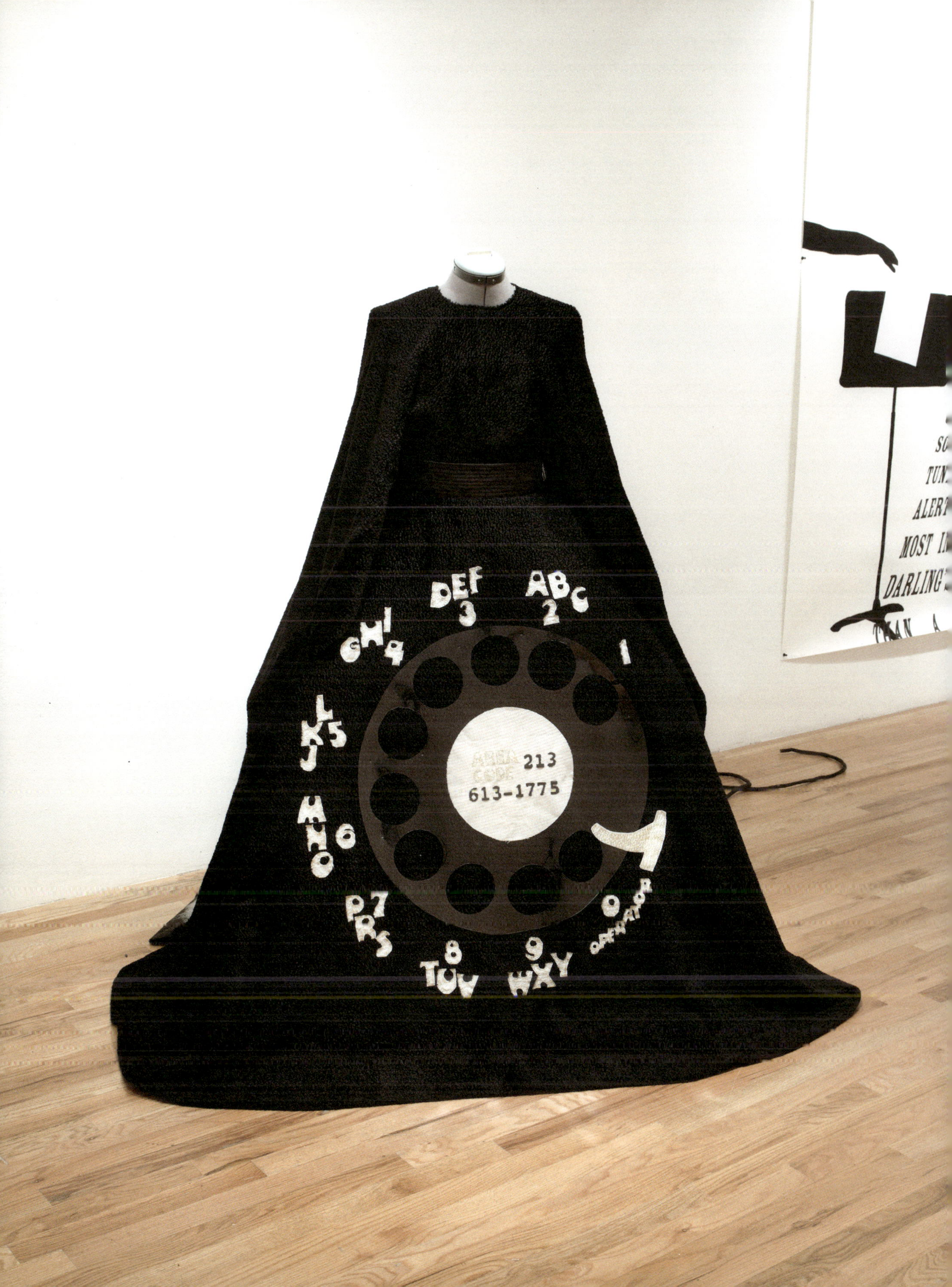
ABC
2
DEF
3
1
GHI
4
JKL
5
MNO
6
AREA
CODE 213
613-1775
PRS
7
TUV
8
WXY
9
OPERATOR
0

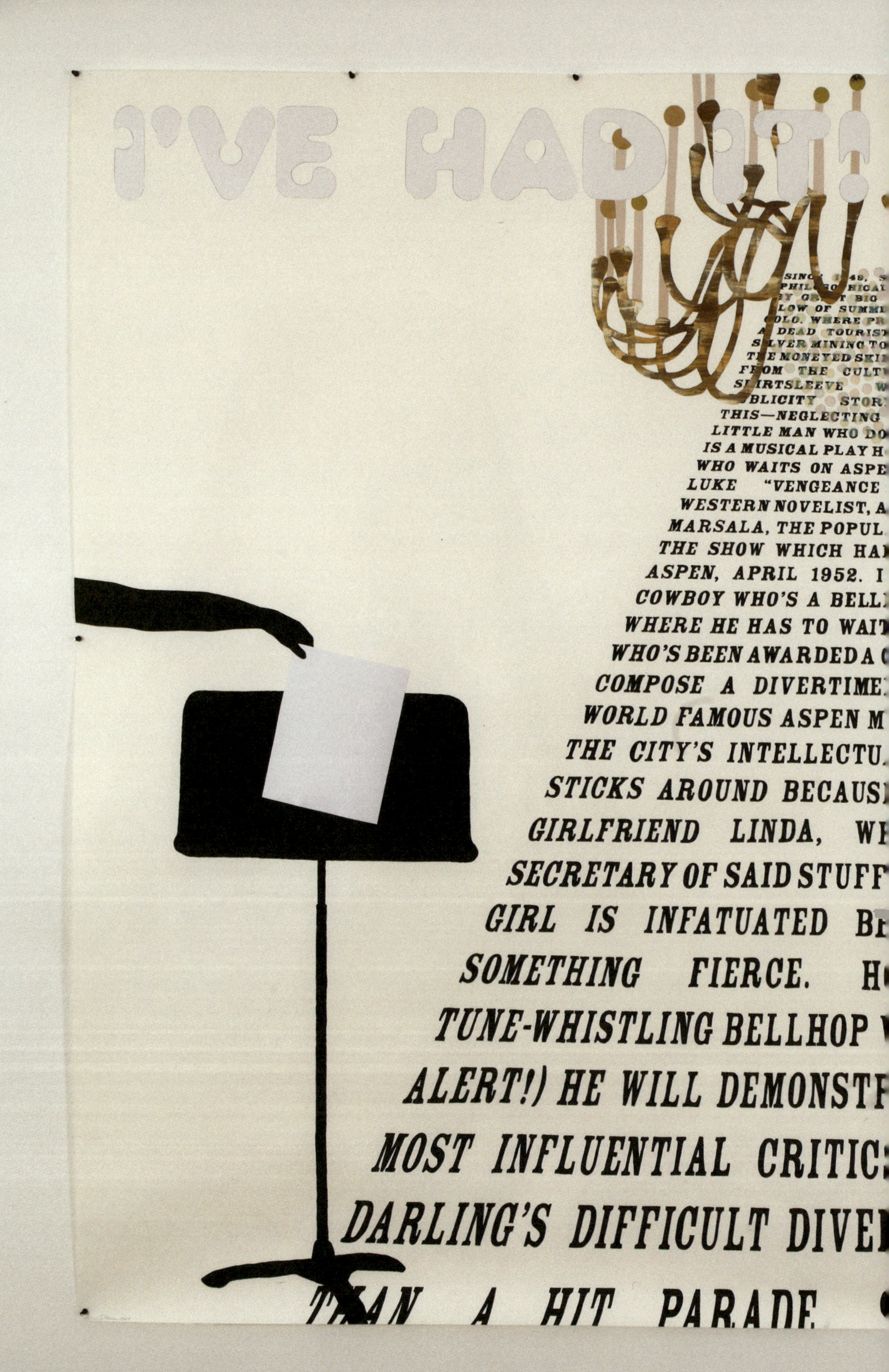
I'VE HAD IT!
SINCE 1949, S
PHILOSOPHICAL
BY GREAT BIG
LOW OF SUMME
COLO. WHERE PR
A DEAD TOURIST
SILVER MINING TO
THE MONEYED SKI
FROM THE CULT
SHIRTSLEEVE W
PUBLICITY STOR
THIS—NEGLECTING
LITTLE MAN WHO DO
IS A MUSICAL PLAY H
WHO WAITS ON ASPE
LUKE "VENGEANCE
WESTERN NOVELIST, A
MARSALA, THE POPUL
THE SHOW WHICH HA
ASPEN, APRIL 1952. I
COWBOY WHO'S A BELL
WHERE HE HAS TO WAIT
WHO'S BEEN AWARDED A
COMPOSE A DIVERTIME
WORLD FAMOUS ASPEN M
THE CITY'S INTELLECTU
STICKS AROUND BECAUS
GIRLFRIEND LINDA, W
SECRETARY OF SAID STUFF
GIRL IS INFATUATED B
SOMETHING FIERCE. HO
TUNE-WHISTLING BELLHOP
ALERT!) HE WILL DEMONSTR
MOST INFLUENTIAL CRITIC
DARLING'S DIFFICULT DIVE
THAN A HIT PARADE.

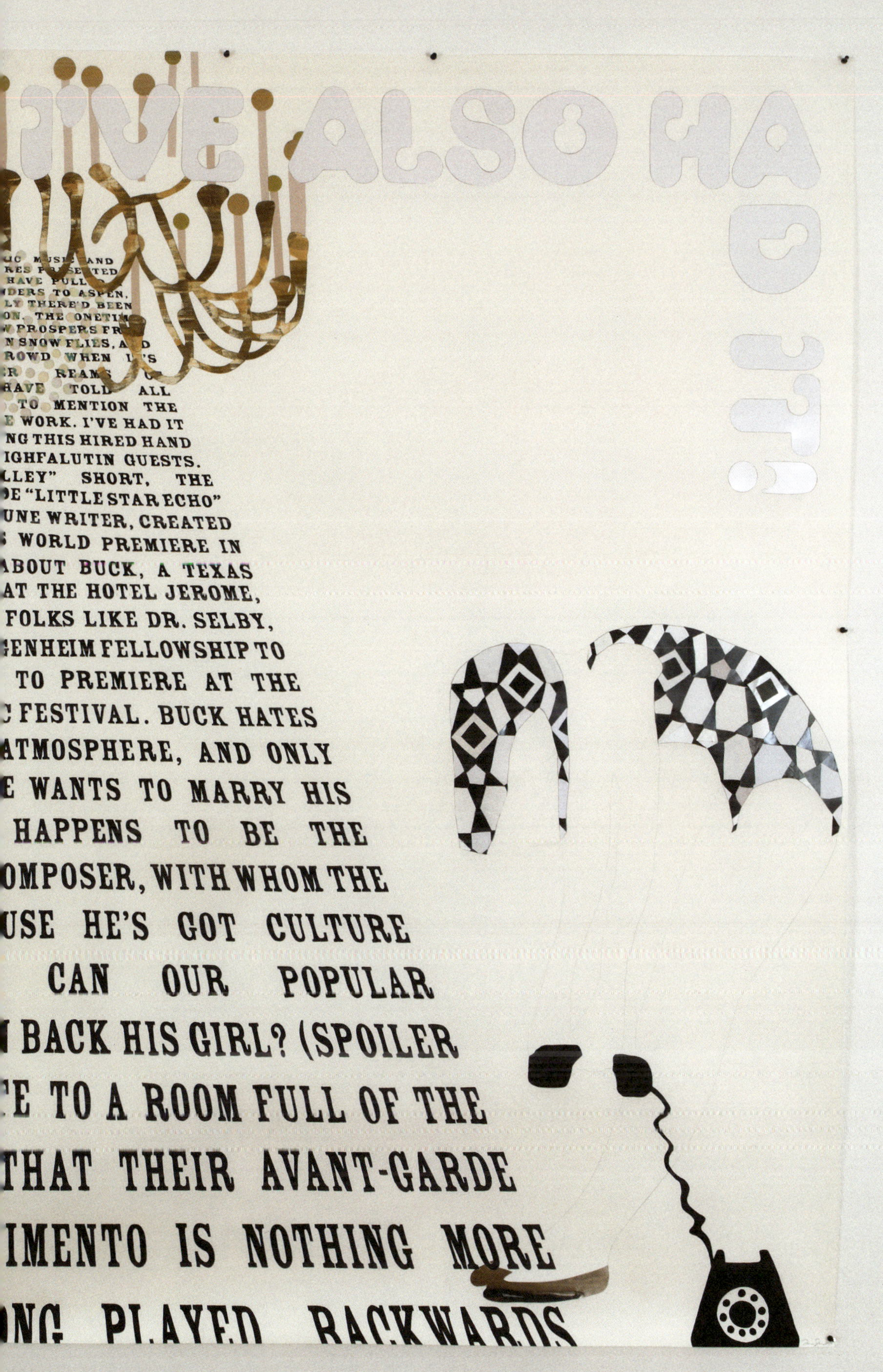
I'VE ALSO HAD IT?
JC MUSIC AND
KES PRESENTED
HAVE PULL
NDERS TO ASPEN,
LY THERE'D BEEN
ON. THE ONETI
N PROSPERS FR
SNOW FLIES, AND
ROWD WHEN I 'S
R REAMS G
HAVE TOLD ALL
TO MENTION THE
E WORK. I'VE HAD IT
NG THIS HIRED HAND
IGHFALUTIN GUESTS.
LLEY" SHORT, THE
E "LITTLE STAR ECHO"
UNE WRITER, CREATED
WORLD PREMIERE IN
ABOUT BUCK, A TEXAS
AT THE HOTEL JEROME,
FOLKS LIKE DR. SELBY,
GENHEIM FELLOWSHIP TO
TO PREMIERE AT THE
FESTIVAL. BUCK HATES
ATMOSPHERE, AND ONLY
E WANTS TO MARRY HIS
HAPPENS TO BE THE
OMPOSER, WITH WHOM THE
USE HE'S GOT CULTURE
CAN OUR POPULAR
BACK HIS GIRL? (SPOILER
E TO A ROOM FULL OF THE
THAT THEIR AVANT-GARDE
IMENTO IS NOTHING MORE
NG PLAYED BACKWARDS

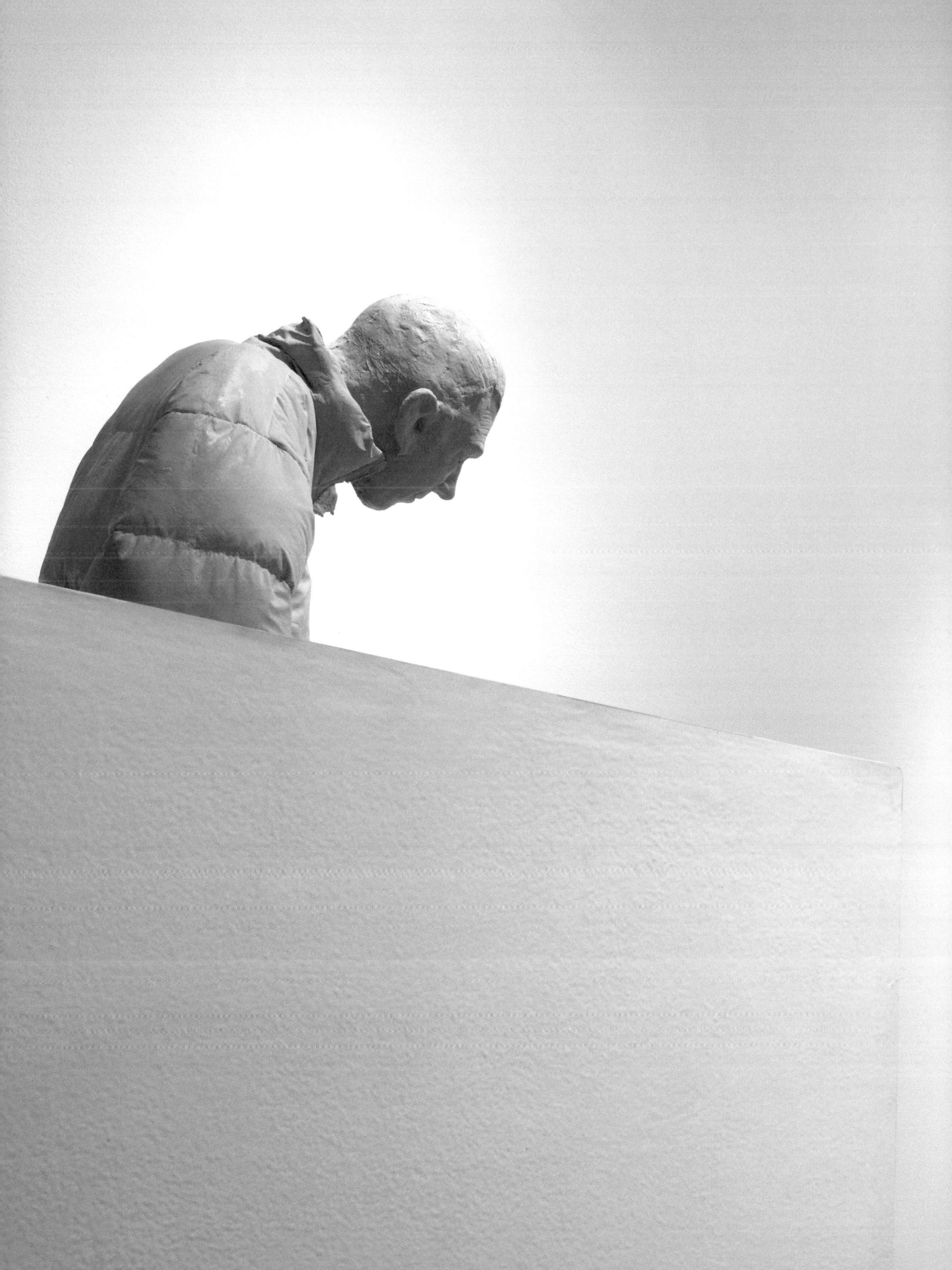

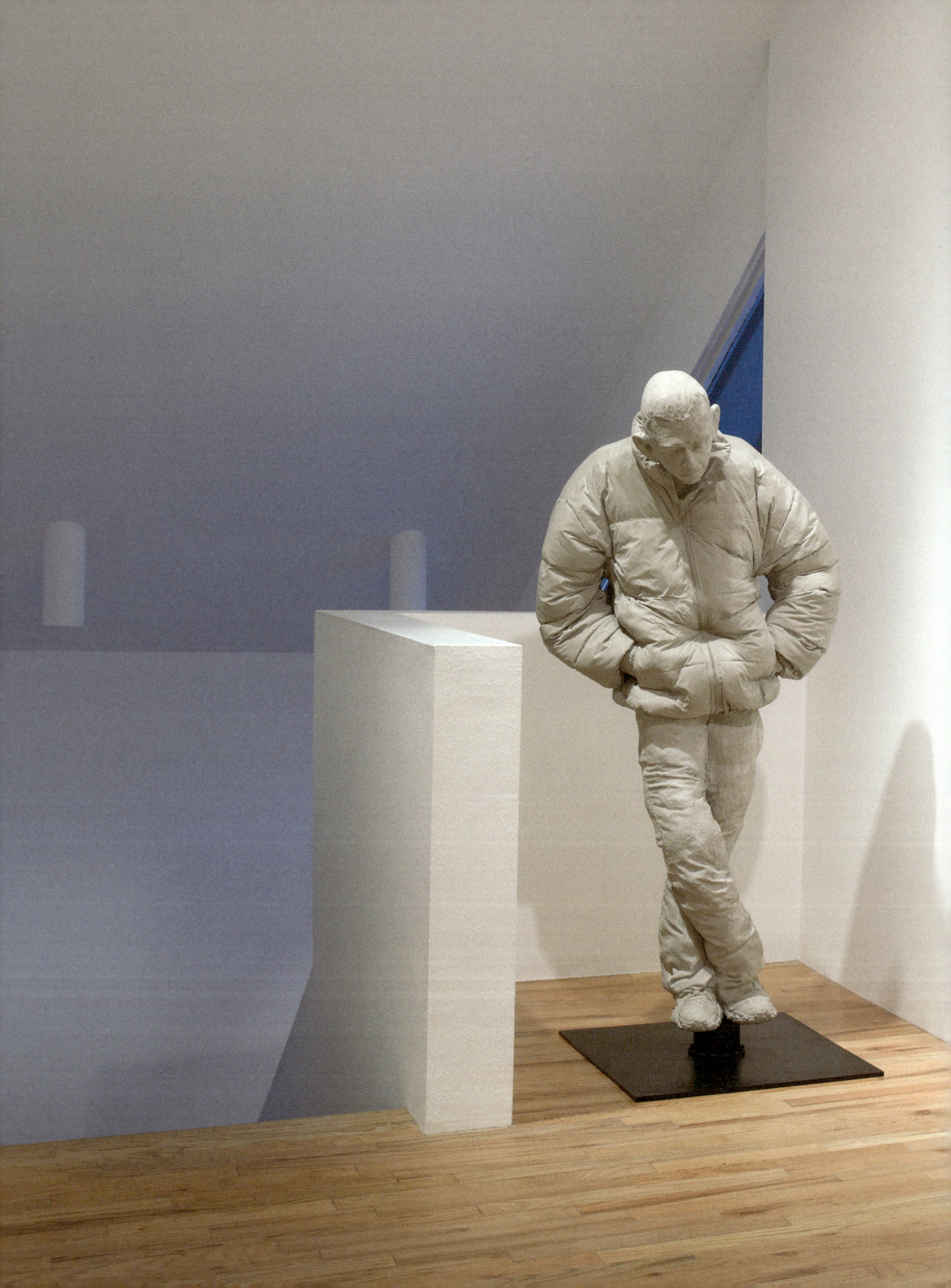

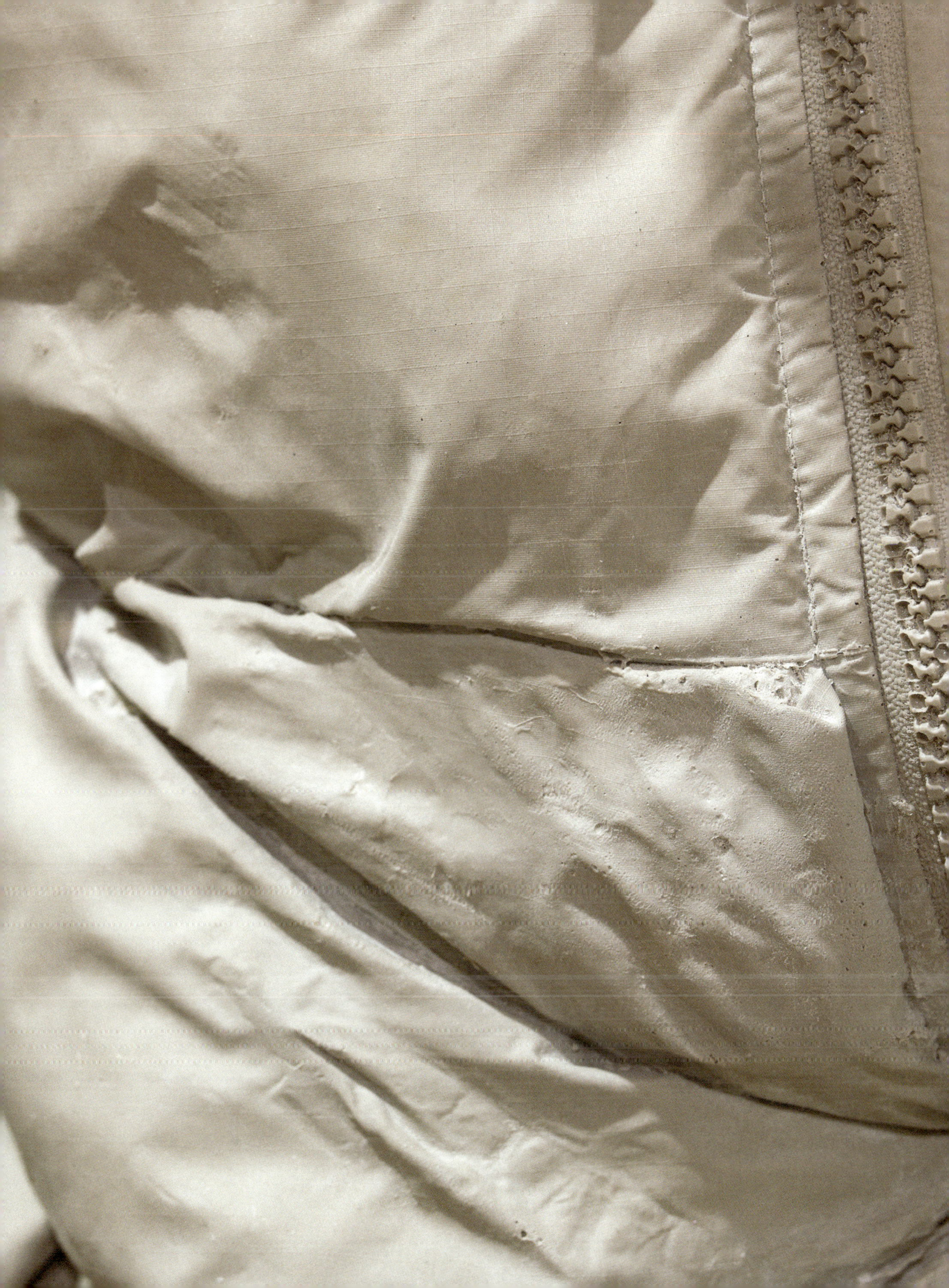

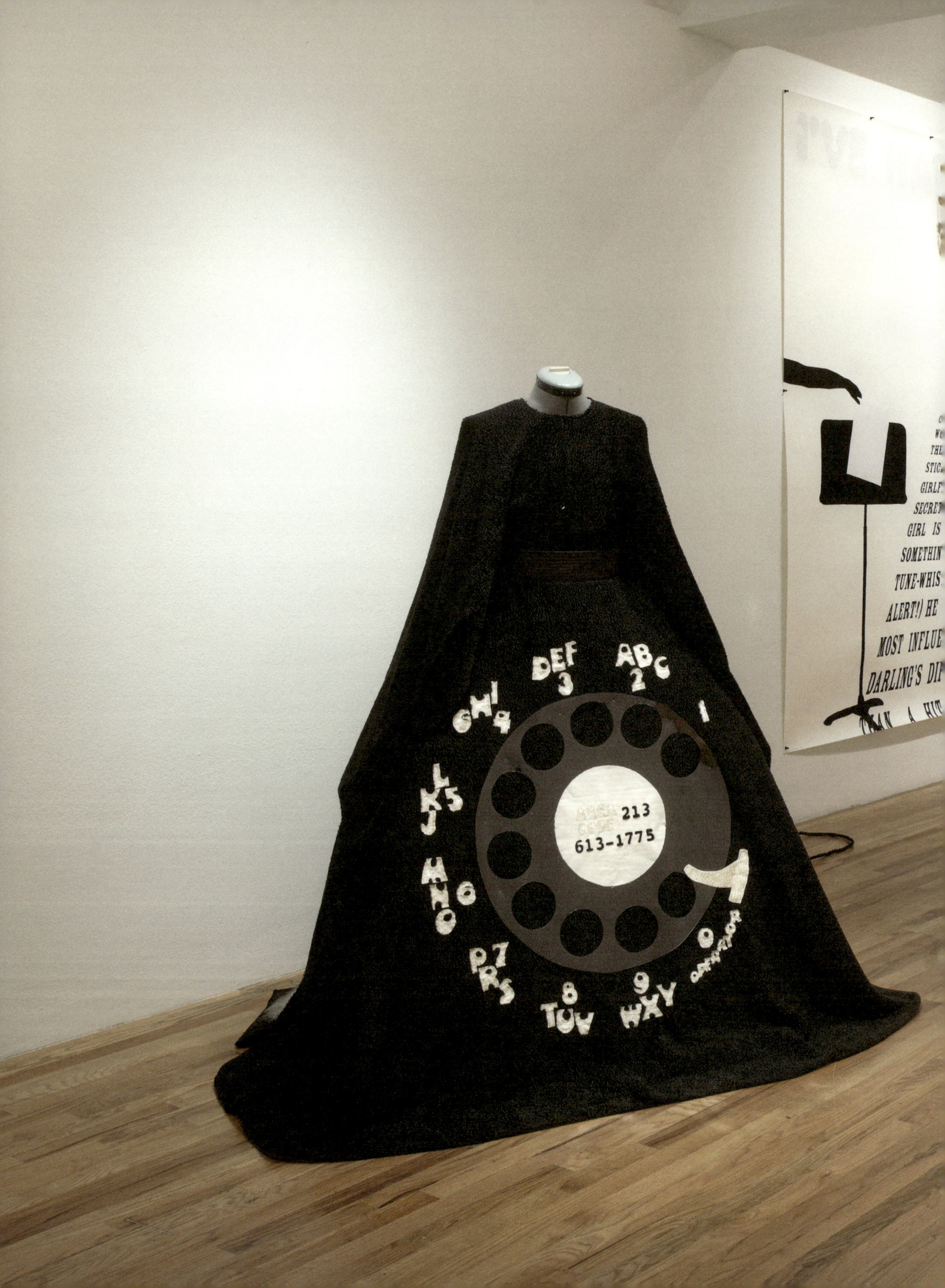

DEF 3
ABC 2
GHI 4
1
JKL 5
MNO 6
213
613-1775
PRS 7
TUV 8
WXY 9
OPERATOR 0

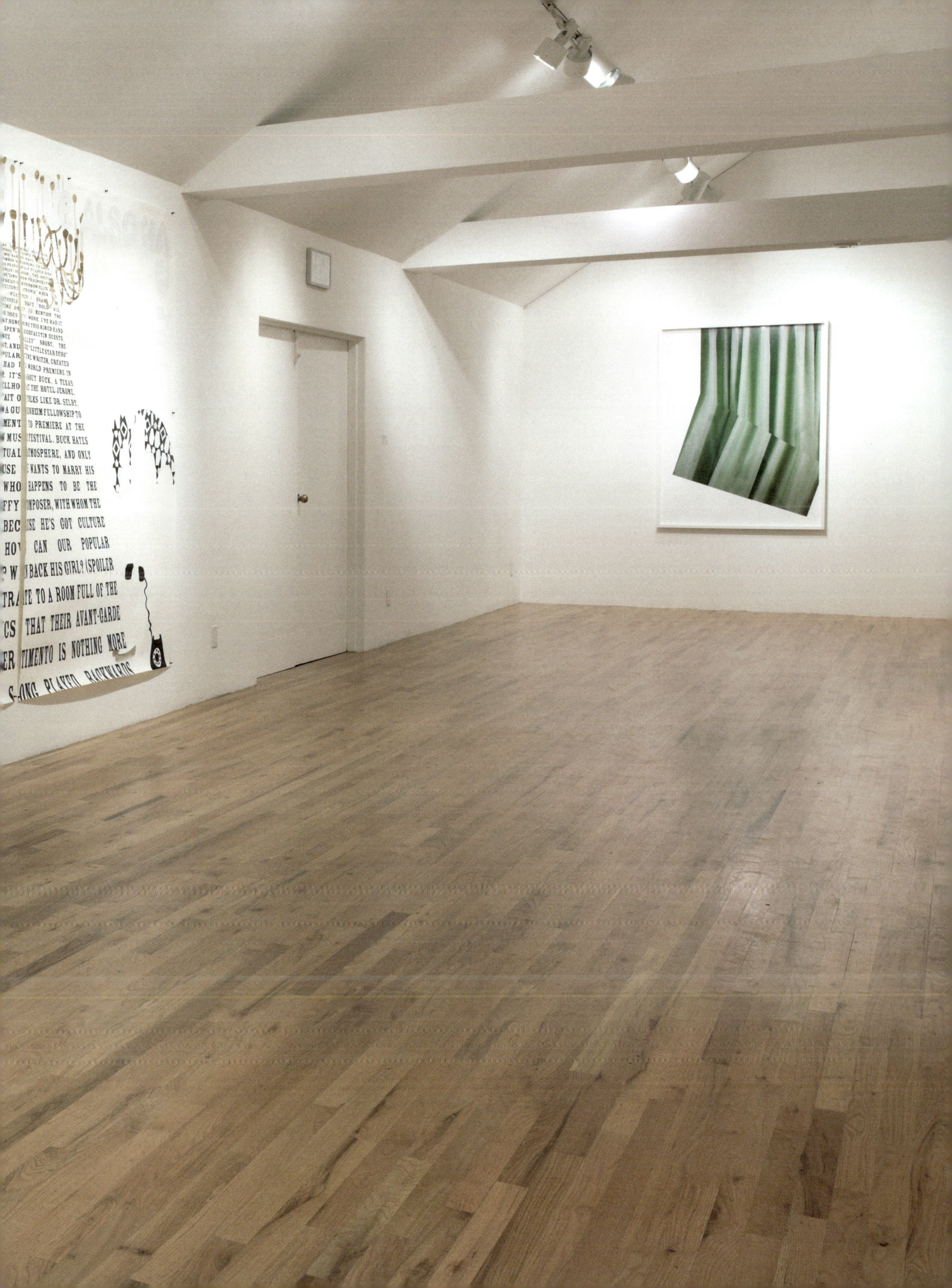

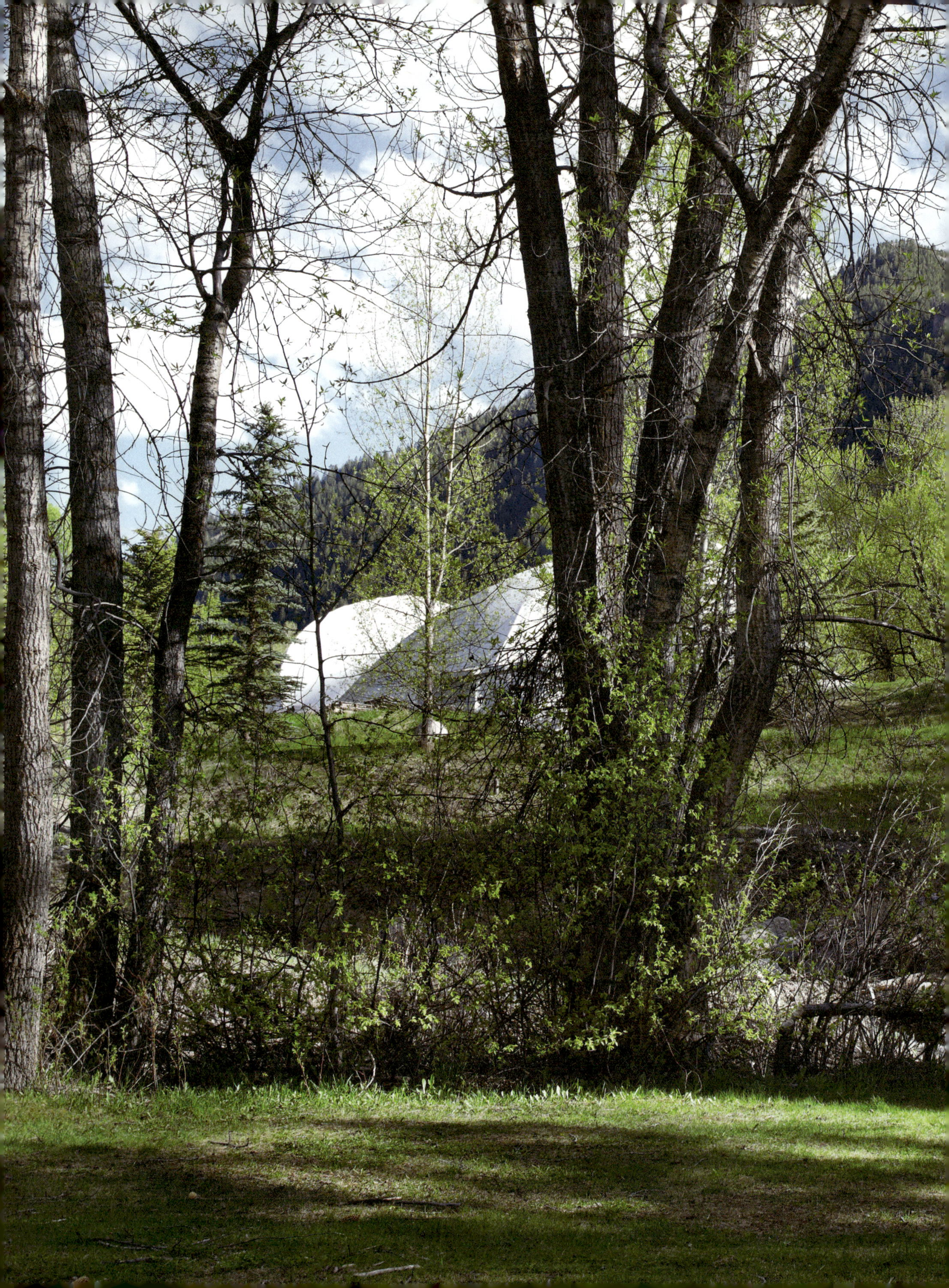

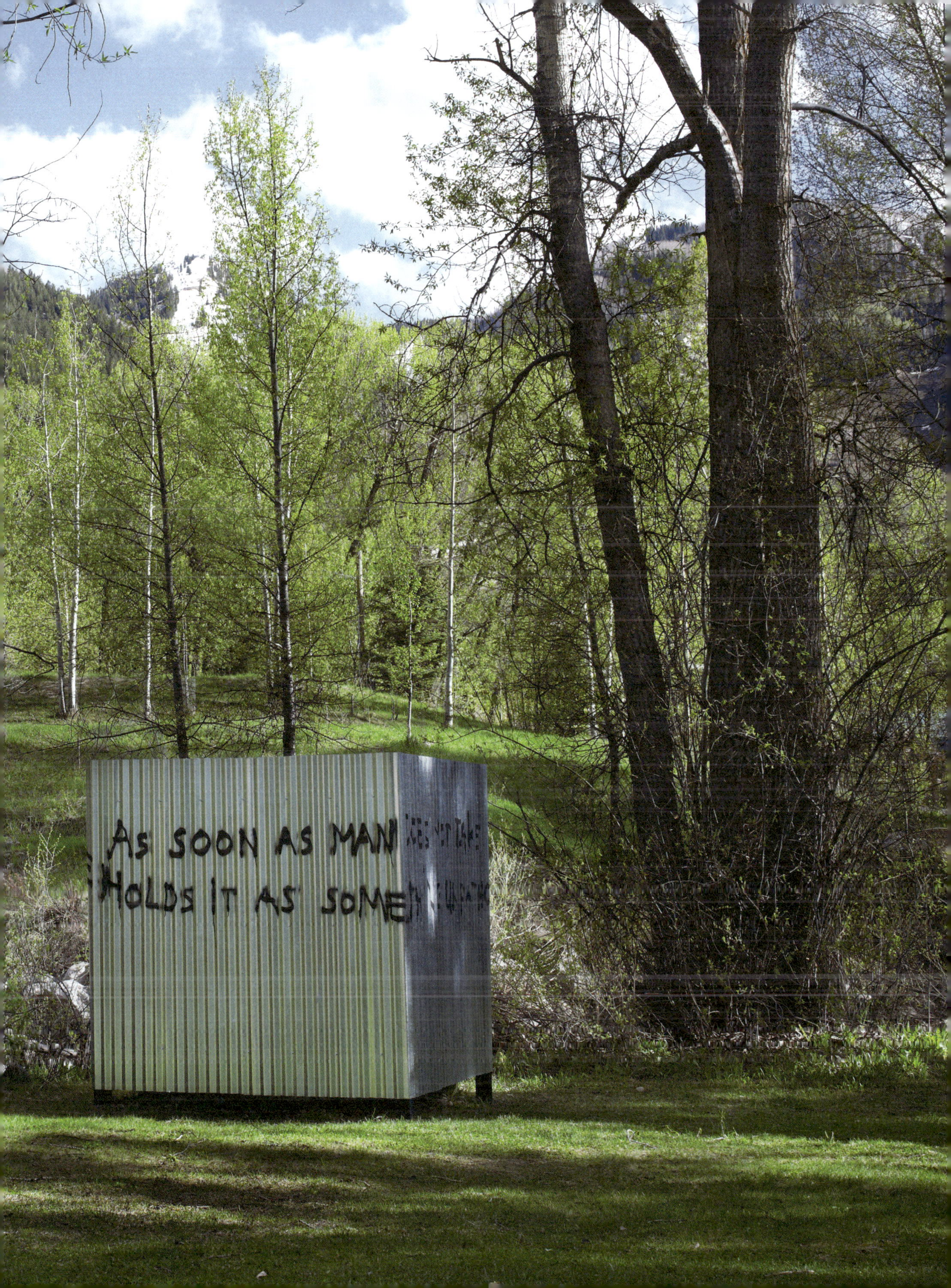
AS SOON AS MAN
HOLDS IT AS SOME

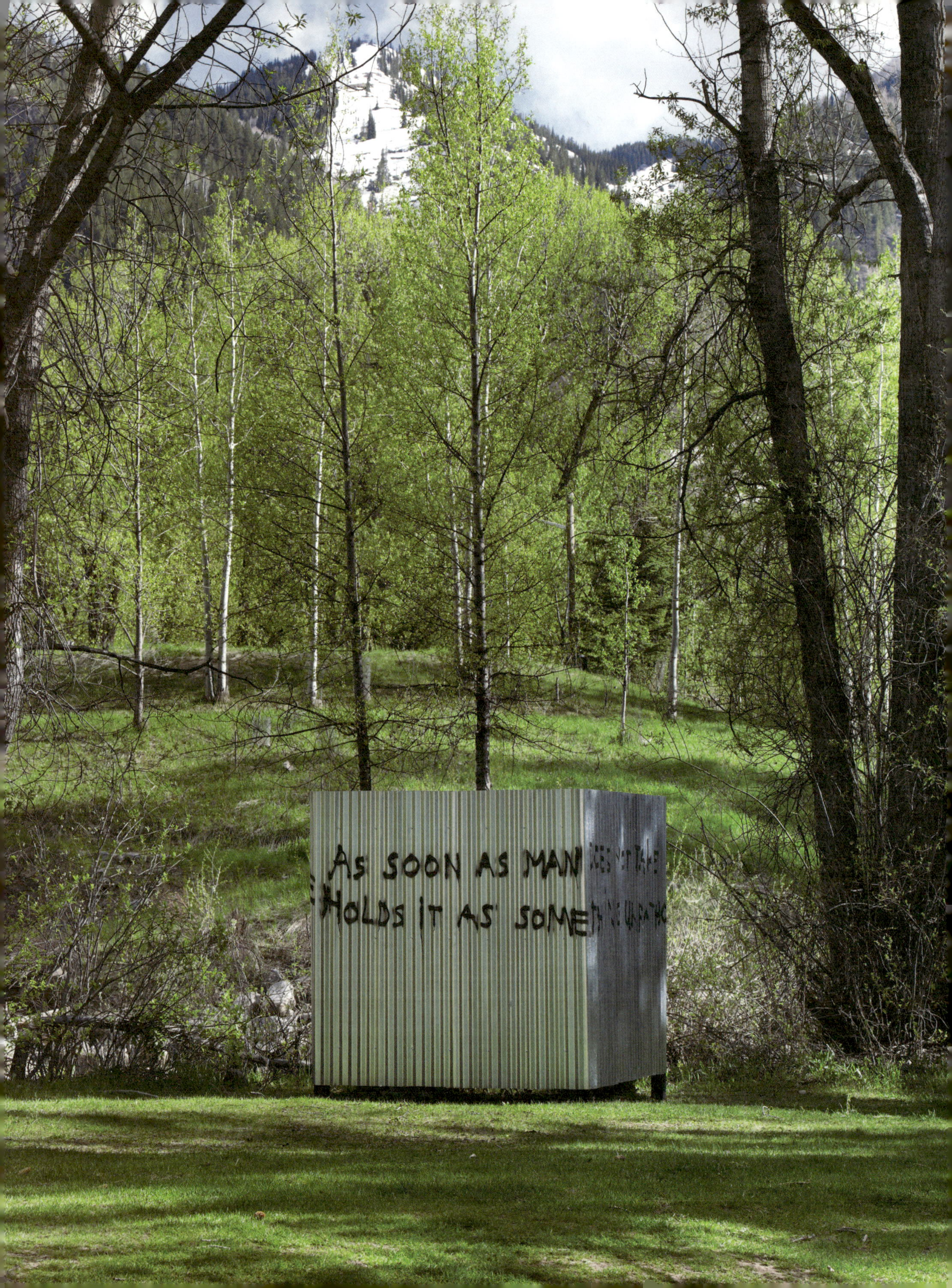

As soon as man
Holds it as someth

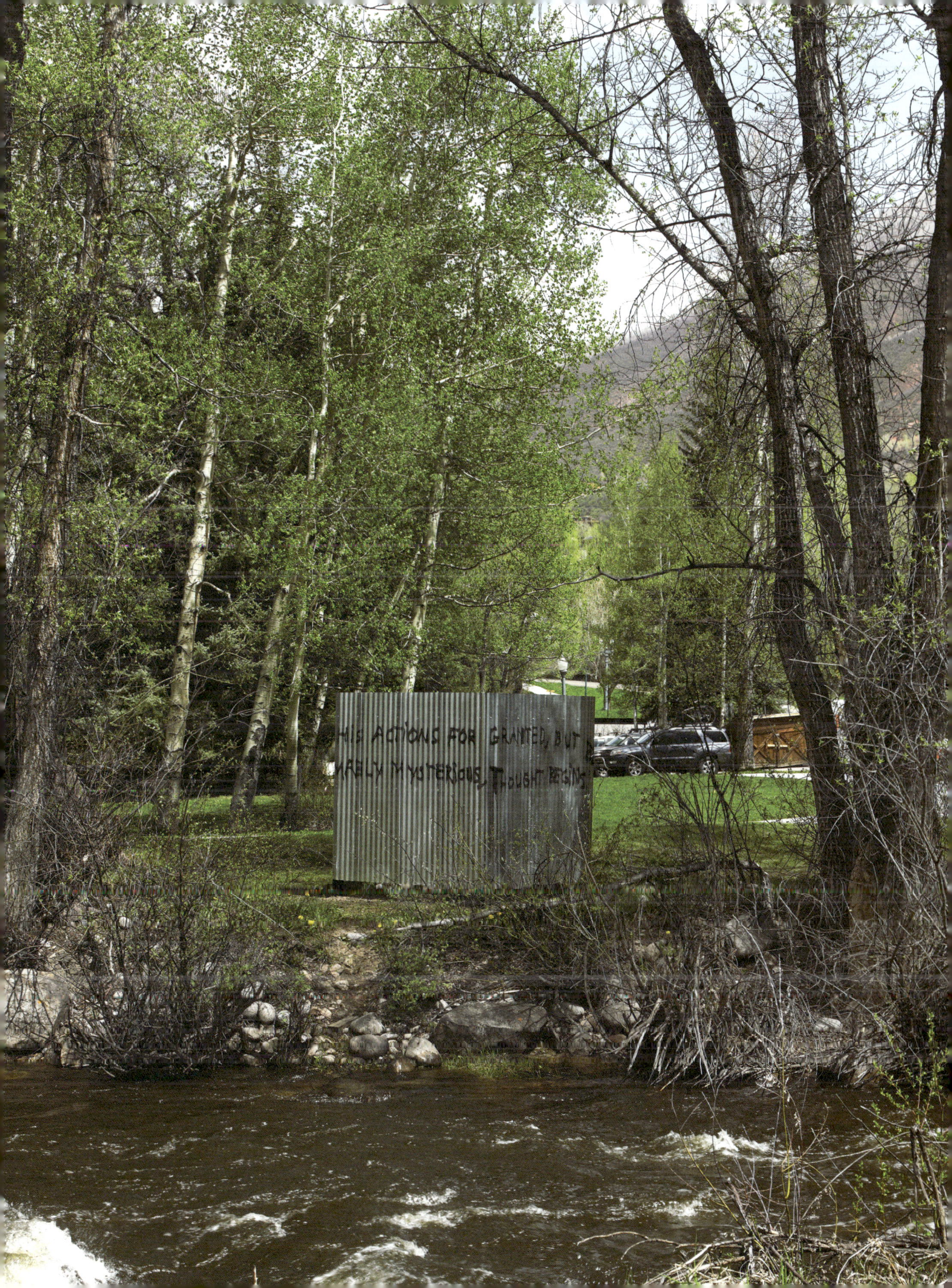
HIS ACTIONS FOR GRANTED, BUT
RELY MYSTERIOUS THOUGHT BEGINS

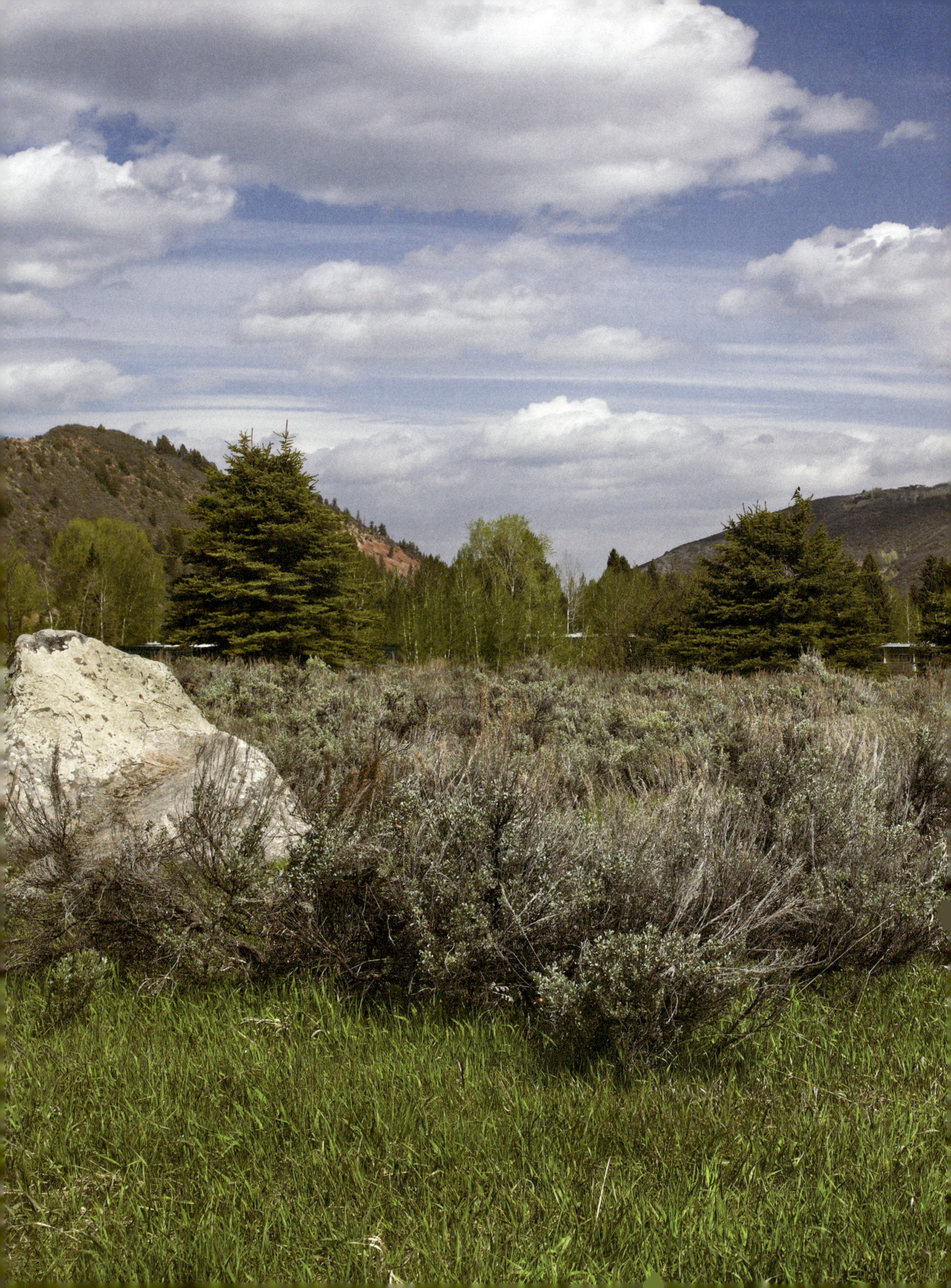

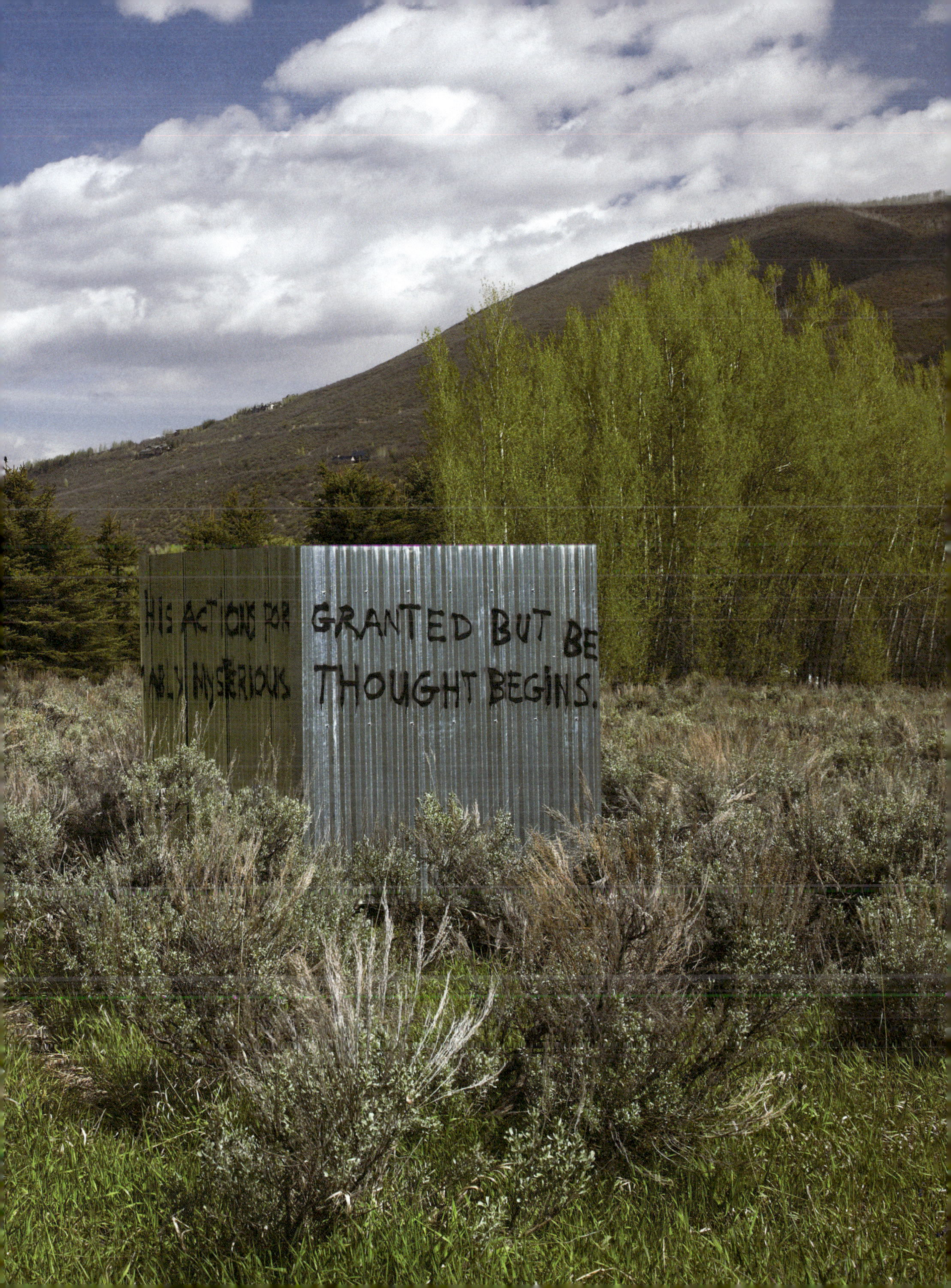
HIS ACTIONS FOR GRANTED BUT BE
NELY MYSTERIOUS THOUGHT BEGINS.

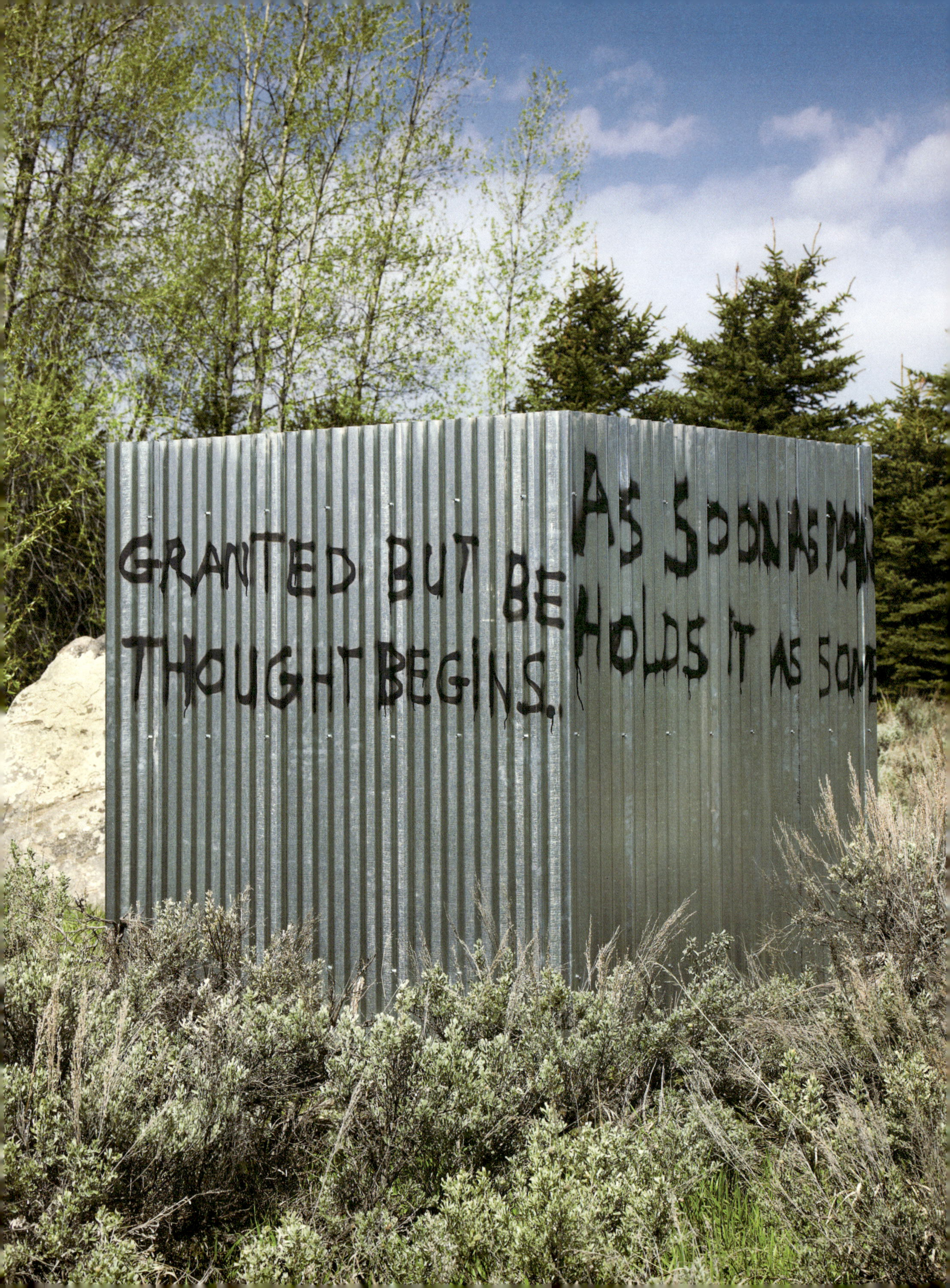
GRANTED BUT BE THOUGHT BEGINS.
AS SOON AS MAN HOLDS IT AS SOME

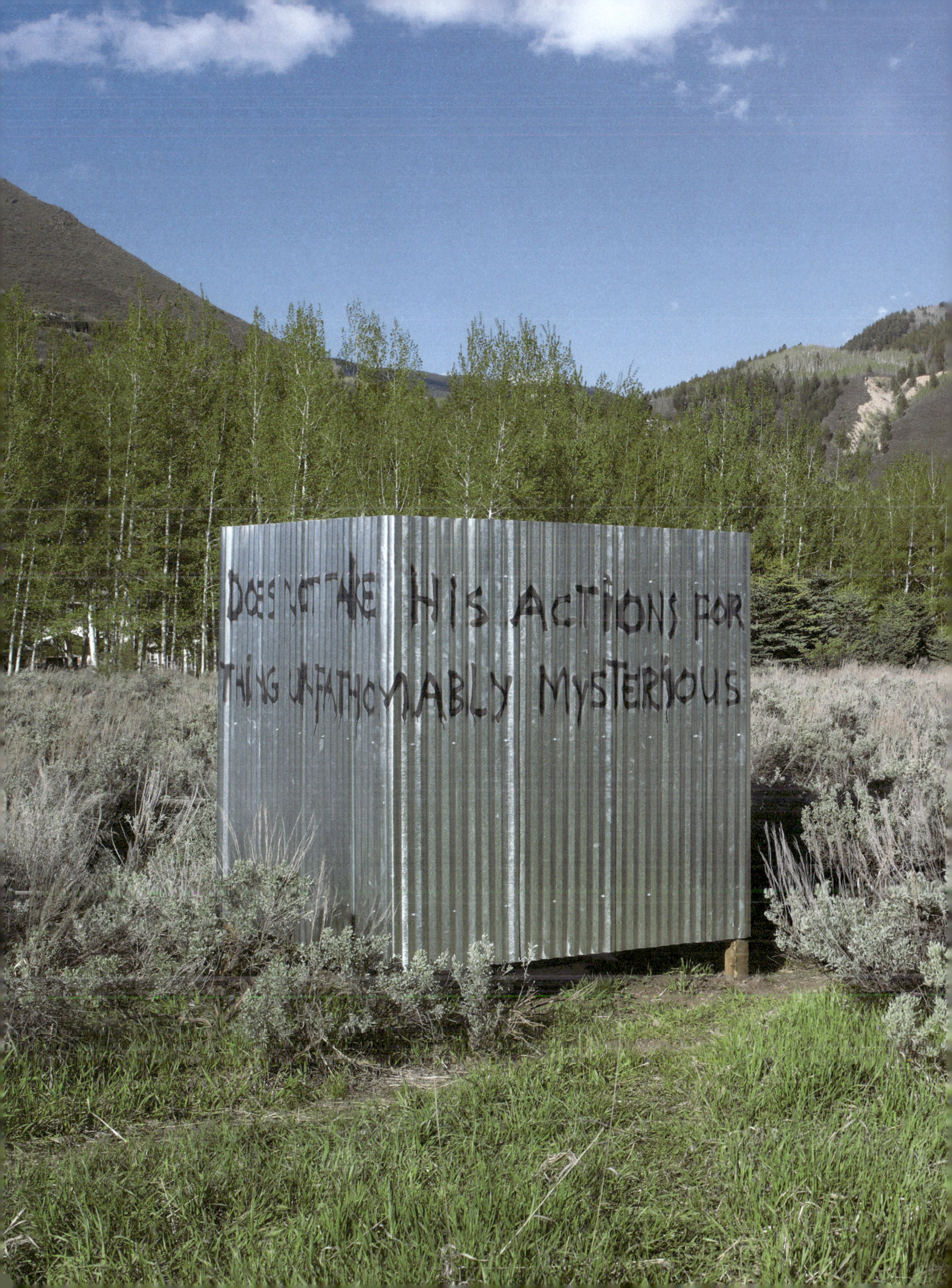
Does not take His Actions for
Thing unfathomably Mysterious

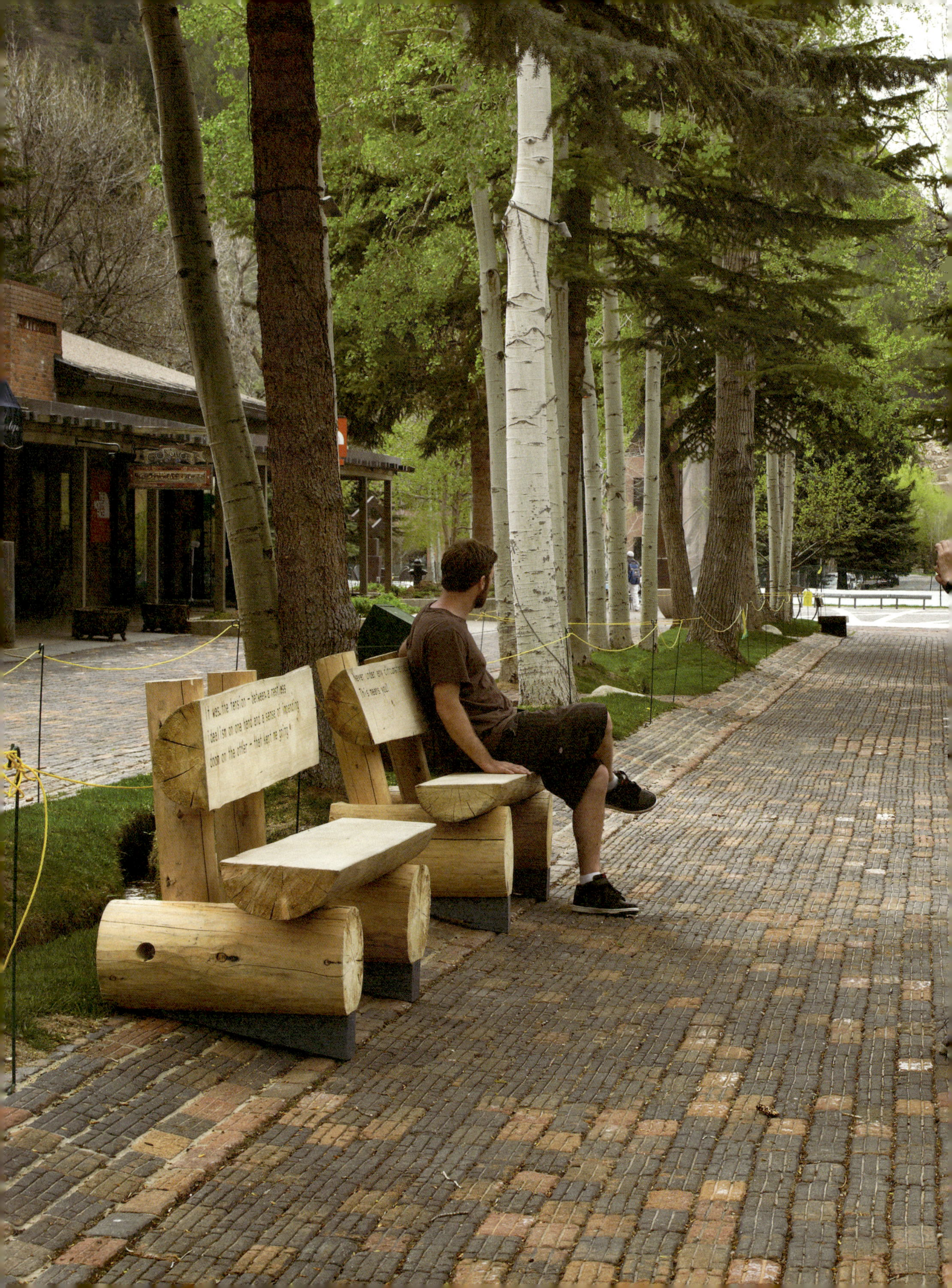
It was the tension – between a restless
idealism on one hand and a sense of impending
doom on the other – that kept me going.
Never ... any circumstance
This means you!

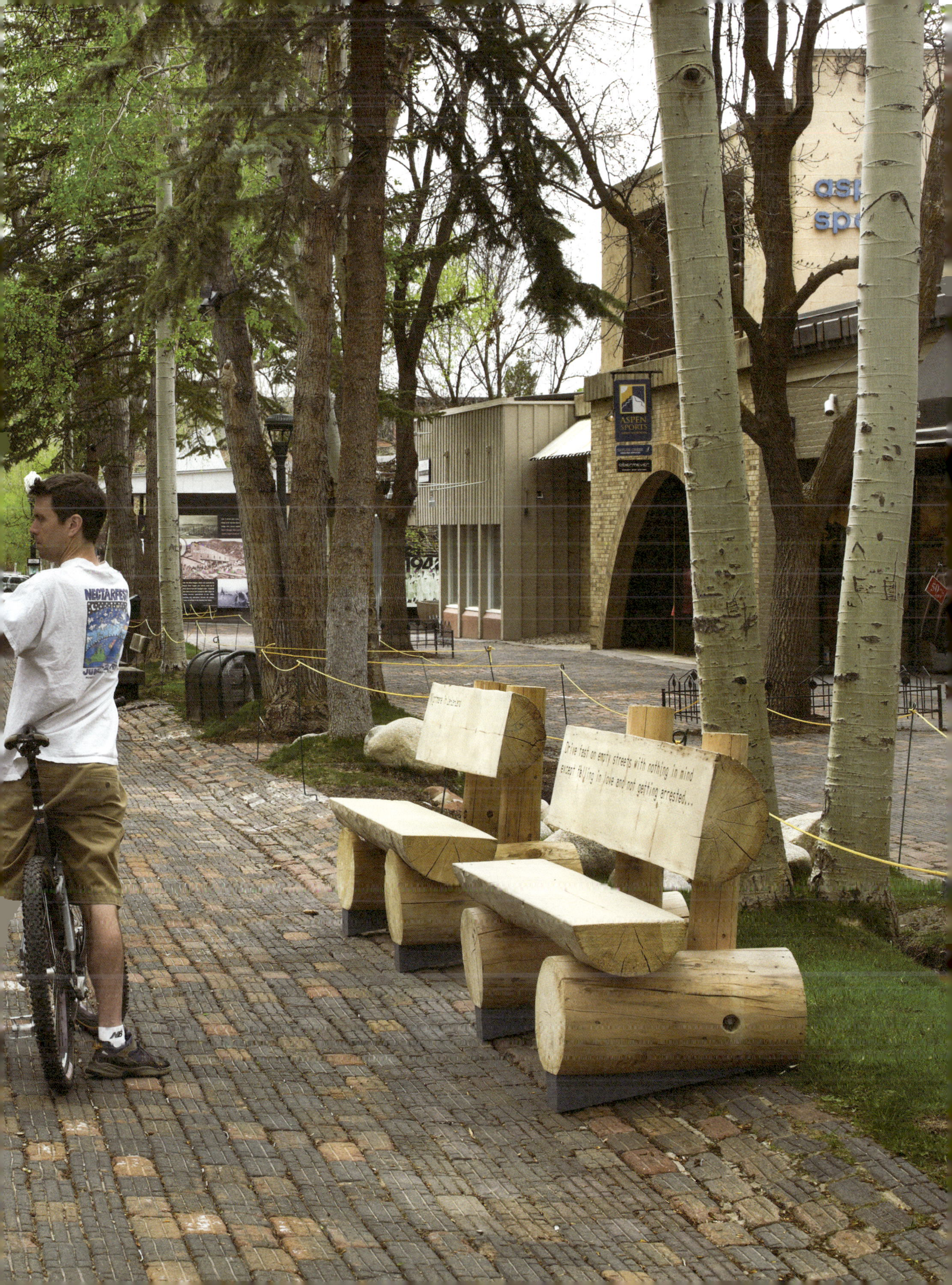

Drive fast on empty streets with nothing in mind
except falling in love and not getting arrested...

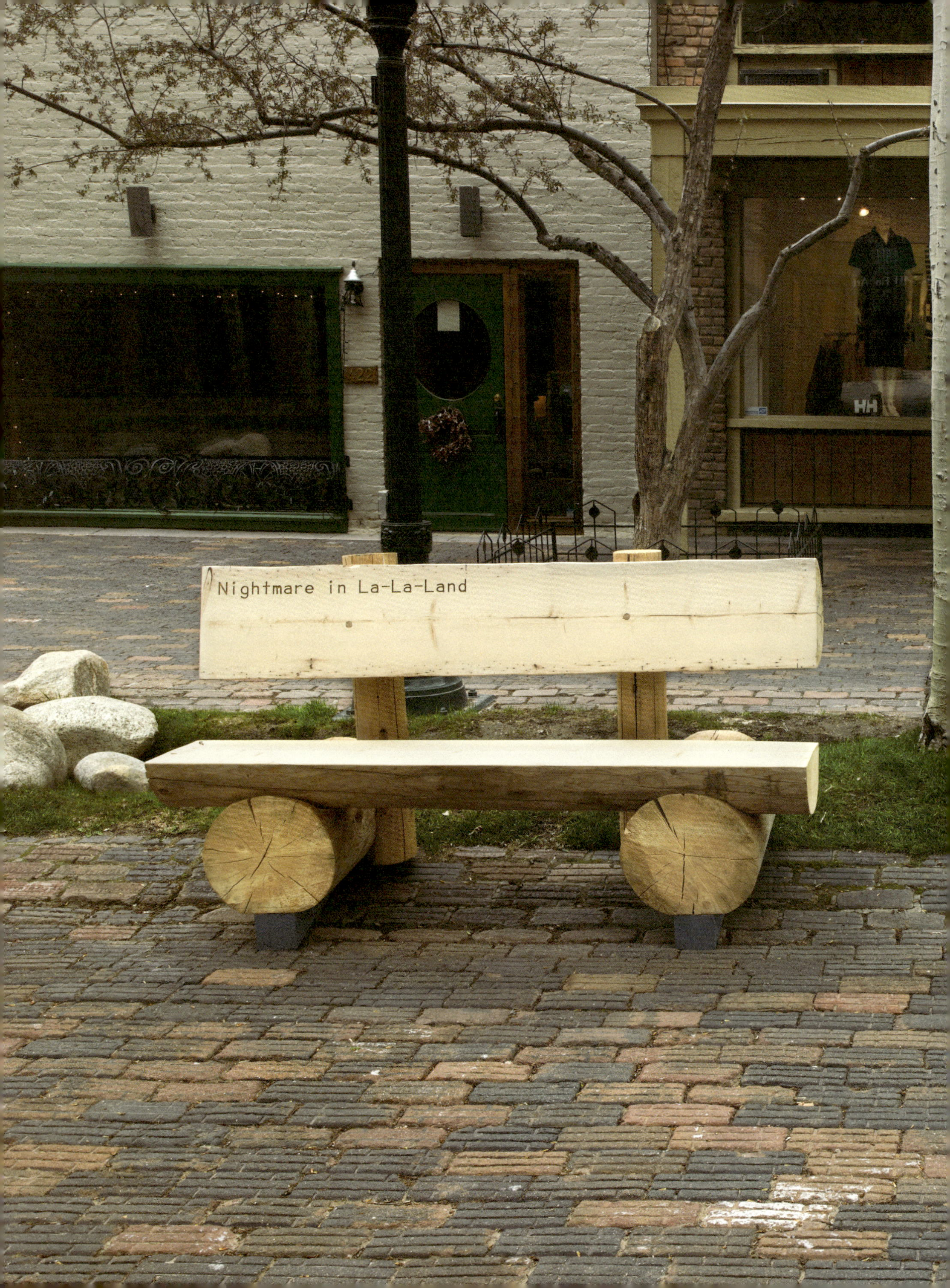
Nightmare in La-La-Land

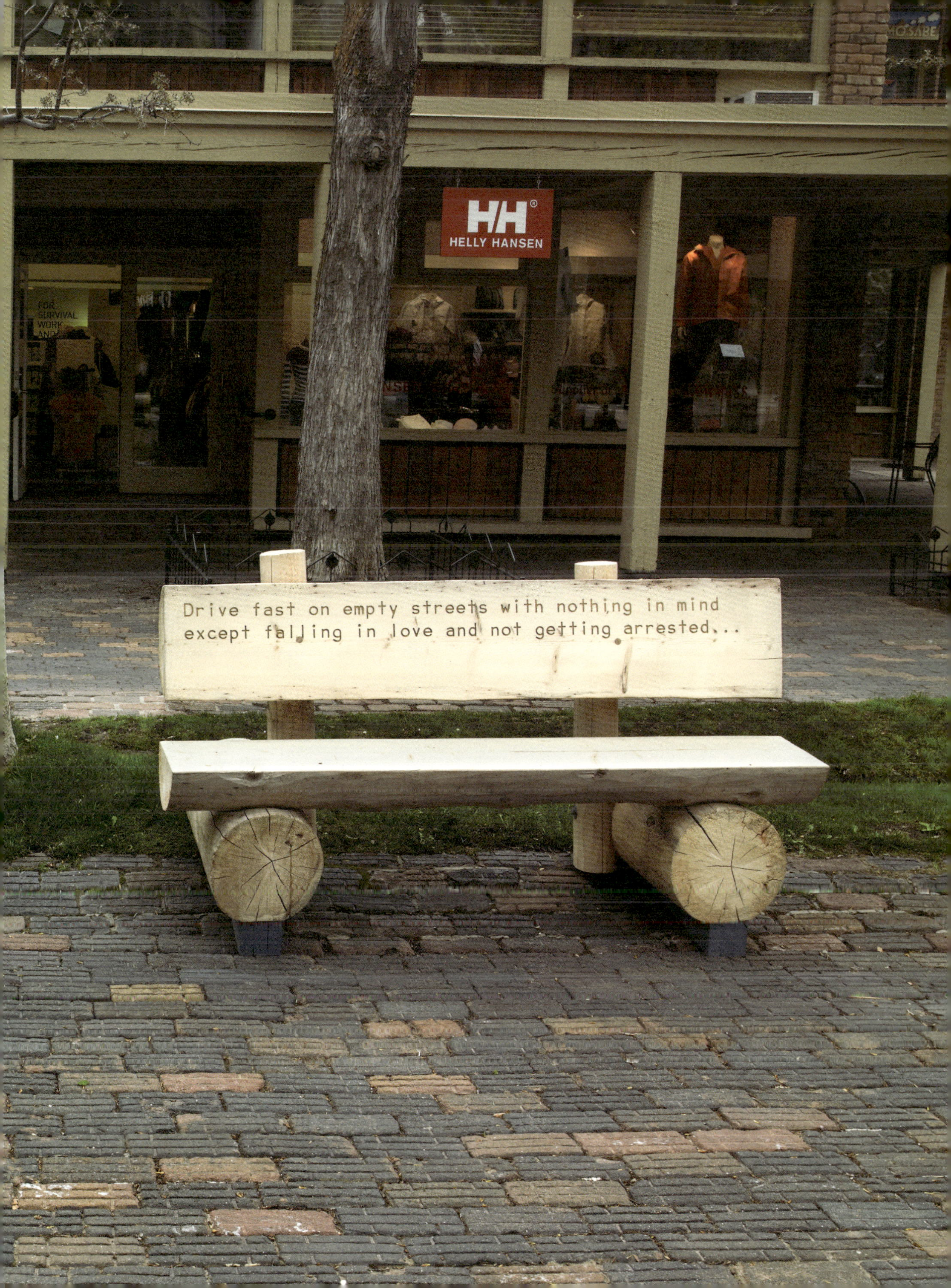

HELLY HANSEN
Drive fast on empty streets with nothing in mind
except falling in love and not getting arrested...

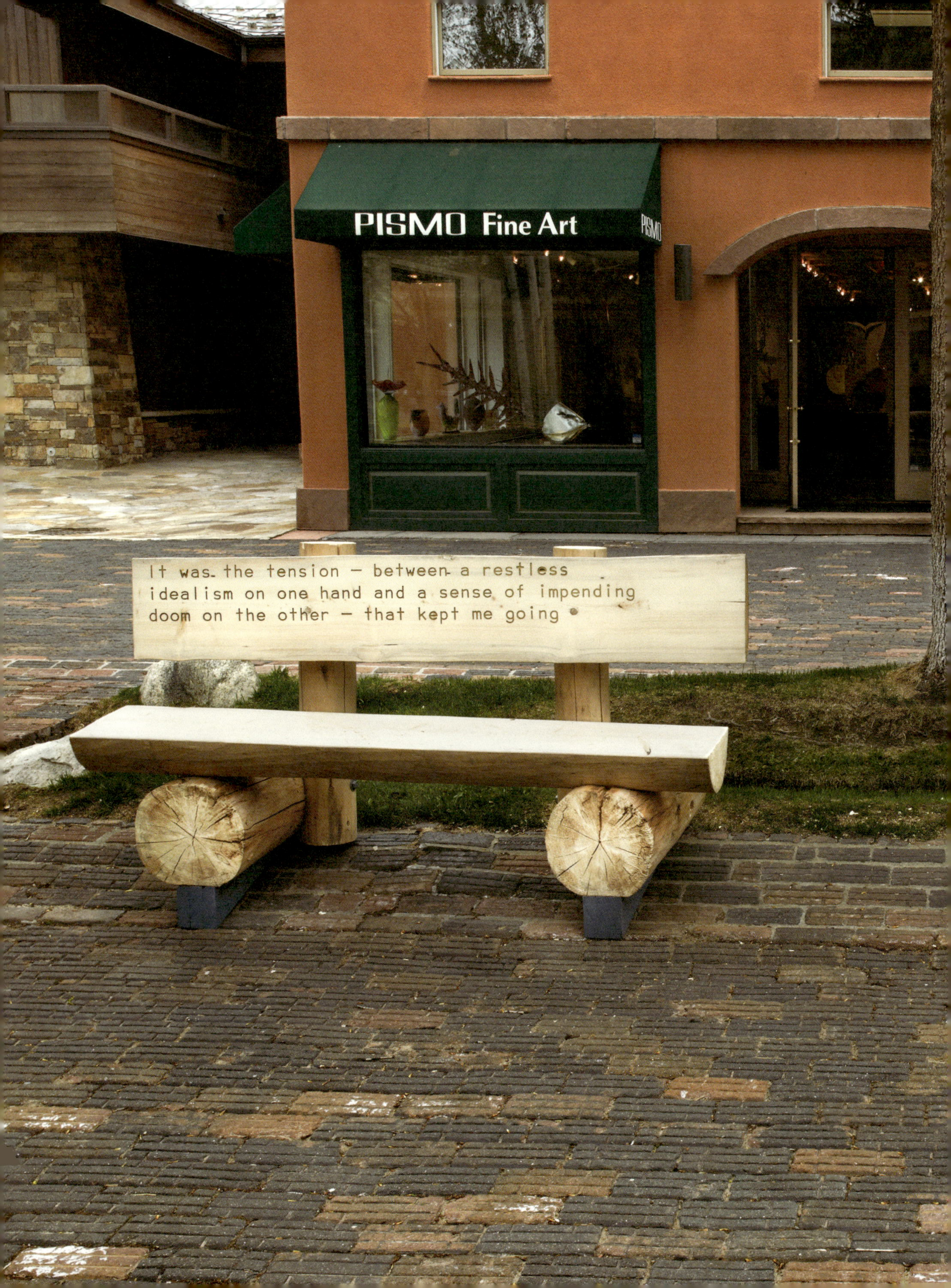

PISMO Fine Art
PISMO
It was the tension — between a restless
idealism on one hand and a sense of impending
doom on the other — that kept me going

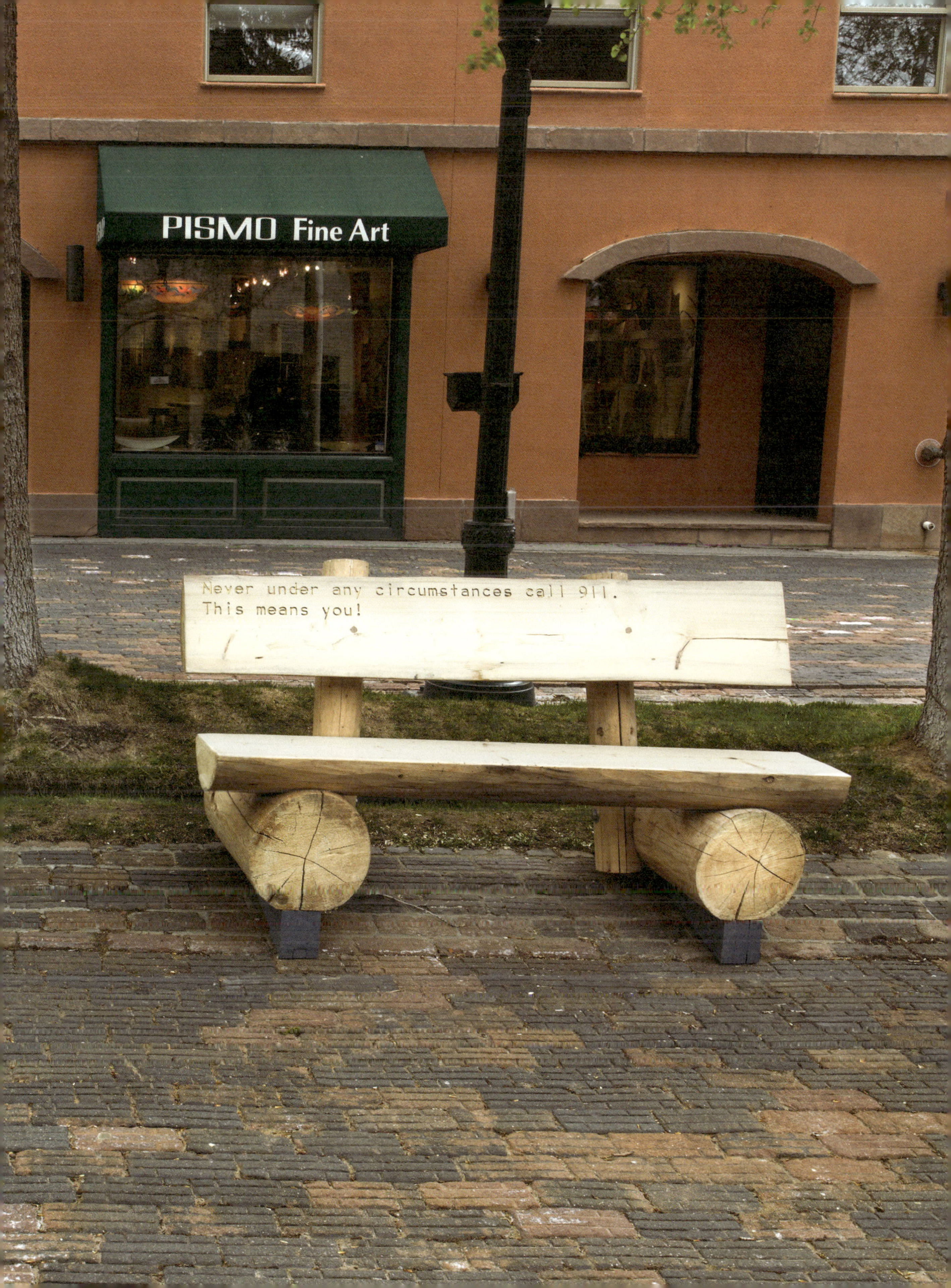

PISMO Fine Art
Never under any circumstances call 911.
This means you!

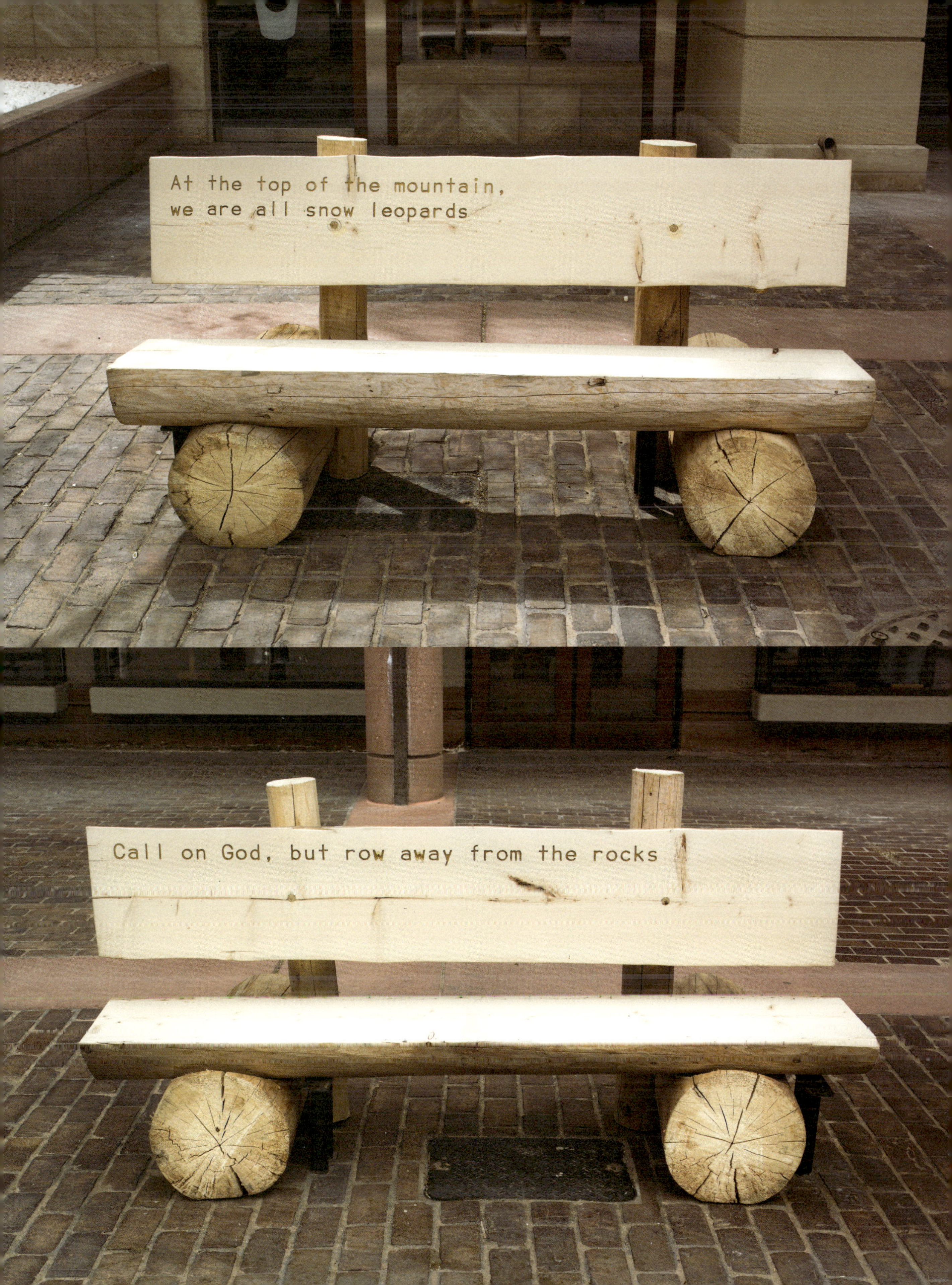
At the top of the mountain,
we are all snow leopards
Call on God, but row away from the rocks

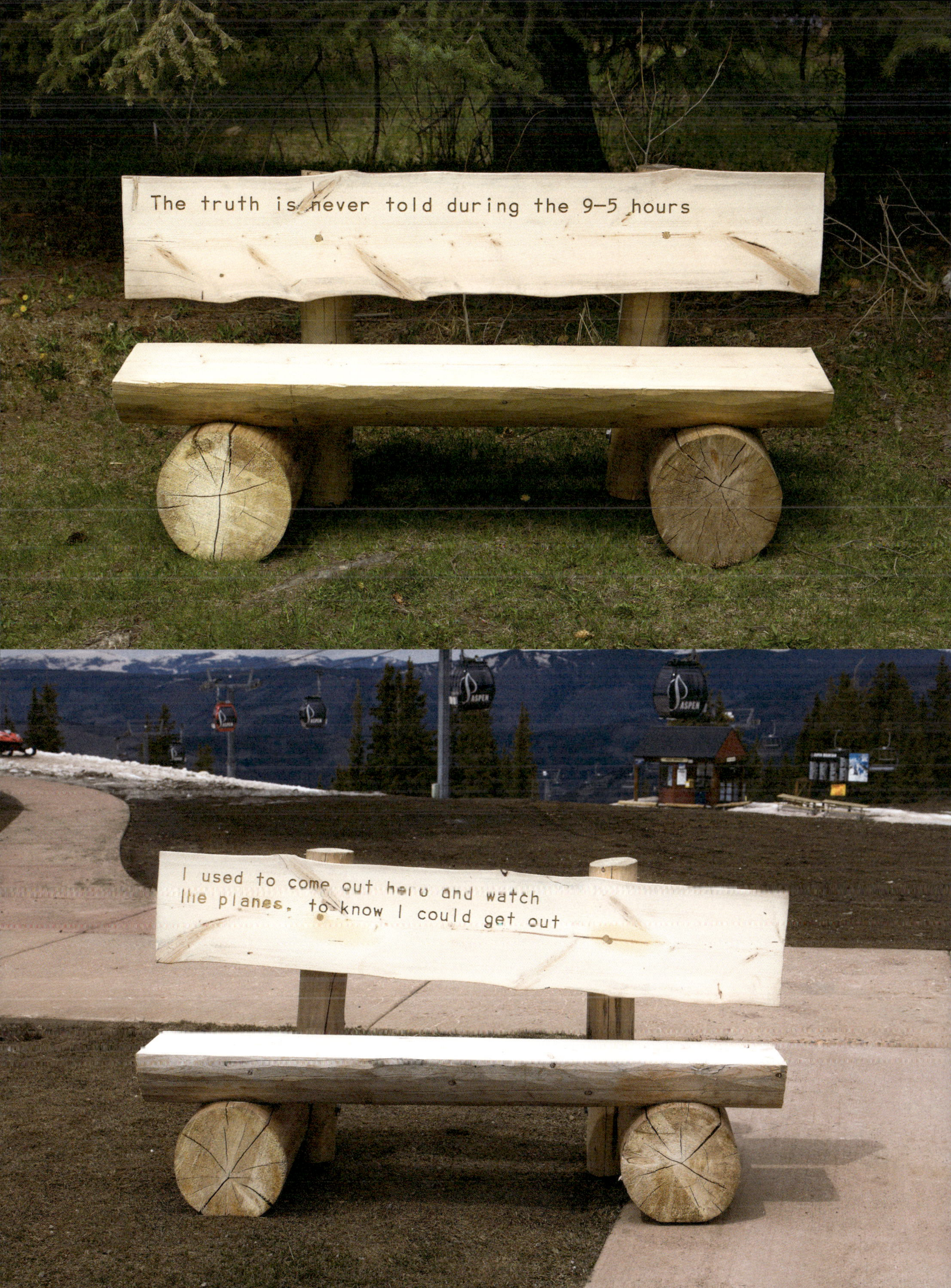
The truth is never told during the 9-5 hours
I used to come out here and watch
the planes, to know I could get out

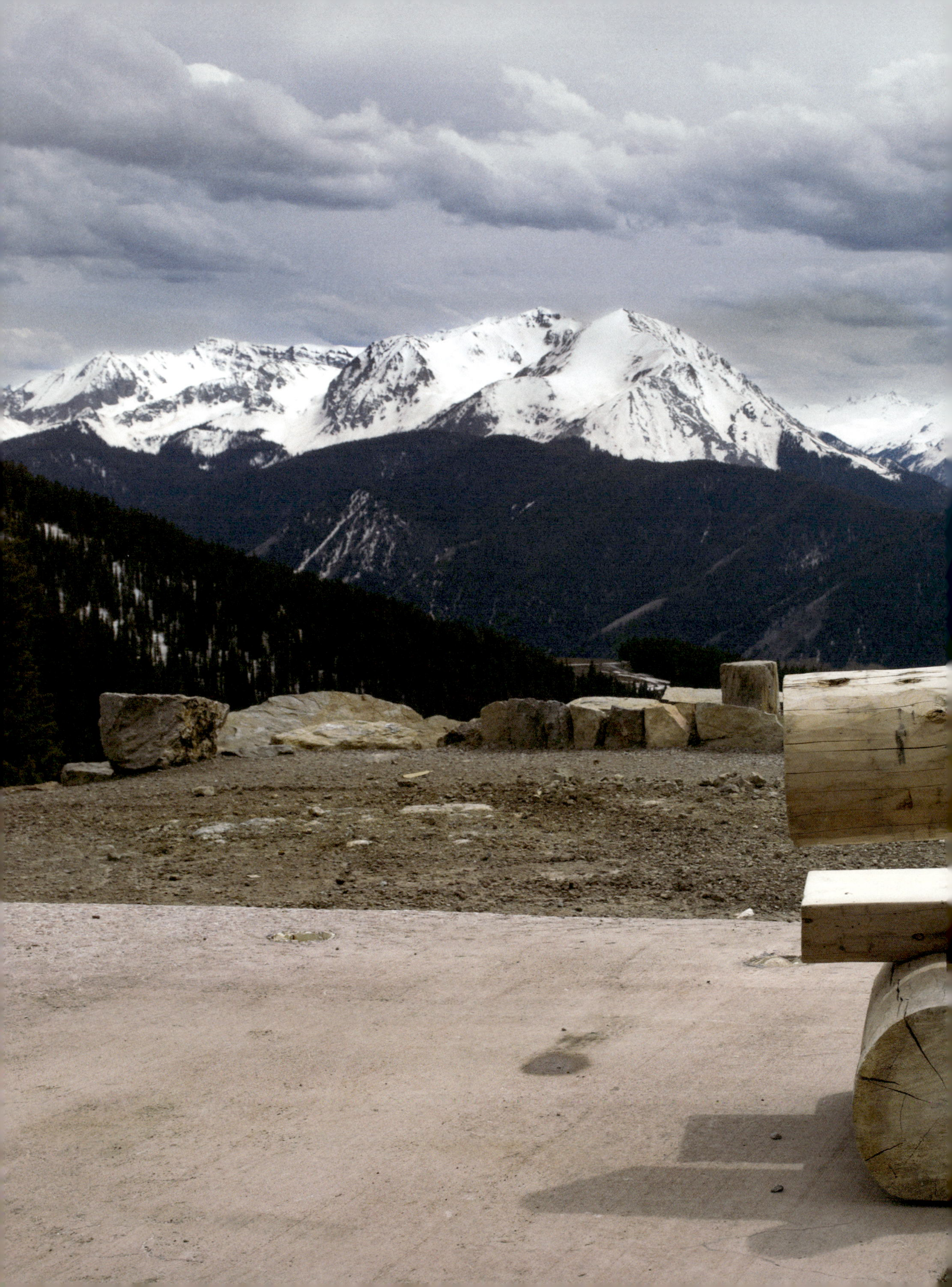

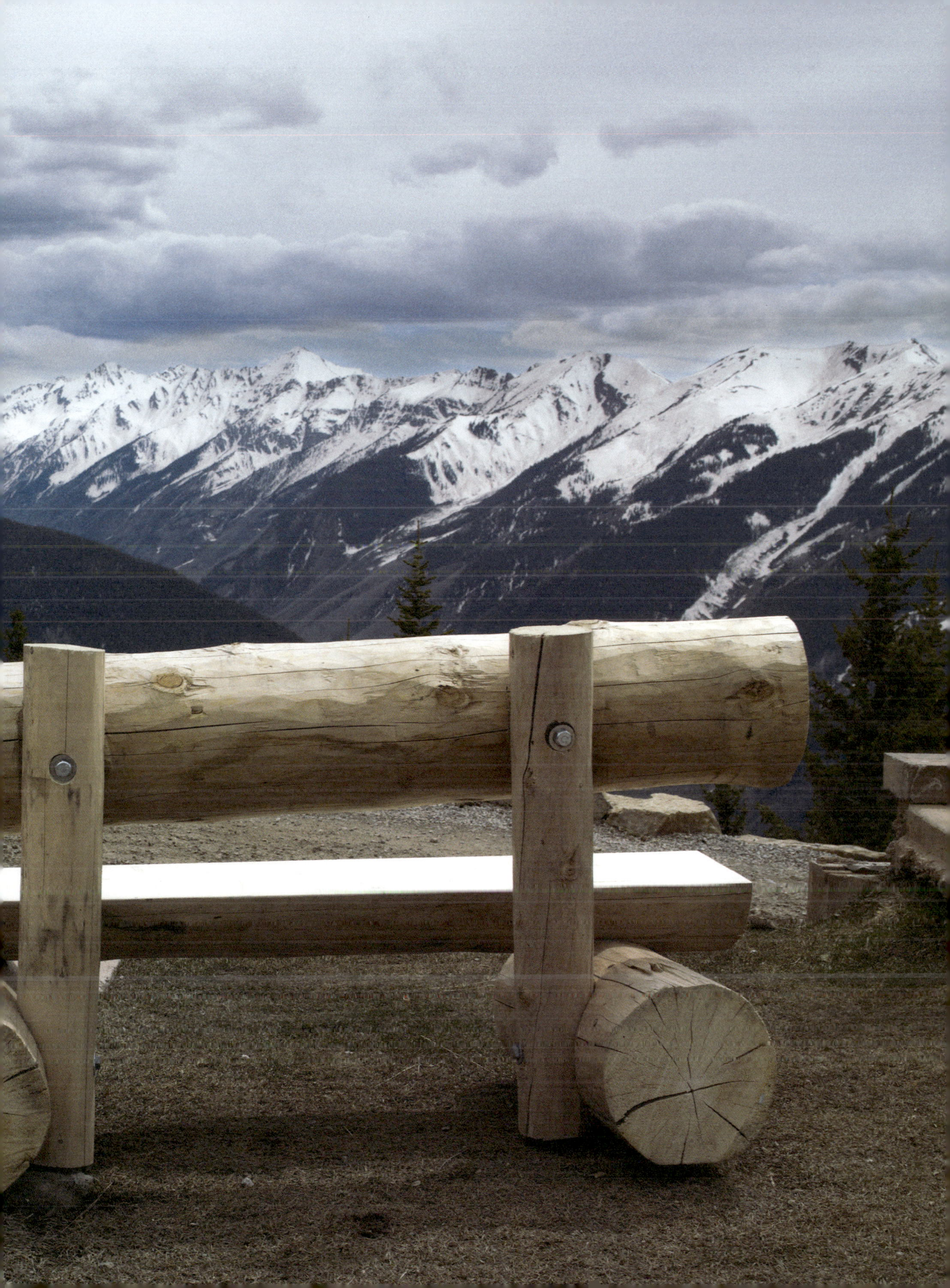

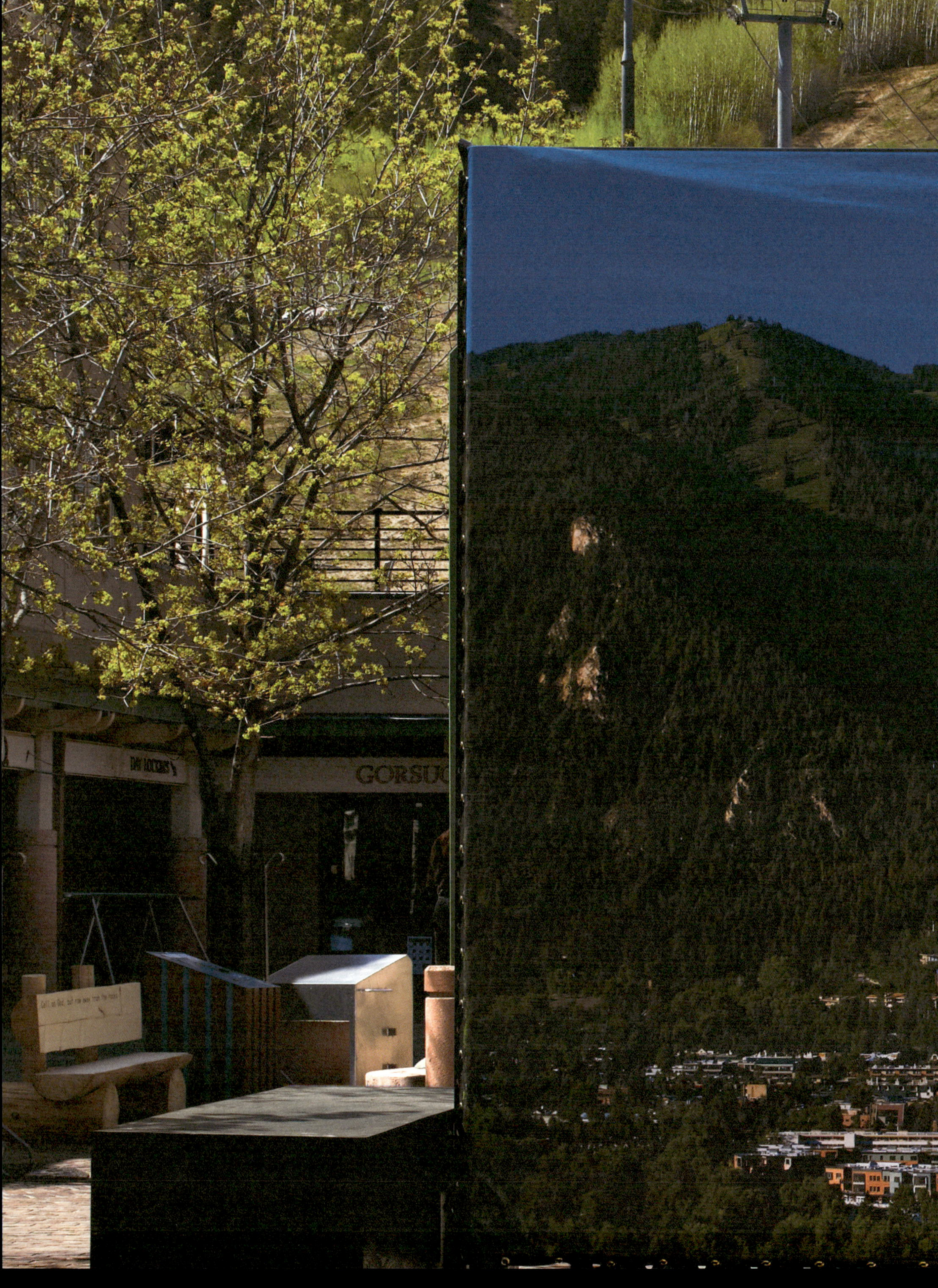

GORSUC

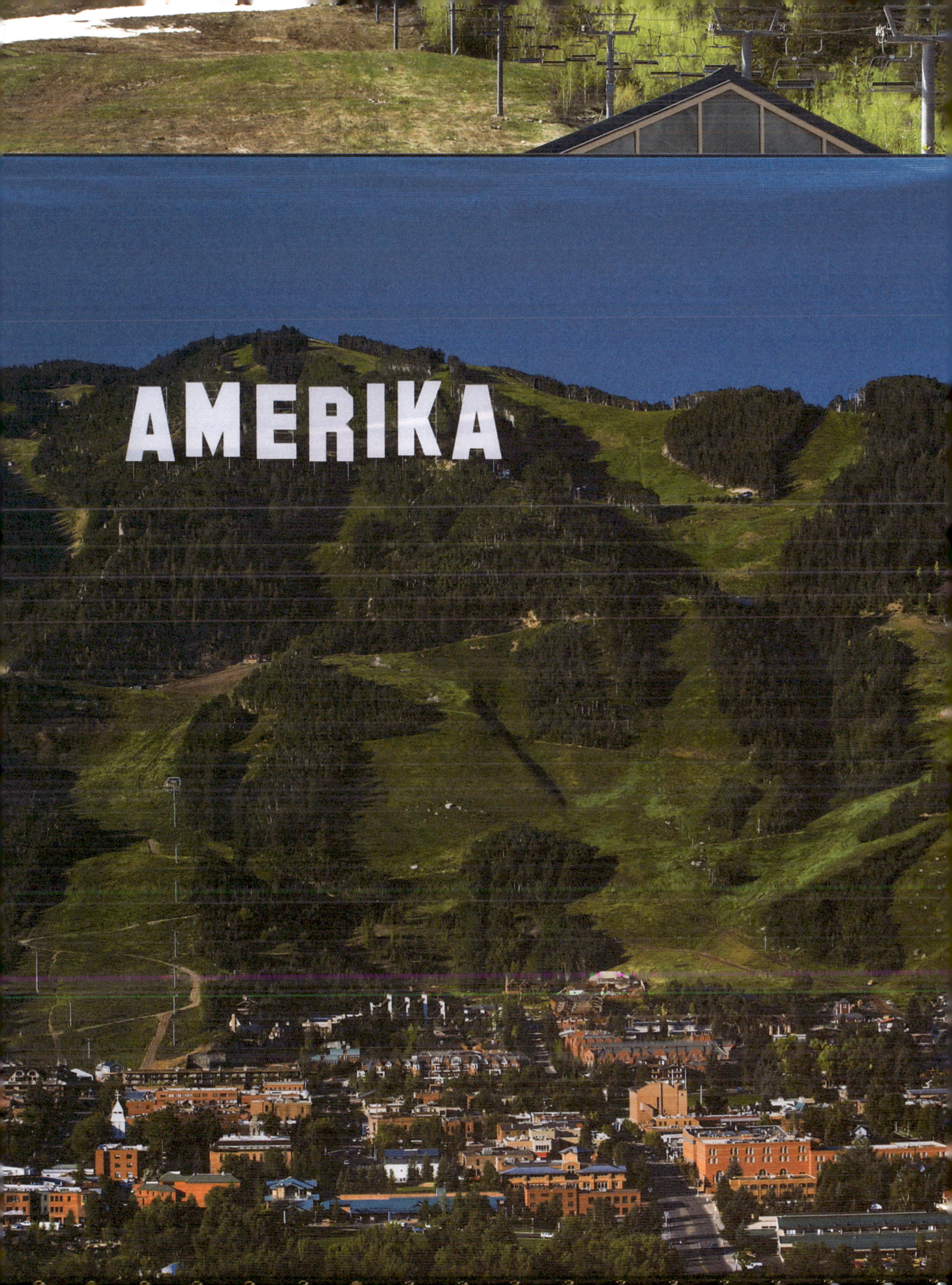
AMERIKA

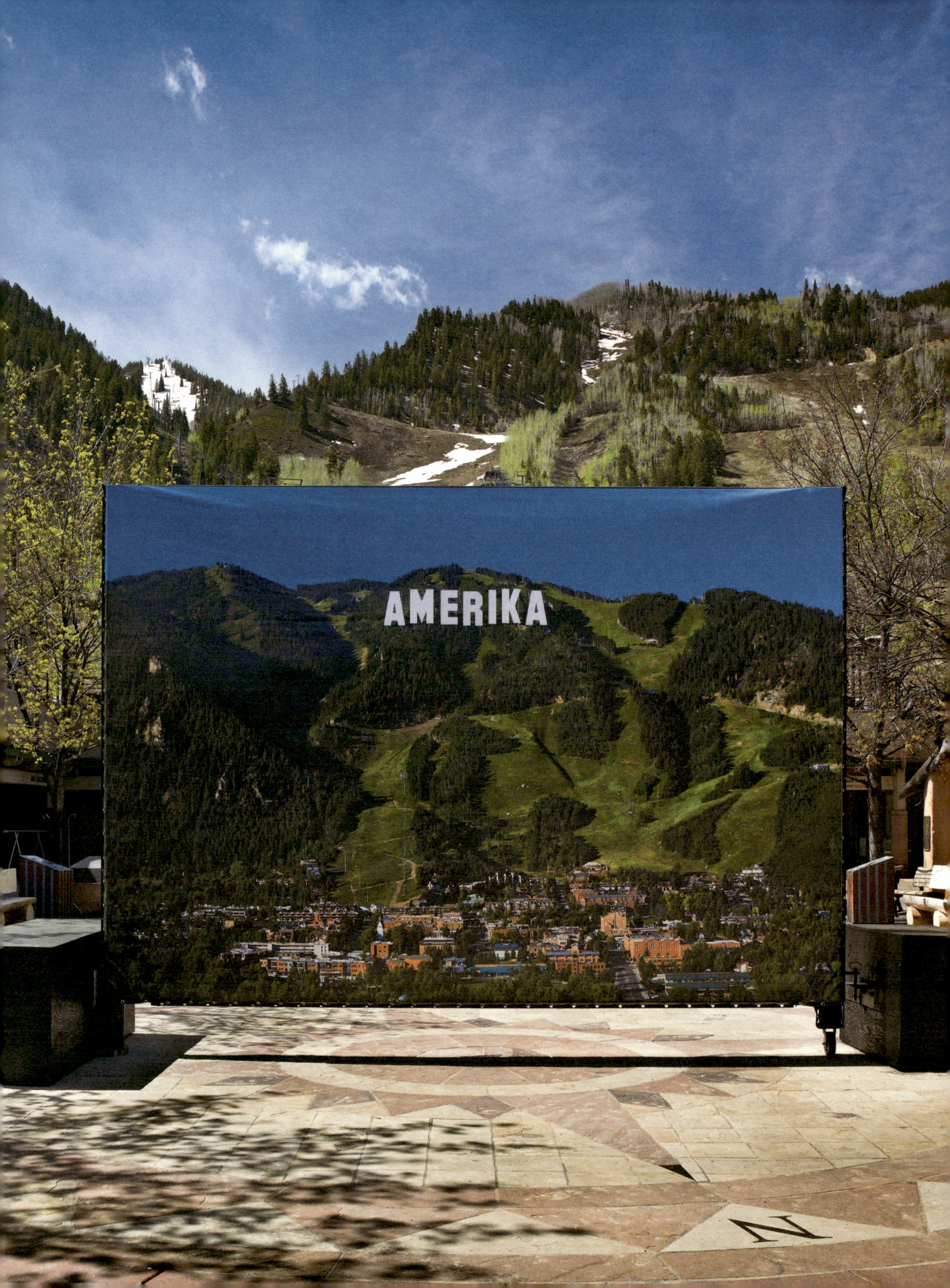
AMERIKA

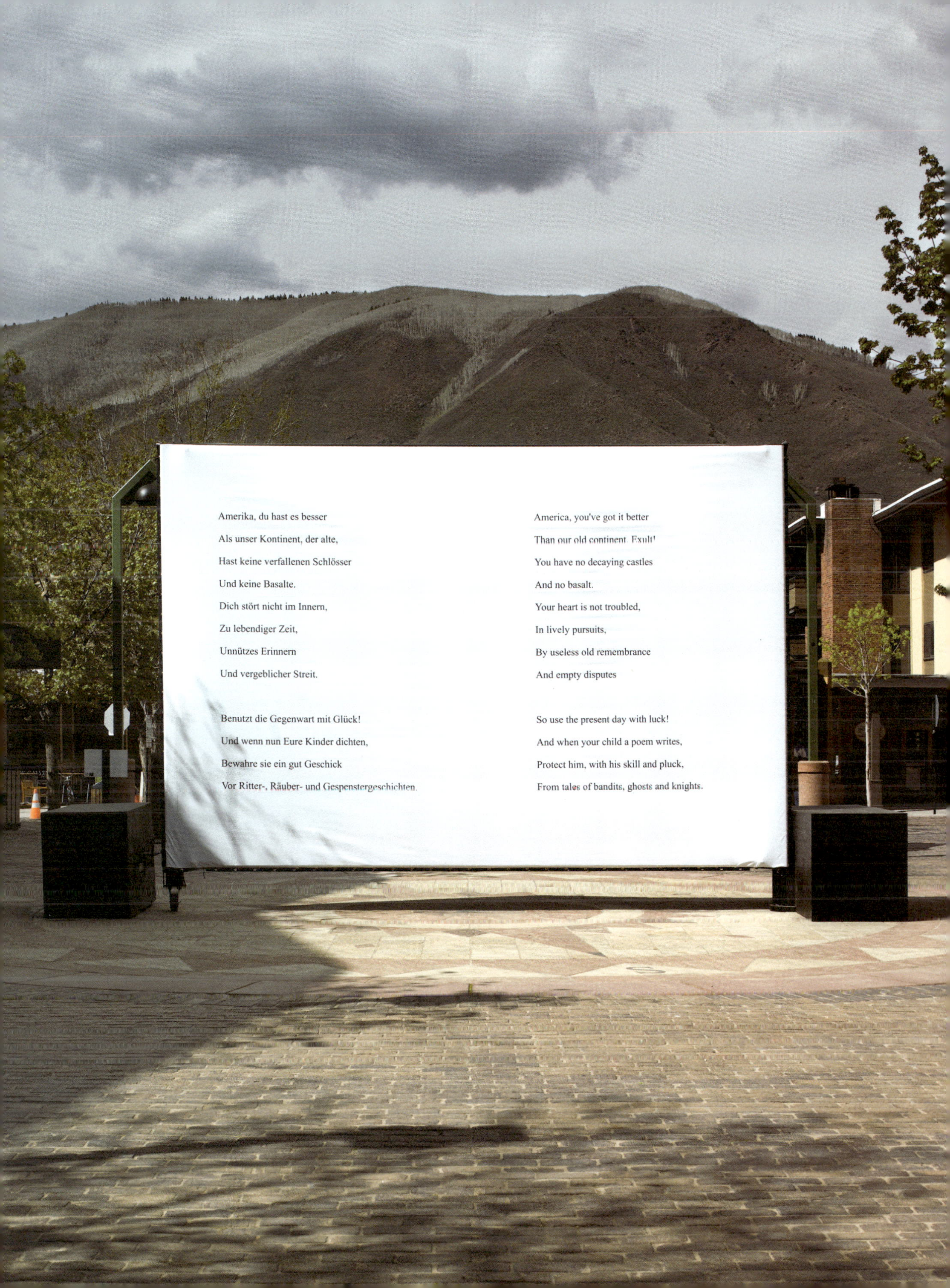
Amerika, du hast es besser

Als unser Kontinent, der alte,

Hast keine verfallenen Schlösser

Und keine Basalte.

Dich stört nicht im Innern,

Zu lebendiger Zeit,

Unnützes Erinnern

Und vergeblicher Streit.

Benutzt die Gegenwart mit Glück!

Und wenn nun Eure Kinder dichten,

Bewahre sie ein gut Geschick

Vor Ritter-, Räuber- und Gespenstergeschichten.

America, you've got it better

Than our old continent. Exult!

You have no decaying castles

And no basalt.

Your heart is not troubled,

In lively pursuits,

By useless old remembrance

And empty disputes

So use the present day with luck!

And when your child a poem writes,

Protect him, with his skill and pluck,

From tales of bandits, ghosts and knights.

It is too late now

Heidi Zuckerman Jacobson

Restlessness is having an uneasy, unsettled heart, mind, or physical body. Empathy is understanding and profoundly associating with the emotions of another. To be restlessly empathetic is to wander among the feelings of others and alternately reflect upon one's own emotions. Restless empathy allows commonalities and differences among people to be highlighted through an interaction with situations or objects. Much as restlessness is difficult to control, empathy cannot be dictated. These open-ended interactions are the goal of the *Restless Empathy* exhibition. They are non-biased, non-prescribed, non-mandatory—yet filled with opportunity.

I have heard that one cannot compare one's inside to anyone else's outside. How well we know ourselves fluctuates, and no one can know the reality of anyone else's mind, body, or spirit. The complexity of knowing both oneself and one's community affects social interactions. Our reality is filled with myriad comparisons of physical beauty, age, weight, and wealth. As such, the emotional exchange between people is often centered on competition and jealousy, rather than empathy. Art can help us examine rigid oppositions or even conflicts.

When the French curator Nicolas Bourriaud published a book entitled *Relational Aesthetics* in 1998, he described what he termed a new movement in art that focused more on the social interaction of art making than on the private practice of the individual artist. Some heralded this change as making art more widely accessible and inclusive. He based his characterizations on what he described as a way of working that resulted from the interests of the individual artists. The artist Tobias Rehberger has said, "An amazing thing in art is that the creation of an artwork always happens within the viewer."[1] In some of Rehberger's early projects, he had the museum attendants at the Städtisches Museum Abteiberg in Mönchengladbach knit sweaters from patterns he created; had the guards at the 1997 Venice Biennale wear underwear designed by the artist; and hired artisans in Cameroon to build classic European Modernist chairs according to his sketches. As Martin Pesch wrote in *Frieze*, "Rehberger is not an artist intent on his own particular mode of expression, but rather a person who, through his art, wants to understand more about the structures and relations in which he works."[2] In general, works associated with *Relational Aesthetics* require the participation of the viewers in various ways, including eating food, adding their objects to a larger installation, or in any other way following directions prescribed by the artist.

Bourriaud defines aesthetics as an idea that sets humankind apart from other animal species. He sees artists as facilitators, rather than makers, and regards art as information exchanged between the artist and the viewer.[3] He proposes that the role of artworks is no longer to form imaginary and utopian realities, but to actually be ways of living and models of action.[4] Consequently, much of the art produced in the 1990s on which he was focused is "open-ended, interactive, and resistant to closure, often appearing to be a work in progress rather than a completed object."[5] Relational art needs the contingencies of its environment and audience, and it is often responsible for creating both.

The critic Claire Bishop details that "this audience is envisaged as a community: rather than a one-to-one relationship between work of art and viewer, relational art sets up situations in which viewers are not just addressed as a collective, social entity, but are actually given the wherewithal to create a community, however temporary or utopian this may be."[6] Art can build, as well as question, communities in a variety of ways. In Jens Haaning's *Turkish Jokes* (1994) (fig. 1), the artist broadcast funny stories told in Turkish through a loudspeaker placed in a public square in Oslo. His effort facilitated the production of a micro-community, one made up of immigrants brought together by collective laughter that may in fact be in direct contrast to daily exile.[7] The development of these temporary groupings is created through the exhibition of art that expresses not only an opportunity to have them form, but also

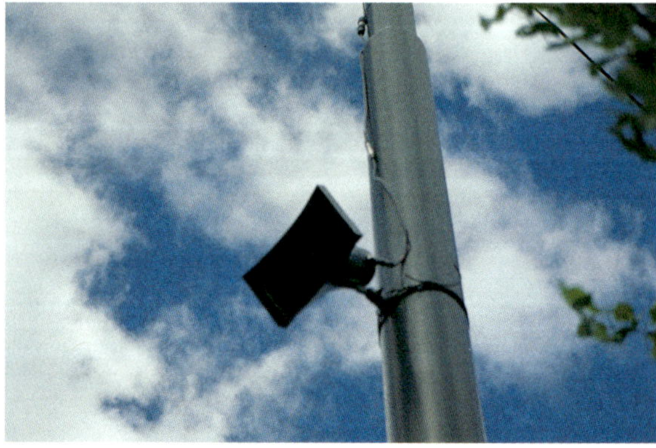

Fig. 1
Jens Haaning
Turkish Jokes, 1994
Installation view in the Turkish area of central Oslo, Norway

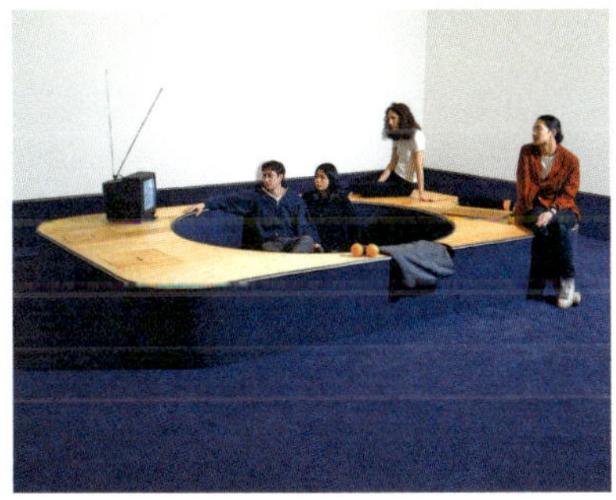

Fig. 2
Andrea Zittel
Prototype for A to Z Pit Bed, 1995
Installation view, Andrea Rosen Gallery, New York, 1995

an interest. The degree of participation required of the viewer by the artist, along with the nature of the works and the models of sociability proposed, all effect the potential exchange.[8]

Bourriaud claims that instead of seeking a "utopian" agenda, late-twentieth-century artists seek only to find provisional solutions in the here and now. Instead of trying to change their environment, these artists are simply "learning to inhabit the world in a better way" because "it seems more pressing to invent possible relations with our neighbors in the present than to bet on happier tomorrows."[9]

Andrea Zittel's long-term project, The A-Z Enterprise, is, however, utopian in that it encompasses all aspects of day-to-day living. Zittel explores home furniture, clothing, and food as sites of an investigation in an ongoing endeavor to better understand human nature and the social construction of needs.[10] *Prototype for A-Z Pit Bed* (1995/2002) (fig. 2) resembles a kind of hot tub for office-like gatherings, though with no apparently clear function. Zittel creates objects that can indeed be functional, but that allow the viewer/user to select and impose any practical application.[11] *The Smock Shop* (fig. 3) is a recent project in which the artist has "given" the pattern for her utilitarian and primary piece of clothing to a variety of artists to use as a means of generating their own income. The pattern has also been placed online as a downloadable PDF so that anyone can make one and wear or sell it.

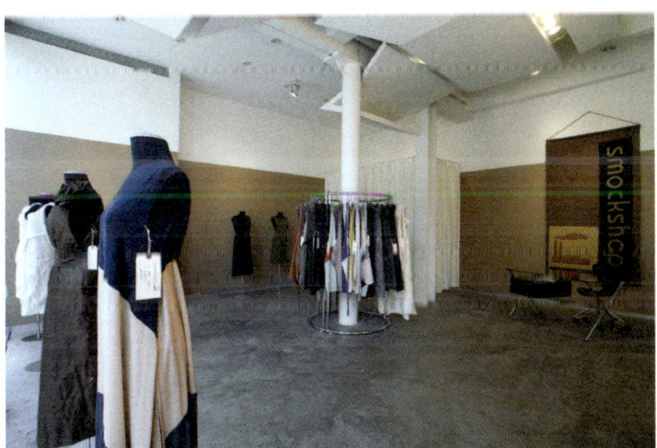

Fig. 3
Andrea Zittel
Smock Shop, 2007
Installation view, Susan Inglett Gallery, New York

Much of this work revives the structural form of artworks produced in the 1960s and 1970s, with the addition of a strong emphasis on the connection between artists and their audience.[12] But art has always been relational in varying degrees. When a viewer encounters a work of art, that exchange, whether visual, intellectual, or physical, creates a space within human relations that can fit, or not fit, harmoniously and openly within the overall system.[13]

In Rikrit Tiravanija's *Untitled (Free)* (1992) (fig. 4), the artist effectively moved the "unseen rooms" of the gallery into the public viewing spaces, including the office, storage, and registration areas. Consequently, the owner and employees of the gallery were on display in the main gallery space. Tiravanija was there too, cooking Thai curry that was offered to gallery visitors. The recipe was also left with the gallery staff, so food was still prepared and distributed when the artist was not there. As the critic Stewart Martin wrote, "Social relations that are usually hidden or subordinate to 'the work' become foregrounded, become the work."[14] I recall seeing the exhibition at 303 Gallery in 1992, and remember the work as having a terrific sense of humor, as well as reflecting the generous hospitality for which Thai culture is known. Yes, Tiravanija insists on interacting with "viewers" in order for his work to be made,[15] but works by the artist that include the sharing of food encompass a camaraderie and inclusiveness that are often absent in subsequent critical accounts.

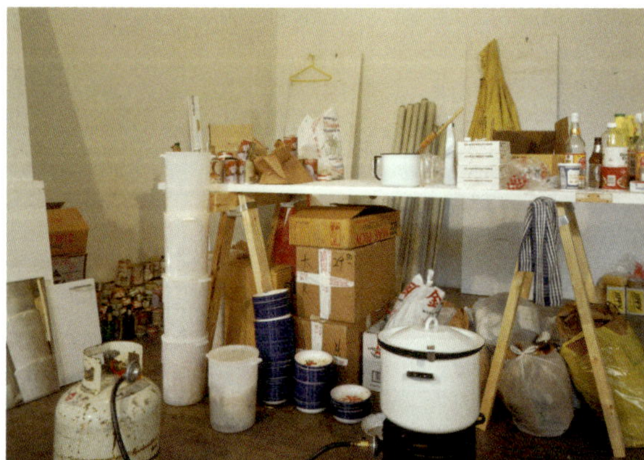

Fig. 4
Rirkrit Tiravanija
Untitled (Free), 1992
Installation view 303 Gallery, New York

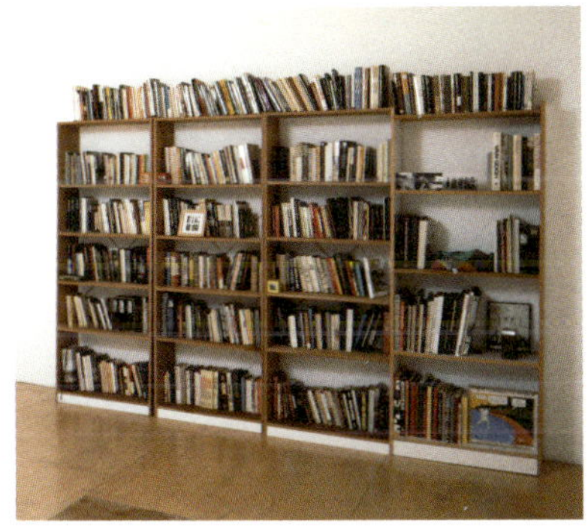

Fig. 5
Jorge Pardo
Portrait of George Porcari, 1995

Jorge Pardo's works straddle the line between art and design. Many of them are objects that have a functional quality. An early work, *Portrait of George Pocari* (1995) (fig. 5), is both practical and conceptual and, like other work associated with Relational Aesthetics, it could not exist without the contributions of its subject. The work is a set of large bookshelves on which all of George Pocari's books are placed. It is a nontraditional portrait that invites "knowing" Pocari through observing the books he collects.[16]

Felix Gonzalez-Torres's work is also included in Bourriard's formulation, but it is perhaps the exception more than the rule. Gonzalez-Torres's practice was diverse and wide-ranging, including a series consisting of elements that were to be taken away by the viewer, primarily stacks of printed paper and candy. These works are unlimited in their quantity, though the decision to replenish them rests with the owner. They are also successful as pure sculptural objects. The interactivity that results from the objects perpetuates through human exchange—they are free to be taken away to homes and offices or, in the case of the candy, unwrapped, placed in the mouths of viewers, and eaten. *"Untitled" (Ross)* (1991) (fig. 6) is a nontraditional portrait by the artist memorializing a specific person, his deceased lover (Ross), including a particular candy the two enjoyed while in Italy.[17] But the work also generously offers the viewer a chance to participate in an intimate moment. The spirit of generosity in Gonzales-Torres's work is built upon by later artists, including some of those included in the *Restless Empathy* exhibition.

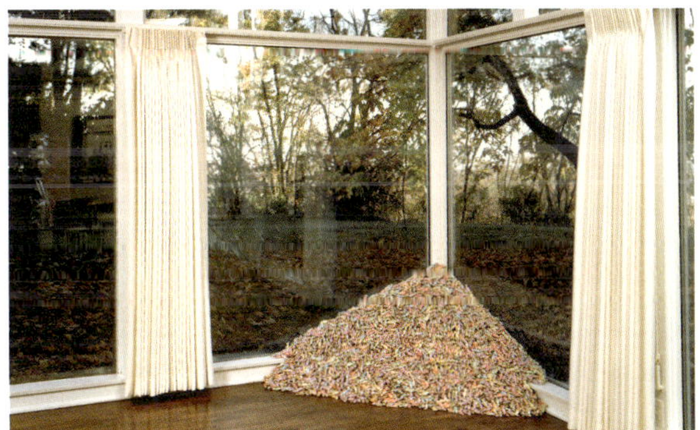

Fig. 6
Felix Gonzalez-Torres
"Untitled" (Ross), 1991
Installation view at the home of Karen and Andy Stillpass, Cincinnati, 1992
© Felix Gonzalez-Torres Foundation

Intimacy was also a factor in a 1974 performance entitled *I Like America* and *America Likes Me*, in which Joseph Beuys lived in a room with a coyote eight hours a day for three days. At the end of the performance the artist hugged the coyote, which had grown quite tolerant of him, and left the space. The work commented, among other things, on the possibilities of harmonious existence.

Within *Relational Aesthetics*, the notion of the viewer "completing" a work of art usually involves a demand placed upon the audience. As such, the viewer becomes instrumentalized within the work itself. Without the interaction/participation of the viewer/participant, the work of art as outlined by the artist would fail to exist. In such cases, art may need the viewer more than the viewer needs the art. Such a relationship is not sustainable.

Restless Empathy includes the work of eight artists— Allora & Calzadilla, Pawel Althamer, Marc Bijl, Lara Favaretto, Geof Oppenheimer, Lars Ø. Ramberg, Frances Stark, and Mark Wallinger—who have created new projects or rethought existing bodies of work and located them throughout the museum and the city of Aspen. While representing a wide range of practices and frames of reference, these artists share a capacity for creating and exploring empathy in unexpected ways. Bringing together artists who approach the idea of the poetic, through material, language, or gesture, *Restless Empathy* examines the complex process of entering the interior world of another—whether artist, viewer, or object—and seeking to make a connection. Rather than use people as a medium, the artists in *Restless Empathy* make markedly generous gestures toward the public, creating a space for unexpected experience through work characterized by a deep sincerity and moments of intimate surprise. *Restless Empathy* can be positioned as a post–*Relational Aesthetics* exhibition, not so much in that the works are in opposition to the earlier strategies, but rather that these artistic efforts have become so completely digested as to allow viewer participation to be a nonchalant occurrence. Artists no longer have to worry that viewers will fail to participate; other forms of engagement, such as restlessly empathetic ones, are suggested.

Allora & Calzadilla's work *Hope Hippo* (2005) was originally commissioned for the 51st Venice Biennale. The work in part responds to the literary and touristic image of Venice as an origin point of humanism. Animals serve a variety of allegorical functions in sculptures around Venice, including Andrea del Verrocchio's equestrian monument to the mercenary general Bartolomeo Colleoni. The artists explain, "In place of a war-horse whose stature is meant to mirror the erect, belligerent body of its human master, [we] summon its monstrous etymological cousin [the] Hippopotamus or 'river-horse,' from the dregs of the lagoon." In contrast to the elevated, enduring materials of classical sculpture, such as marble and bronze, Allora & Calzadilla's creature is created from a natural, "base" material: river mud. The creature's existence is thus finite and vulnerable to the ruinous forces of nature. A volunteer sits atop the hippo at all times, reading a daily newspaper of his or her own choosing. When the sitter reads something believed to be an injustice of any kind, the volunteer blows a whistle. As one person's injustice is another person's truth, *Hope Hippo* plays upon the variegated values held by different members of our society. The sitter does not verbally interact with the audience, leaving viewers to rely on their own perceptions of justice when they hear the whistle.

Geof Oppenheimer also addresses instances of public communication, along with its inherent postures and potential failures. Oppenheim presents two newly commissioned works. The first, *Public Sculpture (Edits)* (2009–10), is a series of nine slip-cast ceramic microphones on stands, recalling those typically found in press conferences and on speakers' podiums. Cast in ceramic, the microphones become formally elegant but ultimately nonfunctional, underscoring the finely crafted yet potentially hollow conditions that currently surround public discourse. A series of wigs top some of the microphones, recalling the perfectly coiffed self-presentation of newscasters and politicians. Formally, the objects and their installation reference the work of the Swiss sculptor Alberto Giacometti. The sculptures appear as part of a unified whole but are separated by an isolating distance. They become contemporary totem figures, simultaneously active and immobile.

The second work, *The Morally Ambiguous Precedent of Abstraction, Police Press Conference, Chicago, Illinois 2008* (2009), is a large photographic abstraction created from an image of a stage curtain taken at a Chicago police press conference. Both works reflect on the mechanisms of stagecraft that dominate public discussion, acknowledging the techniques people use to elicit empathetic reactions from others—not always for altruistic reasons.

The idiosyncratic altruism of Hunter S. Thompson, and specifically his 1970 run for Pitkin County sheriff, inspired Lars Ø. Ramberg's project. Ramberg utilizes the writings of the late journalist as a platform for addressing the concept of empathy. Thompson was a longtime and beloved Aspen resident revered for his life philosophy and lifestyle. He committed suicide at his home in nearby Woody Creek in 2005. Ramberg has created eight memorial benches for Thompson based on the standardized memorial benches that are commonplace throughout Aspen. The first was placed here in about 1977 (although there are no specific records), and the tradition continues to the present. Currently the City of Aspen has placed a moratorium on new benches, as they are uncertain about the number that are actually installed and have another ninety requests on a waiting list.

Ramberg's eight benches are located throughout Aspen: on the grounds of the museum, on Cooper Avenue Mall, on Gondola Plaza, and at the top of Aspen Mountain near the gondola. Each features a quote from Thompson, selected in collaboration with his widow, Anita, machine-engraved into the back of the bench and filled with gold leaf. Neither the benches nor the quotes are visually attributed to Thompson, allowing those who recognize the texts to acknowledge the author, while letting those who do not form their own associations or meanings. The accumulated viewing of the isolated texts adds up to a larger thought. Ramberg states an attraction to what he terms Thompson's "warm anarchism," and he is drawn to the memorial bench form because, unlike traditional memorial markers, these can be sat on and used as a space for contemplation. The project upends the sentimentality traditionally associated with memorializing and offers a slyly satirical approach that recalls the irreverence of its memorialized subject.

Frances Stark's project for *Restless Empathy* also utilizes irreverence and revolves around an Aspen-based musical comedy, *I've Had It!* (1951), which was originally performed at the historic Wheeler Opera House. The musical is about people who work in the service industry in Aspen, and it pokes fun at the "more cultured" audience of the Aspen Music Festival. In *I've Had It!* a bellhop's potential bride gets a job working for a composer who has received a Guggenheim Fellowship to compose a divertimento intended to be performed at the festival. She falls for the composer, annoying the bellhop, and with the help of his bartender friend, the pretentious composer/girl-stealer is exposed as a fraud when the bartender, bellhop, and some bar musicians demonstrate to a room full of important critics that the divertimento is really a hit-parade song played backward.

Stark's project, which will also take place at the Wheeler Opera House, is not, however, a simple restaging of the play, but a performance that engages *I've Had It!* as a regional historical reference, while at the same time formally playing with some of the symmetrical tropes and tensions built into the premise of the musical. Stark's performance uses the description and formal structure of *I've Had It!* to address the complications inherent in rigid distinctions between high and low culture as well as in fraudulence and originality, divisions central to both the play itself and the development of avant-garde artistic strategies in the twentieth century.

Stark herself appears in the performance wearing a telephone costume that comes from a body of work inspired by the Polish writer Witold Gombrowicz's novel *Ferdydurke* (1937), a story about the struggle between social norms and individuality in which the protagonist describes his transformation from a thirty-year-old man into a teenage boy. Reveling in the subversive power of masks and the creative potential of immaturity, the novel is formally echoed by Stark's work in its rich use of pastiche and linguistic play. Stark's interest in the telephone itself springs from its performative qualities. One pretends to focus on the conversation and the person on the other end of the line, but often attention is split as one folds laundry, checks e-mail, or doodles with a nearby pen and paper. At the same time, one never wonders whether the attention of the other is similarly split. As described by David Foster Wallace, the telephone creates a "bilateral illusion of unilateral attention . . . you [get] to believe that you [are] receiving somebody's complete attention without having to return it." [18]

For the performance, Stark has designed a new olio curtain that is also a scrim, thus allowing, through lighting, two simultaneous performances of a Joseph Haydn divertimento written for a double string trio, to be played by two groups in different rooms. The divertimento as a genre was prevalent in the eighteenth century and is notable because it lacks a specific form. Due to its lighthearted tone and social function, it was often used to accompany banquets and other social events. Social implication and play also form a key focus of Stark's work. The often complex and surprising layers of interaction between people, assumptions, associations, and meanings are highlighted in her work for *Restless Empathy*.

Complex interactions of subject and form factor prominently in Pawel Althamer's sculpture. *Guma* (2008) results from the artist's experience teaching "Einstein Seminars," physics classes that he taught for underprivileged youth in his hometown in Poland. The figure depicted in the sculpture is the so-called town drunk, who was often a fixture outside the classroom and occasionally participated—becoming an unofficial mascot for class attendees. When the man died, Althamer created the sculpture as a nontraditional memorial, highlighting the processes by which we remember or eulogize the departed. The figure is a monochromatic gray. Absent of any traditionally representational color, the sculpture metaphorically indicates that its subject is deceased. The detail with which his facial features and clothes are rendered indicates the individualism of the specific human figure captured. The figure is placed on a metal spring that can slightly sway, evoking the bodily movement of an inebriated person. Althamer's representation is both generous and sympathetic, thus seducing the viewer to look at a person potentially overlooked in life.

Lara Favaretto's canvas-covered merry-go-round plays upon the accepted notion of the object as a symbol of youthful fun. Entitled *Cominciò ch'era finita (It began while it was already over)* (2006), Favaretto's version spins so rapidly that it appears out of control. The speed of rotation also causes the canvas flaps installed around its sides to repeatedly and disquietingly strike a column erected in its vicinity. Favaretto's piece harnesses the excitement one feels in seeing an active object in the museum space, the dismay one feels in not being able to participate with it as originally hoped, and the subsequent, yet altered, interest one experiences as a result of the actual interaction with the piece. These alternating responses mirror the circular motion of the carousel. They also map one's emotions after hearing about someone else's challenges, which may start at relief and lead to empathy.

A comparable unfolding of meaning found in Favaretto's work also occurs in that presented by Mark Wallinger. His new site-specific photographic billboard features the ubiquitous Aspen Mountain landscape, over which the text "AMERIKA" is superimposed. The work recalls the famous HOLLYWOOD sign in Los Angeles's Hollywood Hills, as well as references Walter Paepcke's "body, mind, spirit" inspiration, Johann Wolfgang von Goethe, and his 1827 poem "Amerika." Goethe penned the work in the shadows of the United States' adoption of the Monroe Doctrine in 1823, a "hands off" warning to European nations that might be tempted to use interventionist and colonialist tendencies in Central and South America during the volatile years of the early nineteenth century. In "Amerika," Goethe envisions a young nation possessing the potential of existing unfettered to a Europe consumed with historical, political, and cultural determinism as well as mired in notions of autocratic power.[19] Goethe's "Amerika," translated into English, reads:

> America, you've got it better
> Than our old continent. Exult!
> You have no decaying castles
> And no basalt.
> Your heart is not troubled,
> In lively pursuits,
> By useless old remembrance
> And empty disputes
>
> So use the present day with luck!
> And when your child a poem writes,
> Protect him, with his skill and pluck,
> From tales of bandits, ghosts and knights.[20]

Amerika was also the title given to Franz Kafka's unfinished novel by his friend, editor, and literary executor, Max Brod, who assembled the author's incomplete manuscript of the book and published it in 1927, a few years after Kafka's death. The book's genesis was the short story (and the book's first chapter) entitled "The Stoker," which tells the story of a young European man's forced emigration to the United States following a paternity scandal.[21]

The placement of Wallinger's work in front of Aspen Mountain offers the viewer the opportunity to select the "real" landscape of the mountain over the fabricated one, highlighting the difference between looking at, and being in, nature. The inscription of "America" with a K also allows the viewer the chance to move beyond a first impression and assumption of intended meaning.

Marc Bijl's medium itself, spray paint on corrugated metal, responds to assumptions of intention. Bijl's project involves two identical sculptural interventions: six-foot-square corrugated aluminum fences placed around one sculpture on the grounds of the Aspen Art Museum and one sculpture on the campus of the Aspen Center for Physics / Aspen Institute. On each work, the following Albert Schweitzer quote is spray-painted: "As soon as man does not take his existence for granted, but beholds it as something unfathomably mysterious, thought begins."

Schweitzer's only visit to the United States took place in July 1949, when he was featured as a guest speaker at the Goethe Bicentennial Celebration in Aspen. This event began the tradition of gathering great thinkers (as well as great musicians) together in Aspen, and it directly resulted in the founding of both the Aspen Music Festival and the Aspen Institute. Bijl's choice relates to Schweitzer's empathetic understanding of philosophy and self-examination. Rather than viewing philosophy as elitist and removed, Bijl proposes that the practice is accessible and immediate. For him, it is humility in the face of the mysteries of existence, and the process of thinking through these problems for ourselves, that defines the search for truth that unites us as humans. Here again, art proposes commonalities among us.

Formally, the work resembles a construction site that also functions as a philosophical illustration of Nature and Culture being constructed (or renovated or used). By having identical works situated in two different contexts in Aspen, the artist engages the idea of duality as it relates to empathy, as people can have quite different feelings and reactions when encountering the same work, idea, or person in different contexts.

Bourriaud contended that artists cannot waste time betting on happier tomorrows. His formulaic assumptions about the role of artists in society feel truly outdated. Without any real sense of irony, *Restless Empathy* was originally titled *The Friendly Show*. Part of the conceptual appeal of many of the artists and artworks included in the exhibition lies in the multilayered responses that are available in their works. Some may appear off-putting, at least initially: graffiti on construction material, an unmountable carousel, the misspelled name of our country. Through extended looking and an effort past the superficial, however, the viewer's relationship to the object can morph and soften. Commonalities can be found. There is, among all of the artists and artworks, an underlying sense of empathy expressed toward the viewer. The works offer an opportunity to interact; the interaction is not in any way mandatory. Different from traditional works of art where the viewer can interact with the object only visually—say, for example, by standing in front of a painting—the works in *Restless Empathy* are informed by the participatory opportunities described in *Relational Aesthetics* yet infused with a generosity of approach and an open-endedness of involvement. One can choose to sit on a bench, or think about philosophy and life, or read the paper and whistle about injustice, or merely observe others doing so. One can walk among the objects installed around the city or limit their viewing to the museum. There is no right answer. The empathetic choice is, of course, yours.

NOTES

[1] Martin Pesch, "Tobias Rehberger," *Frieze*, no. 29 (July–August 1996), 69.
[2] Ibid.
[3] Tate Collection Glossary, "Relational Aesthetics,"
http://www.tate.org.uk/collections/glossary/definition.jsp?endtryId=634
[4] Nicholas Bourriaud, "Relational Aesthetics," http://www.creativityandcognition.
com/blogs/legart/wp-content/uploads/2006/07/Borriaud.pdf
[5] Claire Bishop, "Antagonism and Relational Aesthetics," http://roundtable.
kein.org/files/roundtable/claire%20bishop-antagonism&relational%20
aesthetics.pdf (October 2004).
[6] Ibid.
[7] Bourriaud, "Relational Aesthetics."
[8] Ibid.
[9] Bishop, "Antagonism and Relational Aesthetics."
[10] http://www.zittel.org/
[11] Stewart Martin, "Critique of Relational Aesthetics," *Third Text* 21, no. 4 (July 2007),
http://www.informaworld.com/smpp/content~content=a781176964&db–all
[12] Chris Cobb, "Relational Aesthetics: Why It Makes So Much Sense,"
http://www.stretcher.org/archives/r3_a/2002_11_13_r3_archive.php
[13] Bourriaud, "Relational Aesthetics."
[14] Martin, "Critique of Relational Aesthetics."
[15] Ibid.
[16] Ibid.
[17] Ibid.
[18] David Foster Wallace, *Infinite Jest* (London: Back Bay Books, 2006), 179.
[19] Mark Wallinger, e-mail message to author, February 17, 2010.
[20] Translated by Daniel Platt.
[21] Wallinger, op. cit., 2010.

Empathetic Objects

Christian Rattemeyer

In 1908, Wilhelm Worringer published his dissertation entitled "Abstraction and Empathy," in which he positioned several oppositional pairs that would serve to illuminate his approach to understanding the history of art in the Western world through a structural analysis. A product of its time in its claims to sweeping generalizations, Worringer's text aims to confront the linearity of the art historical narrative with its cycles of development from primitive to enlightened, and with it to criticize the long-standing privileging of those moments in art history that would be described as classical or neoclassical, from antiquity to the Renaissance to the classicizing styles of the nineteenth century.

Besides Worringer's titular oppositional pair, "abstraction and empathy," he positioned "transcendence and immanence" and "style and naturalism." In his view, transcendence and immanence function as broader social currents, pointing to society's need for art to provide spiritual or cultural guidance as a fixed value in uncertain times (such as religious imagery during the Middle Ages) or society's need for an aesthetic experience of self-recognition, immersion, and play during times of relative calm and plenty (such as the "naturalistic" portraiture of antiquity and the Renaissance that allowed for what Worringer termed "aesthetic pleasure as objectivized self-pleasure"). Out of these broader social needs would arise the aesthetic requirements for abstraction and empathy, in which the former is understood as a distancing device, a reduction to absolute and transcendental values of symmetry, geometry, and order, which could serve as an unchangeable law during times of great uncertainty. (Worringer responded directly here to the felt unrest of his modern time, positioning burgeoning abstraction explicitly not as a de-skilled form of transgression but as a need for eternal order.) Empathy, by contrast, is the urge to identify, to emote directly to forms similar to oneself—most obviously the naturalistic and realistic representation of the natural world in painting and sculpture. The final pair—style and naturalism—might feel most foreign today, but they are simply understood as the formal manifestations of these social needs and aesthetic urges. In the traditional art historical terminology, "style" would be everything that is ornamental and abstract, culturally specific and historically transitional (as in "the Gothic style"), whereas naturalism was simply the ability to achieve representation as close to nature (or its idealized projection) as possible.

Worringer's essay had a considerable impact among artists and cultural critics who wanted to position abstraction as a response to the perils and confusions of the modern world and were drawn to its alignment with the spiritual and esoteric. (It held, for instance, great importance for Wassily Kandinsky.) Classicism, and its ability to offer an emotional connection for the viewer as a form of enlightened self-recognition, was instead devalued as an urge for empathetic immersion available only when a coherent sense of self in the world is available—if not a fallacy, it was at least a luxury.

This desire to eschew an empathetic relationship toward art based on self-recognition, in favor of a model of art as abstract and based on fundamental principles, might be seen as one of the key operative assumptions of the classic avant-gardes, but more importantly for this context, it established an oppositional figure of artistic creation between what might be called "critique" and "affirmation" beyond the confines of style and form. Whereas critique introduces a function of analysis and rejection of a given aesthetic taste—often quite jarringly, as in the wholesale dismissal of everything that came before—affirmation here is understood as a mirroring of the existing world, a radical acceptance of given conditions, both visual and social, through faithful representation.

In the immediate aftermath of World War II, especially in Western Europe, this oppositional formation was explored yet again through an inquiry into the humanist potential of abstraction. The once famous and now forgotten "Darmstädter Gespräche" (Darmstadt Conversations), which took place in the city of Darmstadt between 1950 and 1975, focused on the possibilities of abstraction in representing a human image and were aimed at reconfirming the role of, in the words of the German art historian Werner Haftmann, "world language abstraction." Artists such as Willi Baumeister, who defended abstraction, and Karl Hofer, who argued for a continued relevance of figuration as a way of representing social realities, were pegged against each other in a discussion over art's modernity as measured in its potential for formal innovation and social critique. I am retelling this moment of repositioning of the German—and, by extension, Western European—art world after World War II not only because it had a major ideological impact on exhibitions such as *documenta* (where Haftmann served as adviser and abstraction was championed), but also because it illustrates in hindsight the difficulties of advanced, avant-garde art with the traditional concepts of human representation and identification in the environment of cold-war conflict. The "conversations" established a blueprint of oppositional terms that would remain operative for most of the cold-war period.

Over the last four decades, the oppositional paradigms may have shifted from abstraction and figuration to those of process and object as well as critique and affirmation, as they played themselves out in various forms of dominance and marginality. I do not mean to suggest that any of these practices exist in pure states of either criticality or affirmation, or that a progression from one to the other would suggest a development in the classic teleological sense of historical progress, but rather that these conditions simply constitute other set of dichotomies that shape the field of decision making inherent in any artistic practice and movement. Like the oppositional pairs of abstraction and figuration or narrative and form, critique and affirmation designate concrete choices as well as intellectual temperaments that can help situate an artistic practice in a spectrum of ideas. But whereas critique and affirmation as aesthetic and intellectual artistic choices—as a form of practice—designate an artistic stance, the notion of empathy engages in a more complex relationship between artist and viewer. It proposes, or at least assumes, a form of anticipation on the part of the artist of the impact and effect that the work will produce; often, it actively anticipates and dynamically constructs such effects on the viewer as a core part of its meaning or success.

But empathy should not be understood as simply a feeling toward the audience. Instead of a positioning as either fully apart (as in a stance of critique) or fully immersed (as one of affirmation) in the contexts, forms, discourses, or aesthetics of a given context or institution, empathy suggests a temporary mediation between these poles, an operative role between and awareness of the limits and uses of either position. This does not mean necessarily a sentiment of goodwill, understanding, and moral judgment, but rather a kind of humility, an ability to enact one's own limits (both as a person and as an object) and engage in a practice of ventriloquism. This has a correlation in the field of so-called linguistic empathy, which is understood to make reference to a speaker's point of view, identification with a subject, and so on. Though more prevalent in languages such as Japanese, it exists in English as well, mainly through the use of passive voice, in which the object of an active sentence is rendered as subject, and thus assumes a greater prevalence (and empathetic preference) than in an active linguistic formulation. We are taught to avoid passive sentences, for their indirectness, as well as their resistance to designate the clear protagonist of an event.

In recent considerations of the status of the artworks that might be described as "empathetic," what has developed is a skepticism toward the simple operations of interactivity, social agency, and activism, which has been replaced by more complex rethinking of the role of the art object itself vis-à-vis the viewer. In fact, another common definition of empathy is based on exactly that, a movement toward disabling the distinction between protagonist and object in a given event, an "imaginative projection of a subjective state into an object so that the object appears to be infused with it."[1] To fill an object with feeling, as it were, is precisely not an operation of audience engagement and interactivity, however. Rather, it complicates the status of the object as it positions it to take over parts of the roles and functions of the audience.

One of the most fascinating recent conversations about the changed relationship between art object and audience concerns the exhibition *The Death of the Audience* at the Vienna Secession in 2009, which was curated by Pierre Bal-Blanc, the director of the CAC (Center of Contemporary Art) in Brétigny, France. Asked to review the development of the art of the 1960s to the 1980s through the image of the Secession (which was founded in about 1900 as an artists-driven model for a new institution to display the aesthetic synergies of the time), Bal-Blanc opted to structure his exhibition around what he called "professional outsiders," artists who, though participating in the movements of their time, remain marginal to the dominant practices of the day. But rather than framing the argument in a strict interrogation of center and periphery, canon and addendum, Bal-Blanc chose a discussion by way of relation to the audience:

> PBB: The exhibition needed a title more suitable to the challenge of the artists' works, one that would hold the social implications seen in the transformations of the 1960s. Furthermore, what constitutes the main vector of the 1970s more than (in a continuation of Marcel Duchamp) a redistribution of reception? When Barthes writes about "la mort de l'auteur," it means that the reader is implicated, that the spectator as passive instrument must die and become something else: participant or, as [Jacques] Rancière proposes, "emancipated." Either way, the roles change. To speak about the death of the audience is also to ask whether the death of the author ever occurred.

Instead of arguing for a more active role of the viewer (as would be presumed in his remark about the death of the author), Bal-Blanc raised doubts if the viewer actually ever became more emancipated, or if, in fact, the status of the object changed during the 1970s, so that the viewer could feel more engaged, "emancipated" and involved in the process of the work than would actually be the case. In her interview with Bal-Blanc, the French critic Elisabeth Lebovici pointed to the profound implications of such a reading, and Bal-Blanc's answer was again highly relevant:

> EL: In a way, the show is the opposite of the participatory impulses associated with the art of the 1960s, with kinetic works for instance, or with relational aesthetics in the 1990s, which may be—why not?—the continuation of this participatory movement, a movement also adapted to the enlightened developments of a bourgeois, Western, capitalist culture. But there is a dream of passivity in your proposal; if the walls can slide towards you, why should you move?

> PBB: Yes, and that position is counterbalanced: I like those leaps towards passivity, but when they are succeeded by activity. It's a rhythm, everything is in that rhythm. Interactivity is like industrial domination, a falsely active activity. Like [Slavoj] Žižek, so do I prefer its uncanny double, the term "interpassivity." On the one hand, we have the emancipated spectatorship of Rancière; on the other there is Žižek's interpassivity, a situation in which the object itself takes from you and enjoys for you.[2]

Bal-Blanc pointed precisely toward a process of conflation and complication in the art object itself, as far as it concerns a relationship to the spectator, which he considered a constitutive condition of the most advanced art since the 1970s. As objects get imbued with a sense of their audience and take on responsibility for their viewers, it is they that become empathetic, that enable moments of emotional transference onto their audience.

One hundred years after Worringer claimed that empathy was a desire for self-recognition on the part of the viewer in relation to an art designed to fulfill such needs for representation, the current picture seems inverted, and more complex. Today's objects have not only incorporated the viewer's need for self-recognition—be it in a form of participatory impulses or through more benign forms of figuration and representation—but rather, they have themselves become feeling. When Bal-Blanc used the example of a Robert Breer work—a slowly moving wall that moves through the exhibition space—he only described in the most comically direct ways an artwork approaching its audience; in fact, however, many of the works made today have incorporated the needs of their audience, they have discursively anticipated the hopes for identification and self-recognition, and they are able to presuppose their audience through modes of installation, scale, and choice of materials. Today's artworks, it seems, identify with their audience. The question seems to be: can we return the gaze?

NOTES

[1] *Merriam-Webster's Collegiate Dictionary*, 11th ed.
[2] Elisabeth Lebovici, "The Death of the Audience: A Conversation with Pierre Bal-Blanc," *e-flux*, no. 13 (February 2010), http://www.e-flux.com/journal/view/113

The Promise of Empathy

Matthew Thompson

In May of 2009, political controversy erupted around President Barack Obama's appointment of Sonia Sotomayor to the United States Supreme Court. At issue was President Obama's framing of his nomination, specifically statements such as, "I view that quality of empathy, of understanding and identifying with people's hopes and struggles, as an essential ingredient for arriving at just decisions and outcomes."[1] Attacks from conservatives sharply questioned the place of empathy within the process of judicial decision making, accusing Sotomayor of "applying her feelings . . . when deciding cases."[2] Even though numerous Republicans had previously praised compassion as a judicial attribute, empathy became a partisan issue.[3] Sotomayor was eventually confirmed—though not until after rancorous hearings where empathy was a main point of contention. Empathy promises to be a vital topic of American political discussion for the foreseeable future, with the recent passage of sweeping health care reform and looming debates about immigration reform, as well as another Supreme Court nomination. Empathy just might be dangerous.

George Bernard Shaw once cautioned, "Do not do unto others as you would that they should do unto you. Their tastes may not be the same."[4]

The Golden Rule is a core element of ethical and moral reasoning in Western thought, and a basis for our modern understanding of human rights.[5] Though commonly attributed to Jesus in the Gospel of Matthew, there are analogous expressions across cultures, and it is a common standard by which culturally disparate groups resolve conflicts.[6] Within the field of evolutionary biology, the related concept of reciprocity is seen as the evolutionary basis of cooperation, on which our species depends.[7] As Shaw so incisively pointed out, there is a danger in attempting to extrapolate universal principles from personal experience. Empathy is more complicated than we think.

Empathy is most simply stated as an emotional connection between individuals. As Shaw's criticism makes clear, however, empathy involves the imaginative leap of seeing the world from another's perspective.[8] It is a mode of projection.

In 1873, Robert Visher first articulated a central role for empathy within aesthetics. His concept of *Einfühlung* (literally, "feeling-in") endeavored to explain the physical responses that paintings trigger within viewers. Toward the end of the nineteenth century, other art historians, including Heinrich Wölfflin and Aby Warburg, developed Visher's concepts, describing not only how the viewer was implicated physically in the work, but also how this physical response interacted with an emotional response to the work.[9]

This mode of embodied analysis, however, was at odds with the dominant understanding of the aesthetic as advanced by Immanuel Kant: that disinterestedness is the hallmark of the aesthetic, which is inherently contemplative and spectatorial.[10] In fact, twentieth-century art history largely eliminated the emotional, the empathetic, and the noncognitive bodily response from its scope of inquiry. This privileging of a fully cognitive, disembodied approach coalesces in the writing of Clement Greenberg. And although in the 1970s a "new art history" emerged, turning to historical, social, and cultural analysis of art production and reception, it still largely ignored precognitive responses.[11]

Recently, there has been vigorous academic interest in questions of embodiment and empathy. Numerous conferences have focused on empathy as a transdisciplinary phenomenon, citing research in the social sciences and the arts, as well as the natural sciences, such as evolutionary biology and neurophysiology. There are striking similarities in how each conference or seminar describes the timeliness of empathy, declaring this an "age of empathy," citing its popularity in academic journals and best-seller lists, its central role in current political discussion—in effect, outlining empathy as a larger cultural project.[12] Whether this combination—being a valued research end in a variety of disciplines, besides having greater social and political relevance because of the fundamental role it plays in "how people conduct their lives on a daily basis, and how they define themselves in relation to others, to government, and to society as a whole"[13]—is sufficient enough to determine if empathy is a cultural project like the Enlightenment is outside the scope of this text. But it can be contextualized as part of a much larger drift in western thought toward a greater focus on social interaction and embodied experience.

If artwork both reflects and absorbs the material reality (in the economic as well as physical sense) of the context in which it is produced, a genealogy of the present moment can help untangle the increasingly complex ways in which contemporary art is engaging with the social in form and content. It will also provide a basis for thinking about how our evolving understanding of embodiment and empathy affects its reception.

A split between mind and body was first articulated by René Descartes, giving primacy to the rational mind as the basis for existence. For Descartes, the senses are inherently unreliable, and deductive reasoning, solely a property of the immaterial mind, is the basis for knowledge of the world.[14] This primacy of rationality characterizes the Enlightenment. And while much Enlightenment thought focused on the individual—from Descartes's conception of the mind to the focus on individual liberties in the American Declaration of Independence and the French Declaration of the Rights of Man and of the Citizen—the economic changes resulting from the transition from feudalism to capitalism, along with the invention of the printing press, created new spaces of social exchange.

In his analysis of the "bourgeois public sphere," the German sociologist and philosopher Jürgen Habermas outlined the social conditions that allowed Enlightenment ideas to spread. This included a "realm of communication marked by new arenas of debate, more open and accessible forms of urban public space and sociability, and an explosion of print culture."[15] Crucially, Habermas defined the public sphere as being essentially egalitarian and focused on "common concern."[16] The formation of this social space was precipitated by the public discussion of literature in journals and in cafés, with a popular interest in sentimental novels and moral weeklies: literature that revealed the interior self and emphasized an audience-oriented subjectivity.[17] In both literature and politics, Habermas described the public significance of private social interaction.[18]

The gradual move away from feudalism toward capitalism resulted in the switch to machine-based manufacturing in the Industrial Revolution, which precipitated a new focus in thinking about labor as a collective experience, from Karl Marx to Henry Ford. As an urban industrial economy began to overtake a rural agrarian one, new social classes formed, and populations began to concentrate heavily in cities. The rise of the middle class coincided with a consumer revolution and the beginnings of mass consumption, and the consumer became another group at the focus of social thought. Although newspaper ads appeared as early as 1704, the first advertising agency was not formed until 1812 in the United Kingdom, and 1850 in the United States.[19] By 1908, the Harvard Business School had opened, ensuring that these methods of thinking about collectivity—in terms of labor and consumption—became formalized as areas of academic study. Around the middle of the twentieth century, rigorous modern methods of studying consumer behavior began to emerge.[20]

Beginning with the abolitionist movement in the late eighteenth century, and continuing through debates about women's suffrage in the nineteenth and early twentieth centuries, the social welfare policies of the New Deal in the 1930s, the civil rights movement in the 1950s, and the ongoing struggles for gay rights beginning in the 1970s, concerns have been articulated about the liberty of various marginalized social groups. Many of these struggles focused on the fundamental rights of groups to participate in society. This provides a sharp contrast to the concern for individual liberty expressed in the revolutionary era.

This is, admittedly, an American-centric perspective, and is anything but exhaustive, but hopefully it demonstrates the material changes that affected how we think about and talk about group behavior, and the increasingly complex ways we analyze social space. Analyses of aesthetics and art history, however, by and large deny the social, along with any embodied analysis, well into the 1970s. But if we examine art making, particularly in the twentieth century, I would argue that, in many respects, it follows this increasing focus on the social and becomes progressively more attenuated to the embodied experience of the viewer.

There are early precedents for bodily engaging the viewer in more or less direct ways. The formation of the Cabaret Voltaire in Zürich in 1916 created a social space for interdisciplinary artistic events. While they were not conceived necessarily as discrete works, they certainly provided a model for event-based practices like those of Allan Kaprow (fig. 7), whose first Happenings took place in 1959. In Europe at about the same time, both Piero Manzoni and Yves Klein dealt directly with issues of performance and viewer participation. These works differed significantly from traditional theatrical performance structures in that they were far more temporally and structurally open-ended. Manzoni's *Living Sculptures* (c. 1961), for example, consisted of the artist signing people's bodies and declaring them living works of art.[21] And, although the oft-reproduced image of Manzoni signing a female nude implies the use of models, with Manzoni's signature and the appropriate certification, anyone could become a living sculpture.[22] Klein, too, folded live female nudes into the language of painting with his *Anthropometries* (1960), but it is *Le Vide* (1958) (fig. 8) where the viewer is implicated most directly. In the work, Klein emptied a Paris gallery and gave tours of immaterial psychic energy he had "imbued" into the space.[23]

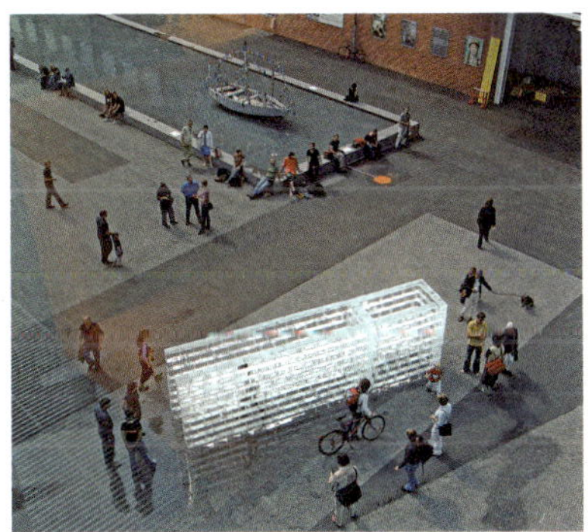

Fig. 7
Allan Kaprow
Fluids, 1967/2005

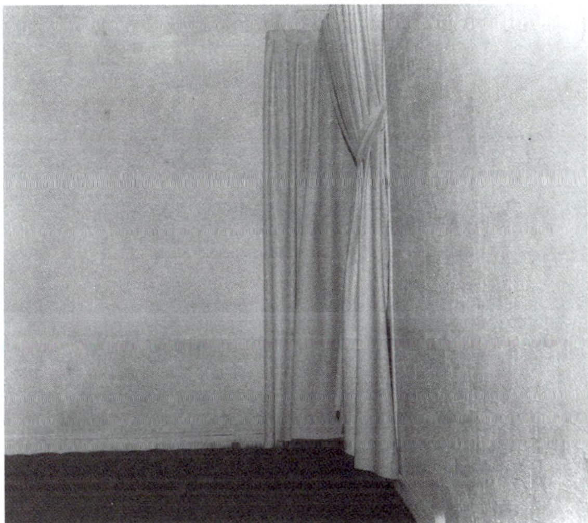

Fig. 8
Yves Klein
Le Vide, 1958
Exhibition *La Spécialisation de la sensibilité à l'état matière première en sensibilité picturale stabilisée*, Iris Clert Gallery, Paris, France, April 28 – May 5, 1958
© 2010 Artists Rights Society (ARS), New York / ADAGP, Paris

organized in New York. Fluxus grew out of experimental music, with a number of its associates, including Kaprow and George Brecht, meeting in a 1958 class on experimental composition taught by John Cage at the New School for Social Research.[24] Brecht began to concentrate on and develop the aesthetic experience as an intimate situation. His event scores from this period reframed everyday actions as performances, occasionally engaging the viewer with imaginary or impossible experiments with everyday situations.[25] For instance, the score for *Three Lamp Events* (1961) (fig. 9) simply reads "On.Off. / Lamp / Off.On," while the more oblique *Flute Solo* (1962) calls for "Disassembling / Assembling." These actions and thought experiments described by the event scores recall similar devices present in the work of conceptual artists such as Robert Barry, whose work provoked a search for a realm beyond the visible, depending on a viewer to enact them.[26] Take, for example, *It Has Order* (1969–70), in which the following eight sentence appear on four otherwise blank pages: ". . . it has order . . . it is always changing . . . it is affected by other things . . . it affects other things . . . it is not confined . . . it is not in any specific place . . . it can be presented, but go unnoticed . . . to know of it is to be part of it."[27]

Presence and absence were also central to Land art of the late 1960s and early 1970s, especially Robert Smithson's ideas of site and non-site, where objects in the gallery removed from a natural location refer to that location, through what Smithson termed "dimensional metaphor."[28] Land art also created a precedent for outdoor sculptural works that truly engage their context. Although initially these interventions were formal or phenomenological, Land art began to engage the site as social-political space in the work of artists such as Hans Haacke and Gordon Matta-Clark.

The works and writings of American Minimalist sculptors such as Carl Andre, Donald Judd, and Robert Morris in the 1960s proposed a new relationship to the spaces in which they were exhibited and the viewers who encountered them. Morris, in fact, was one of the first writers to consider the "new sculpture" in phenomenological terms, referring to its "public mode" and the "extended situation" it creates,[29] directly engaging the embodied experience of the viewer.

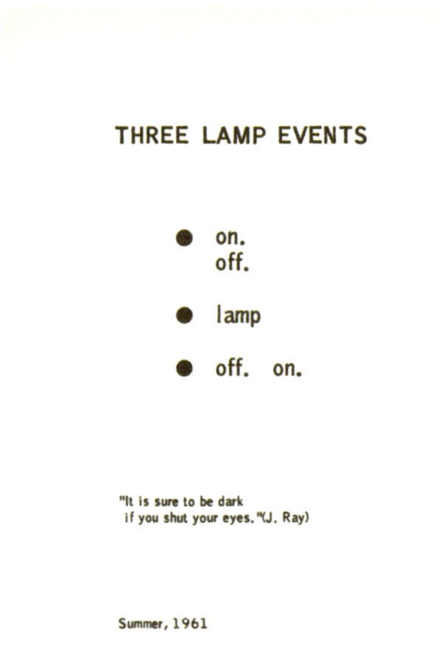

THREE LAMP EVENTS

on.
off.

lamp

off. on.

"It is sure to be dark
if you shut your eyes."(J. Ray)

Summer, 1961

Fig. 9
George Brecht, Selection from Water Yam, 1963/1965
© 2010 Artists Rights Society (ARS), New York / VG Bild-Kunst, Bonn

Though anticipated by the Gutai group in Japan in the mid-1950s, performance art as such first appeared in the United States in the early 1960s. Much canonical early performance, including the work of Carolee Schneemann, Chris Burden, Vito Acconci, and Marina Abramovic, explicitly engaged with notions of embodiment, in terms of both the experience of the viewer and the literal presence of the body of the artist. Duration and endurance were central to a number of performances in the 1970s, like Burden's *Five Day Locker Piece* (1971) (fig. 10), where he locked himself inside a small locker for five days with only five gallons of water, or Abramovic's *Freeing the Voice* (1975), in which she screamed until she lost her voice. Tehching Hsieh, in *One Year Performance 1980–1981*, punched a time clock every hour, on the hour, for an entire year.

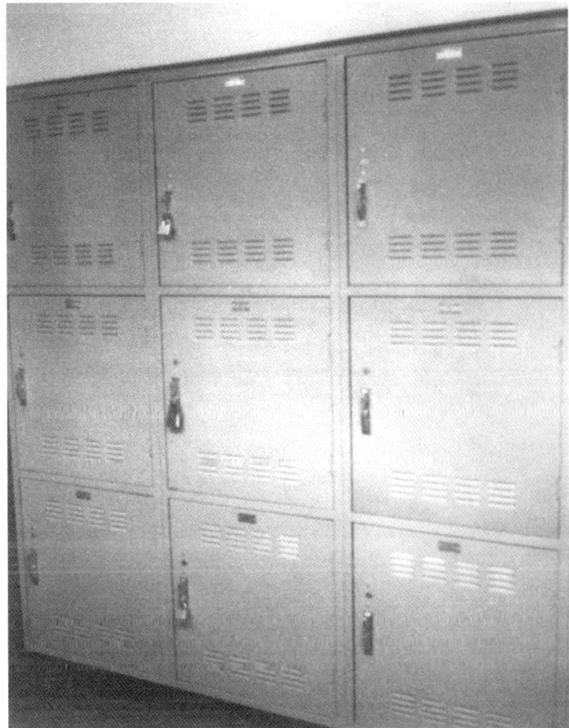

Fig. 10
Chris Burden
Five Day Locker Piece, 1971

In the late 1960s, and continuing into the 1970s, artists such as Bruce Nauman used video cameras as an extension of their own bodies.[30] Sony's 1967 release of the Portapak, the first portable video recorder, made video readily available to artists. Andy Warhol had already begun to work with film earlier in the decade, playing with temporal experience in works like *Sleep* (1963) and *Empire* (1964). But with video, artists had a much cheaper and more immediate medium with which to engage time. In the 1980s, the potentials of the technology were expanded, and video and installation merged into immersive environments.[31] Artists also began to take existing media as a raw material, part of larger trends of appropriation that can be loosely located within DIY, punk, and activist traditions.[32] These redirections of existing imagery spoke directly to the collective experience of visual culture. Later in the decade, these practices become intertwined with bricolage, what the French anthropologist Claude Levi-Strauss called "'the science of the concrete," the handling, adapting, and piecing together of *things*."[33]

This represents only a partial catalogue of developments in contemporary art that provided precedent for and contextualized a so-called social turn in the art from the early 1990s to the present. The form and content of these works have been variously described as being dialogue, sociability and the space of human relations, acts of service provision, and interests in collectivity, collaboration, and direct engagement with specific social constituencies.[34] Unfortunately, much of the critical discussion about these practices has been limited to a dissection of the claims made for the works, the ethics of how specific communities are engaged, or whether or not the works are politically resistive or complicit. These certainly cannot be the sole criteria by which to experience, interpret, and judge works of art. As Claire Bishop argued, "The conceptual density or artistic significance of the respective projects are sidelined in favor of an appraisal of the artists' relationship with their collaborators."[35] She also pointed to a disturbing trend of artists privileging "authorial intentionality (or a humble lack thereof) . . . over a discussion of the work's conceptual significance as a social or aesthetic form."[36] Critical attention has moved from the gallery to the press release.

The French curator Nicolas Bourriaud pointed to "a theoretical discourse complete with shortcomings" as an impediment to the legibility of relational practices.[37] I tend to agree, but would argue in the other direction: we have a lack of thoughtful discussion about the function of empathy and the embodiment of the viewer, a way of thinking about the private, independent space along with the sphere of social relations. Art can engage collective reception and interaction, while at the same time opening opportunities for individual experiences. We should endeavor to understand.

American pragmatism of the 1930s, especially John Dewey's thinking about aesthetic experience, sought to reconcile the mind-body split of Descartes and reinvigorate the disinterested aesthetics of Kant.[38] For Dewey, meaning and knowledge were generated through experience, and through our understanding and perception of the interaction between a disembodied "receptivity" and an embodied "action."[39] It is in this conversation between consciousness and the objects of consciousness, between the inside and outside, that our reality emerges. Dewey found aesthetic engagement to be the paradigmatic form of meaningful experience.[40] It was also, in his mind, deeply affective, as through perception "our own experience is re-oriented," becoming "far more efficacious than the change effected by reasoning because it enters directly into attitude."[41] There is a striking resonance here with how the German art critic Jörg Heiser used the term *circulation* as "a shorthand for the ways in which the fluctuating relations between forms (from both inside and outside art) co-define the relations between artist and their audience."[42]

Social relations have become an interdisciplinary concern and, in many ways, as much a medium for commerce as for contemporary art. The terms used in a number of projects associated with *Relational Aesthetics* bear a striking resemblance to the language of globalization and marketing trends, and their structure recalls elements of the service industry.[43] There is a prevailing platitude that technological advance is eroding the social fabric by increasingly isolating individuals and creating individually attenuated experiences. But at the same time there is prevalent academic and popular interest in the way groups behave, especially with regard to users of systems or consumers. Interactivity, the illusion of personal free choice, and empowerment—*my*space and *you*tube—are branding strategies. Marketers are relying on ever more sophisticated methods of collecting and analyzing data based on usage habits. Amazon knows what you want to read before you do, but as a result of a complex algorithm based on the decisions of people who have made similar decisions in the past: not by knowing you, but by abstracting you.

As computers and connected devices embed more deeply in the mechanics of our lives, we are faced with more interfaces, and hence an explosion in resources put toward interface design. Our trips to the airport, the bank, the gas station, and the grocery store are increasingly automated, and our aggregated actions will most likely be quantified and reintegrated into the interface. Interfaces depend on protocol to send information over distributed networks. So our lives are more and more infused with protocol. The Internet relies on protocol. Our mobile phones rely on protocol. Networks and protocol exhibit "an explicit tension between freedom and control . . . for protocol to enable radically distributed communications between autonomous entities it must deploy a strategy of universalization and homogeneity . . . it must promote standardization in order to enable openness."[44]

Social networking, increasingly leveraged for marketing and profit, figures equally (and is nauseatingly prominent) in news reports and business books. *The Tipping Point*, *The Wisdom of Crowds*, *Here Comes Everybody*, and *Freakonomics* are circulating these ideas on the best-seller racks. We are subsumed by demographic thinking. Perhaps we should spend less time thinking about aggregates of action, and more time thinking about each other.

The aesthetic experience cannot be tracked or measured, cannot be rationally projected from available data. It is, following Dewey, "a mode of production not found in charts and statistics, and it insinuates possibilities of human relations not to be found in rule and precept, admonition and administration."[45]

On Saturday, March 20, 2010, the day before the final vote was to come on sharply contested health care legislation, protesters spat on a member of Congress and shouted racial and homophobic slurs at supporters of the bill. Members of Congress who voted for the bill received death threats and were the victims of vandalism. Representative James E. Clyburn of South Carolina, the highest-ranking black lawmaker in the House of Representatives, received an anonymous fax showing the image of a noose.[46] We are living amid a crisis of civility.

For Dewey, incivility stems from the fact that "human beings are divided into non-communicating sects." Empathy, not manners or social mores, is at the core of civil discourse. He used empathy as the benchmark for any society,[47] and the experience of art was for him a crucial mode of engendering it. Dewey added an embodied, empathic dimension to Modernism's blend of socially progressive thought and aesthetic introspection. And the centrality of aesthetic experience and the promise of empathy present in his thinking feel vital at the present moment. These are fraught times if empathy itself can be politicized. According to Dewey, "our first imitations of wide and large redirections of desire and purpose are of necessity imaginative."[48] By letting the rich interactions opened up by contemporary art expand our imaginative capacities, we can open ourselves to the promise of empathy.

NOTES

[1] President Obama's comment about empathy was widely quoted without the context of his subsequent remarks: "I will seek somebody who is dedicated to the rule of law, who honors our constitutional traditions, who respects the integrity of the judicial process and the appropriate limits of the judicial role. I will seek somebody who shares my respect for constitutional values on which this nation was founded and who brings a thoughtful understanding of how to apply them in our time." Press Briefing, The White House Office of the Press Secretary, May 1, 2009, http://www.whitehouse.gov/the_press_office/Press-Briefing-By-Press-Secretary-Robert-Gibbs-5-1-09/

[2] Andrew Burns, "Sotomayor Starts Taking Hits from Opposition," Politico.com, May 26, 2009, http://www.politico.com/news/stories/0509/22965.html

[3] http://mediamatters.org/research/200905260048

[4] George Bernard Shaw, Man and Superman (Cambridge: University Press, 1905), 181.

[5] See, for example, the Universal Declaration of Human Rights, adopted December 10, 1948, by the General Assembly of the United Nations, http://www.un.org/en/documents/udhr/

[6] Walter T. Stace, *The Concept of Morals* (New York: MacMillan), 1–3, 93–98.

[7] See, for example, Martin A. Nowak, "Five Rules for the Evolution of Cooperation," *Science* 314, no. 5805 (2006): 1560–63; and Frans de Waal, "The Evolution of Empathy," *Greater Good Magazine* (2010), http://peacecenter.berkeley.edu/greatergood/2010/january/De_Waal.php

[8] Roman Krznaric, *Empathy and the Art of Living*, 6. http://www.romankrznaric.com/Art%20of%20Living/Time%20and%20the%20Art%20of%20Living%202400907.pdf

[9] David Freedberg and Vittorio Gallese, "Motion, Emotion, and Empathy in Esthetic Experience," *Trends in Cognitive Sciences* 11, no. 5 (2007): 198.

[10] Martin Jay, "Somaesthetics and Democracy: Dewey and Contemporary Body Art," *Journal of Aesthetic Education* 36, no. 4 (2002): 56.

[11] Jonathan Harris, *The New Art History: A Critical Introduction* (New York: Routlege, 201), 3–5.

[12] See, for example, "The Promise of Empathy," University of Iowa, 2003; "Seminar on Empathy," Indiana University Bloomington, ongoing; "Perspectives on the Body and Embodiment," University College Dublin Body Conference, 2007; "The Barnard Interdisciplinary Conference on Embodiment: Translating Embodied Mind Approaches for the Next Decade," Barnard College, 2010.

[13] Press release, "The Promise of Empathy," University of Iowa, 2003, http://www.uiowa.edu/~poroi/seminars/empathy_conf/empathy%20description.pdf

[14] See his *Meditations on First Philosophy* (1641), especially the first and third meditations.

[15] James Van Horn Melton, *The Rise of the Public in Enlightenment Europe* (Cambridge: Cambridge University Press, 2001), 4.

[16] Jürgen Habermas, *The Structural Transformation of the Public Sphere* (Boston: MIT Press, 1991), 36–37.

[17] David Randall, "Ethos, Poetics, and the Literary Public Sphere," *Modern Language Quarterly* 69, no. 2 (2008): 221.

[18] Melton, *Rise of the Public*, 10.

[19] See http://adage.com/century/timeline/index.html

[20] D. G. Brian Jones and Eric H. Shaw, "A History of Schools of Marketing Thought," *Marketing Theory* 5, no. (2005): 239–81.

[21] Jay, "Somaesthetics and Democracy," 41.

[22] Barry Schwabsky, "Piero Manzoni," *Artforum* 37, no. 9 (1998), http://findarticles.com/p/articles/mi_m0268/is_n9_v36/ai_n27533121/

[23] Jay, "Somaesthetics and Democracy."

[24] Fluxus had a similar grounding in Europe, where the German serialist composer Karlheinz Stockhausen taught a composition course in Darmstadt attended by LaMonte Young and Nam June Paik. See Hannah Higgins, *Fluxus Experience* (Berkeley: University of California Press, 2002), 1–2.

[25] Yves-Alain Bois, "George Brecht, Museum Ludwig, Cologne," Artforum 45, no. 8 (2006): http://findarticles.com/p/articles/mi_m0268/is_8_44/ai_n18764245/

[26] Peter Eleey, *The Quick and the Dead* (Minneapolis: Walker Art Center, 2009), 32.

[27] Jorg Heiser, "Robert Barry," *Frieze*, January–February 2004, http://www.frieze.com/issue/review/robert_barry/

[28] Robert Smithson, "A Provisional Theory of Non-Sites," in *The Collected Writings* (Berkeley: University of California Press, 1996), 364.
[29] Ivy Cooper, "Being Situated in Recent Art: From the 'Extended Situation' to 'Relational Aesthetics,'" *Janus Head* 11, no. 2 (2009): 334–36.
[30] Michael Rush, *Video Art* (London: Thames and Hudson, 2007), n.p.
[31] John Hanhardt, "The Discourse of Landscape Video Art: From Fluxus to Post-Modernism," in *American Landscape Video*, ed. William Judson (Pittsburgh: Carnegie Museum of Art, 1988), 70.
[32] Lane Relyea, "Your Art World: Or, the Limits of Connectivity," *Afterall* 14 (Autumn/Winter 2006): 4.
[33] Ibid., 5.
[34] See Nicolas Bourriaud, *Relational Aesthetics* (Paris: Le Presses Du Réel, 1998), 113; Steven Henry Madoff, "Service Aesthetics," *Artforum* 47, no. 1 (September 2008): 165; and Claire Bishop, "The Social Turn: Collaboration and Its Discontents," *Artforum* 45, no. 6 (February 2006): 178.
[35] Bishop, " Social Turn," 181.
[36] Ibid.
[37] Bourriaud, *Relational Aesthetics*, 7.
[38] Eugene Halton, "Pragmatism," in *Encyclopedia of Social Theory*, ed. George Ritzer (Thousand Oaks, Calif.: Sage Publications, 2004), 5–6.
[39] Howard Cannatella, "Dewey's Art as Experience" (paper presented at the Philosophy of Education Society of Australasia Conference, 2007), 7.
[40] Jay, "Somaesthetics and Democracy," 56.
[41] John Dewey, "Art as Experience," in *The Philosopher's Handbook*, ed. Stanley Rosen (New York: Random House, 2000), 274, as quoted in Mary Jane Jacob, "In the Space of Art," *Buddha Mind in Contemporary Art*, ed. Jacquelynn Baas and Mary Jane Jacob (Berkeley: University of California Press, 2004), 167.
[42] Jörg Heiser, quoted in William Straw, "The Circulatory Turn" (unpublished proofs), 25, in The Wireless Spectrum: *The Politics, Practices and Poetics of Mobile Media*, ed. Barbara Crow, Michael Longford, and Kim Sawchuk (Toronto: University of Toronto Press, 2010).
[43] See, for example, Relyea, "Your Art World," 3–4, and Pat MacIntyre, "(More or Less) Democratic Forms: Relational Aesthetics and the Rhetoric of Globalization," *Anamesa* 5, no. 1 (Spring 2007), 44.
[44] Kate Southworth, "Transformative Practices: The Aesthetics, Ethics, and Politics of Social Relations" (paper presented at the International Symposium on Electronic Art, 2009), 3.
[45] Jay, "Somaesthetics and Democracy," 55.
[46] Carl Hulse, "After Health Vote, Threats on Democrats," *New York Times*, March 24, 2010, http://www.nytimes.com/2010/03/25/health/policy/25health.html
[47] Cannatella, "Dewey's Art as Experience," 5.
[48] Ibid., 4.

Allora & Calzadilla

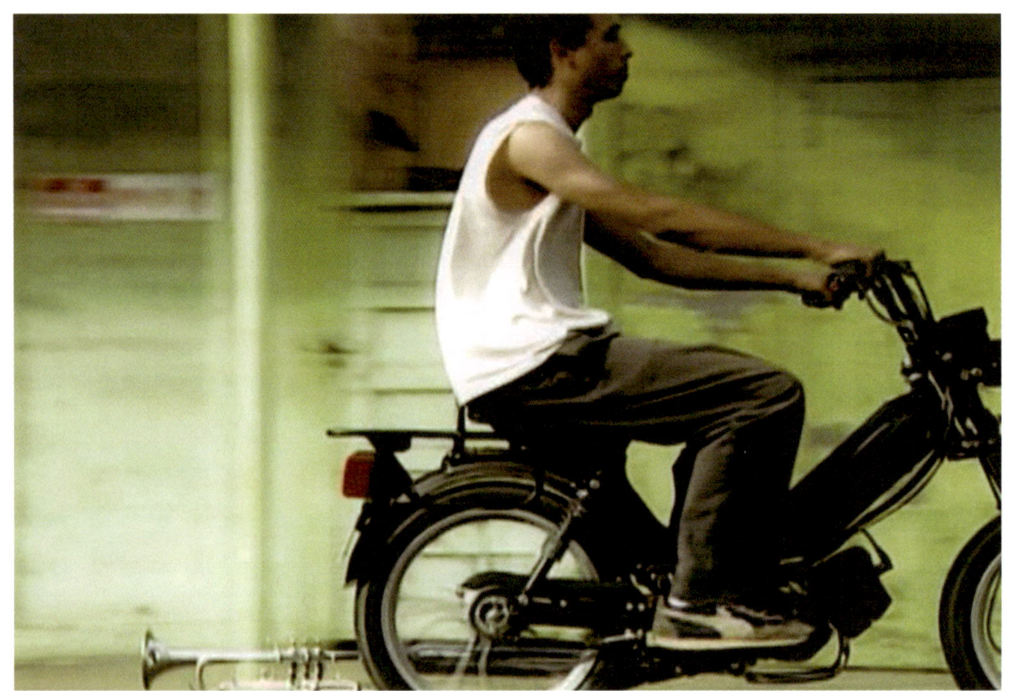

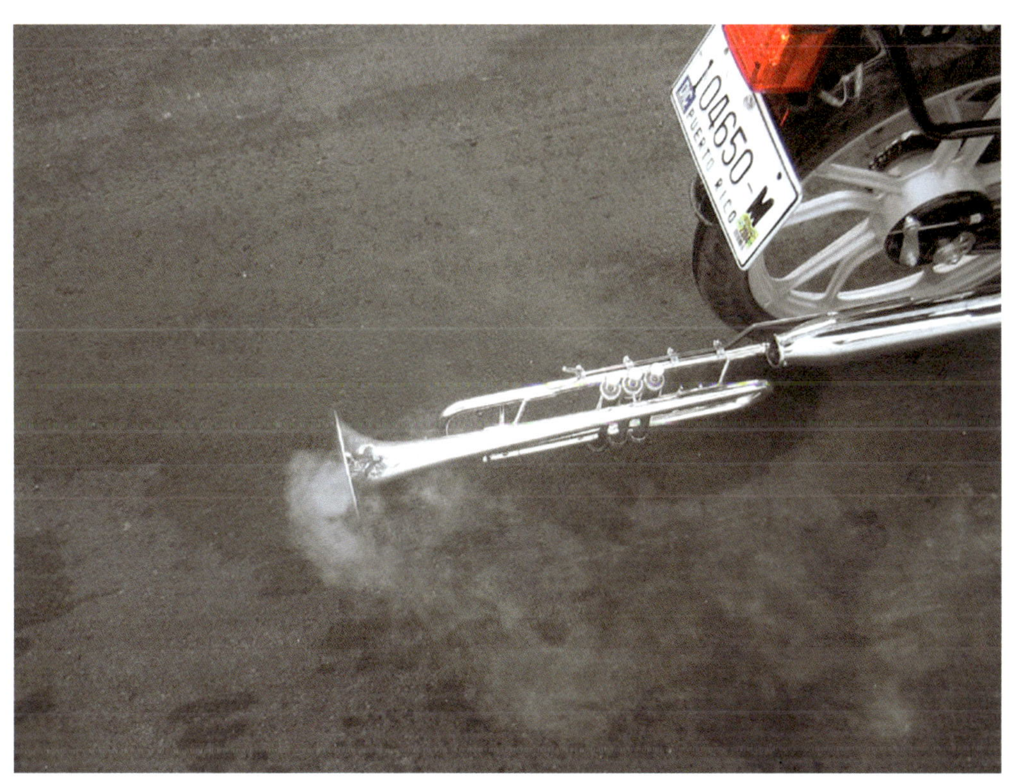

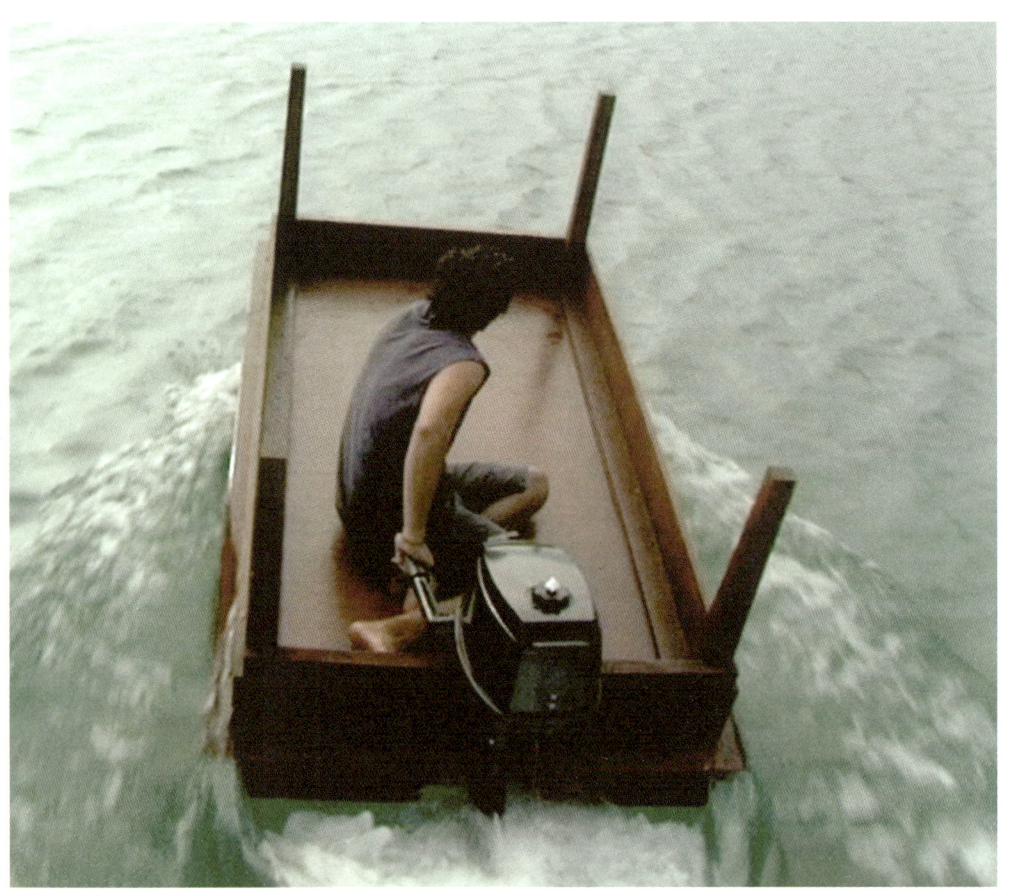

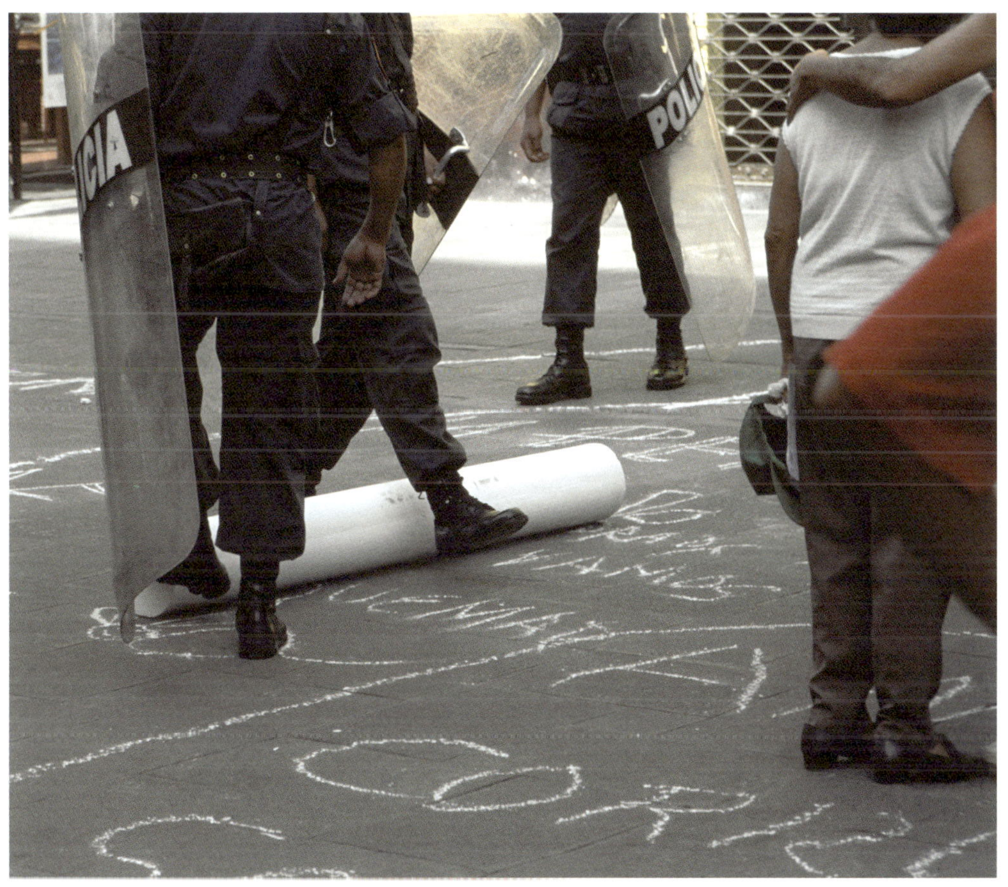

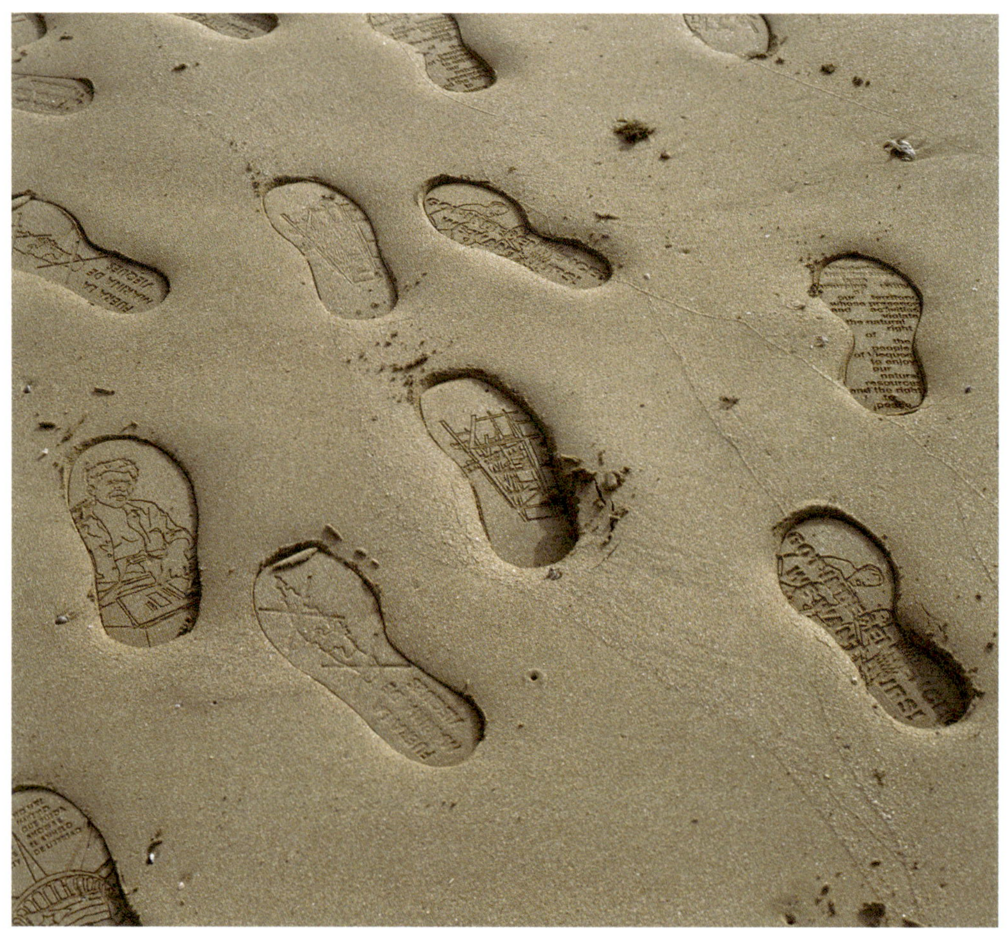

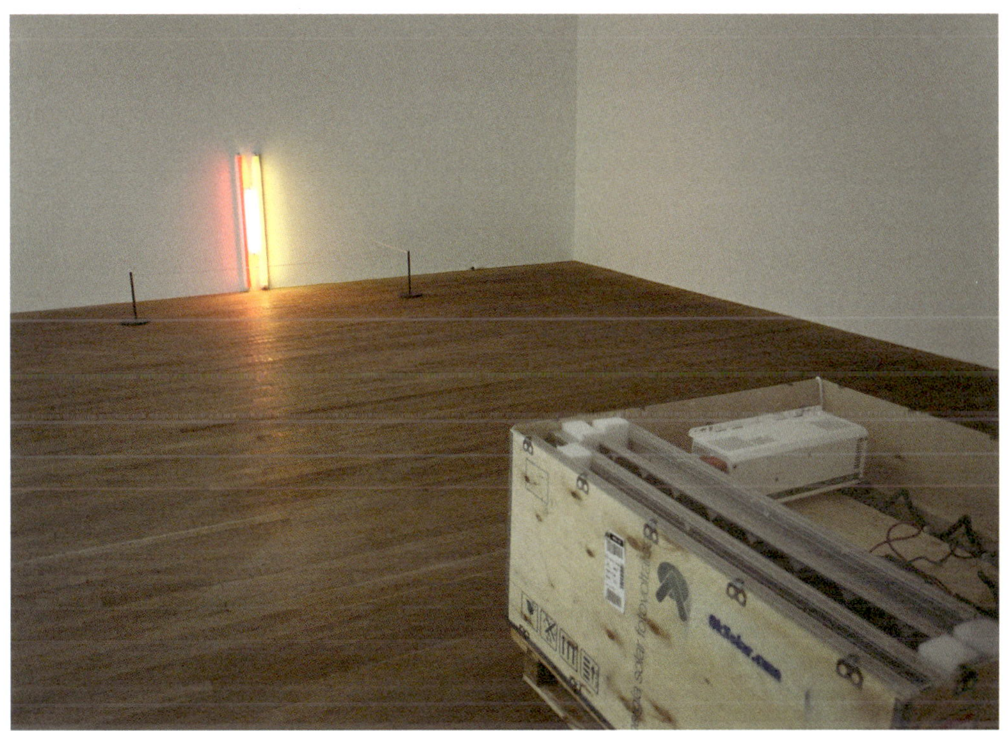

IT PROVIDES (CON)
IT PROVIDES (CON)
IT PROVIDES (CON)
IT PROVIDES (CON)

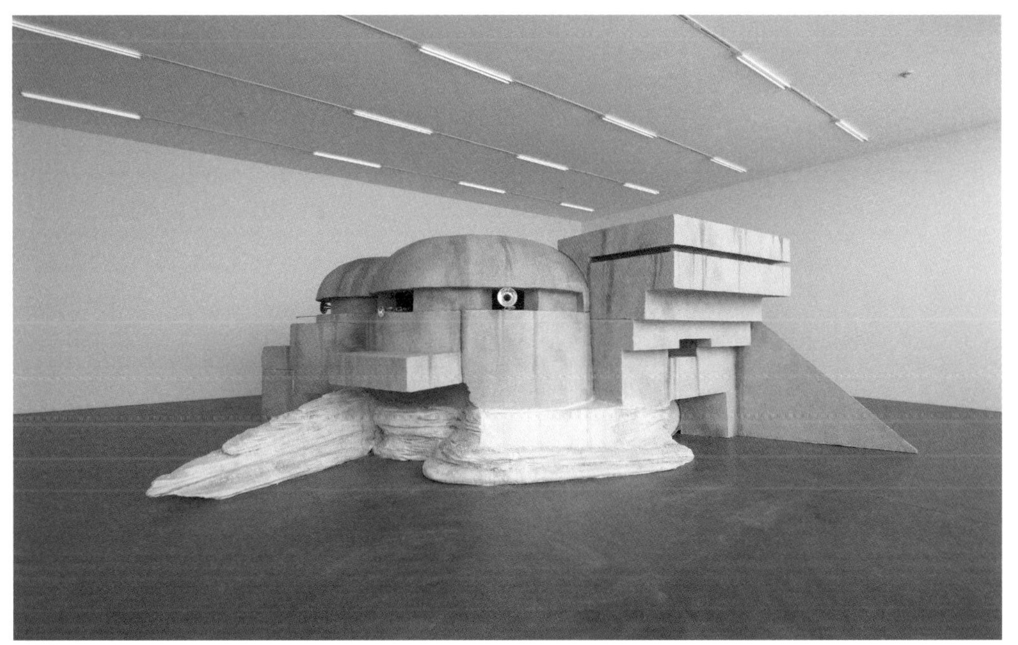

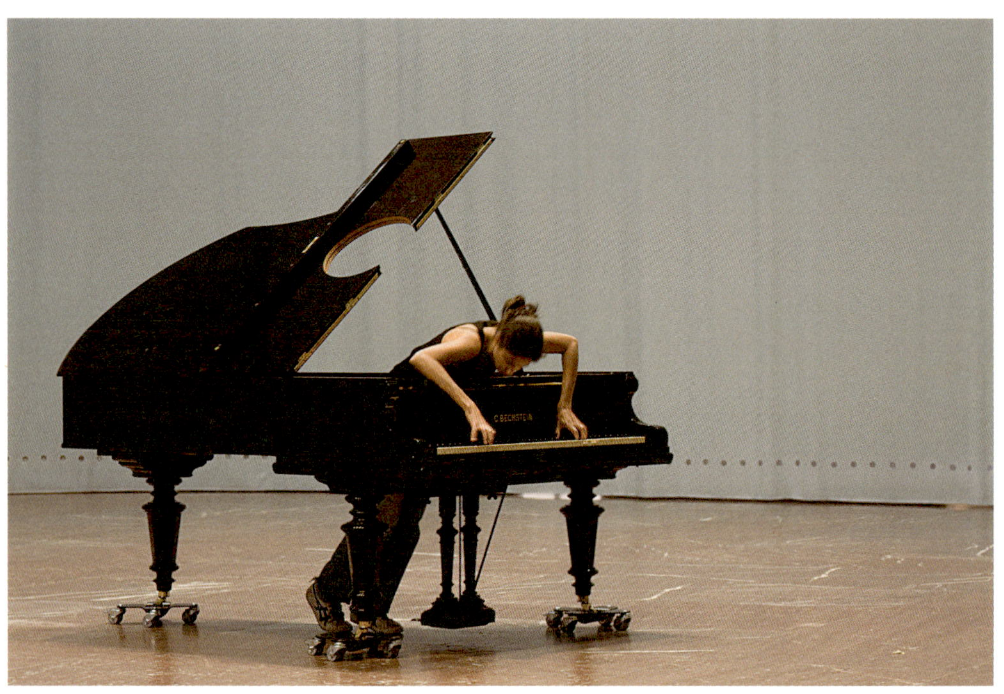

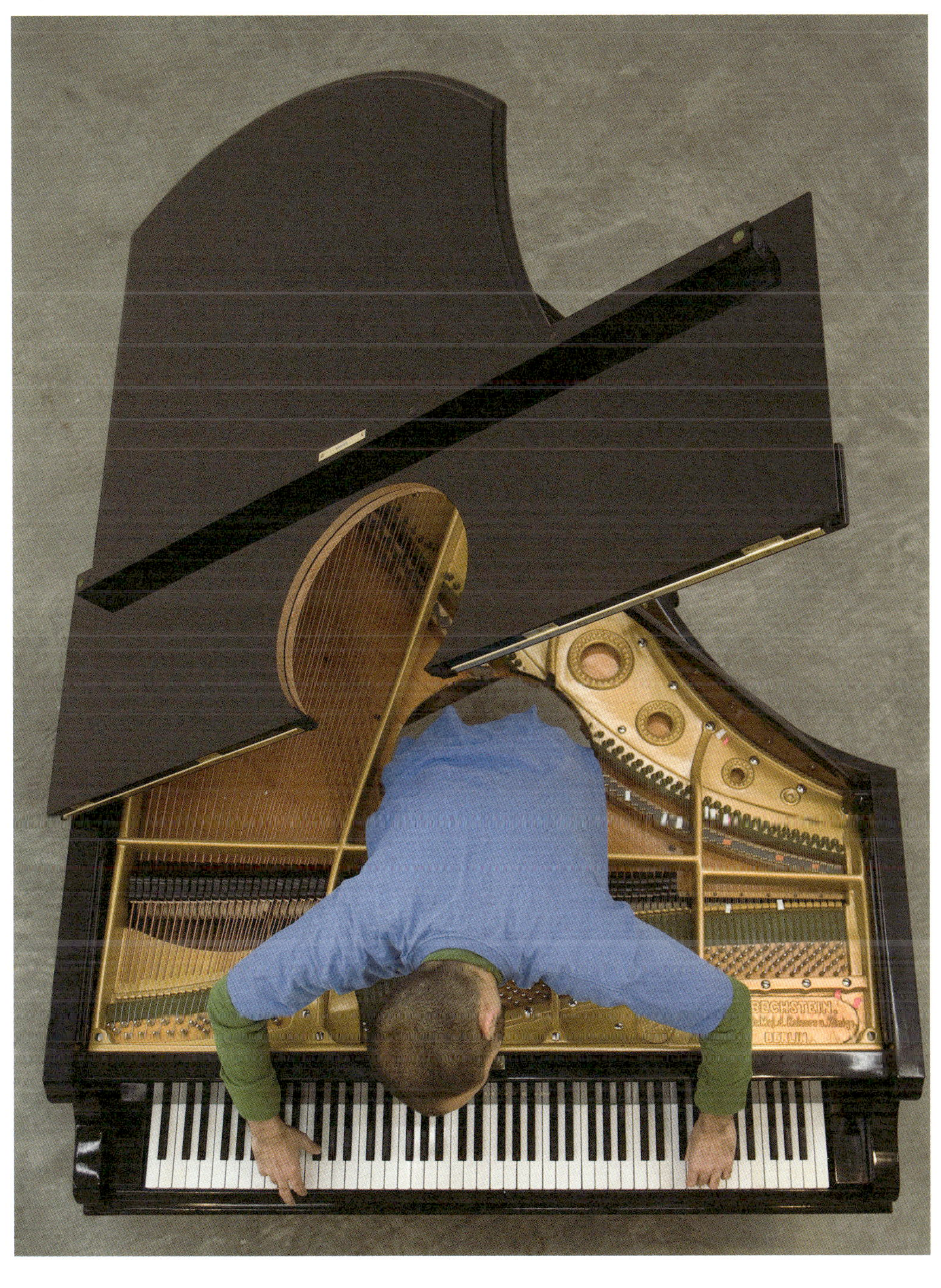

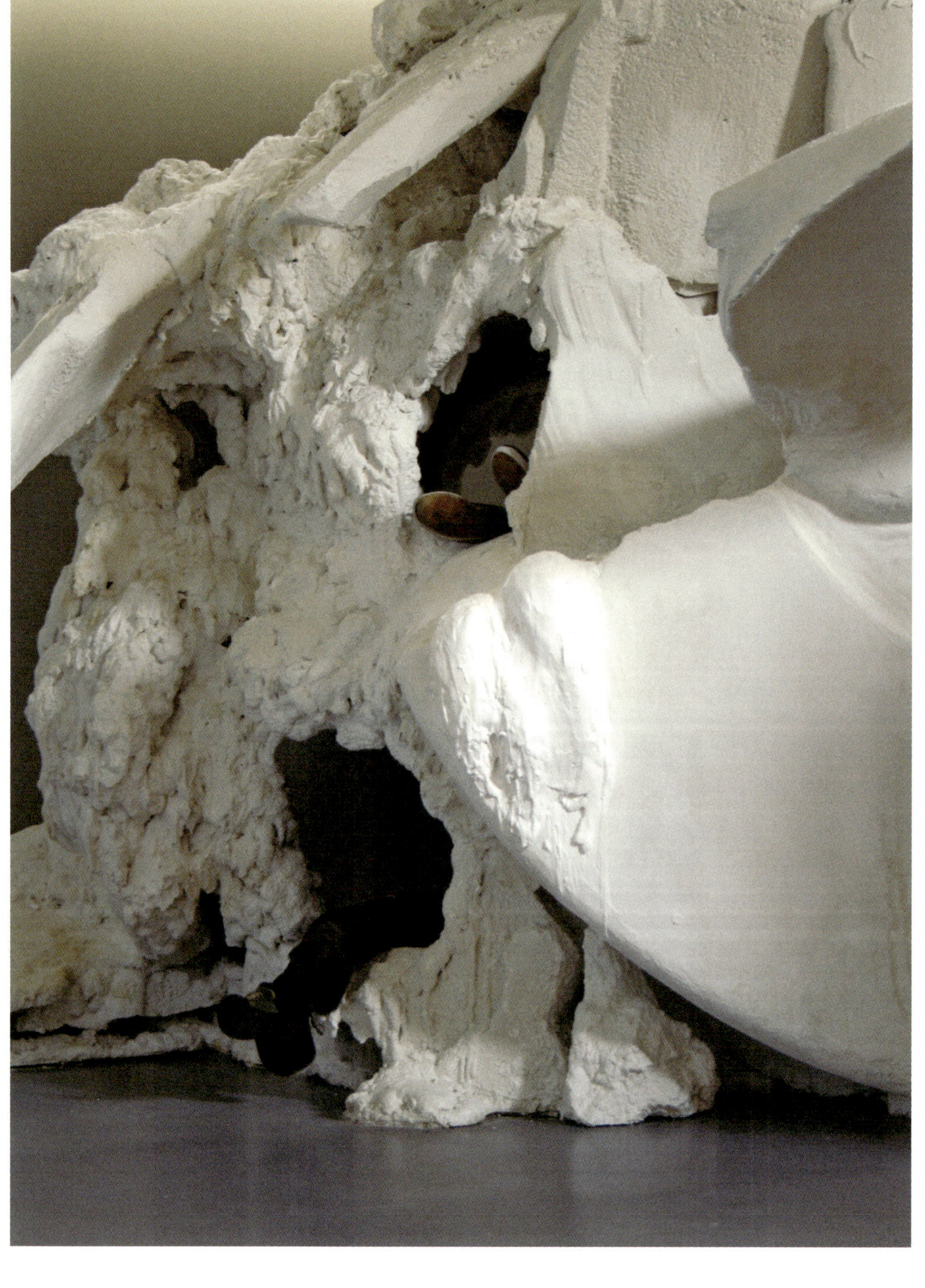

Pawel Althamer

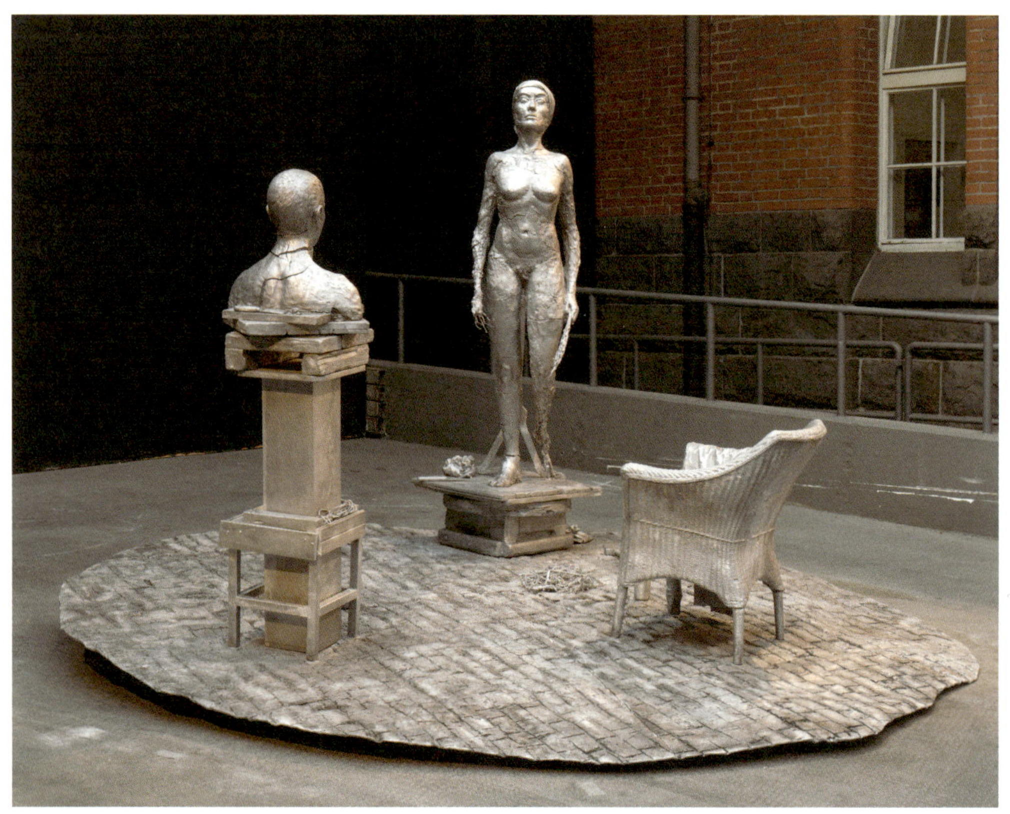

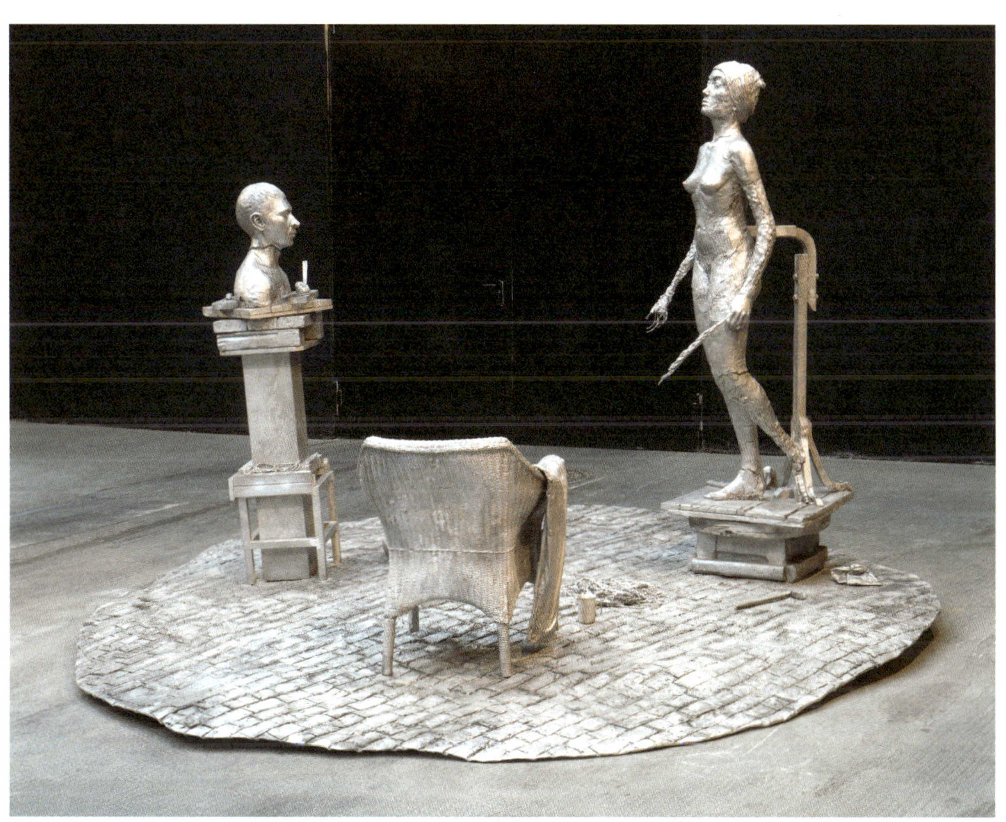

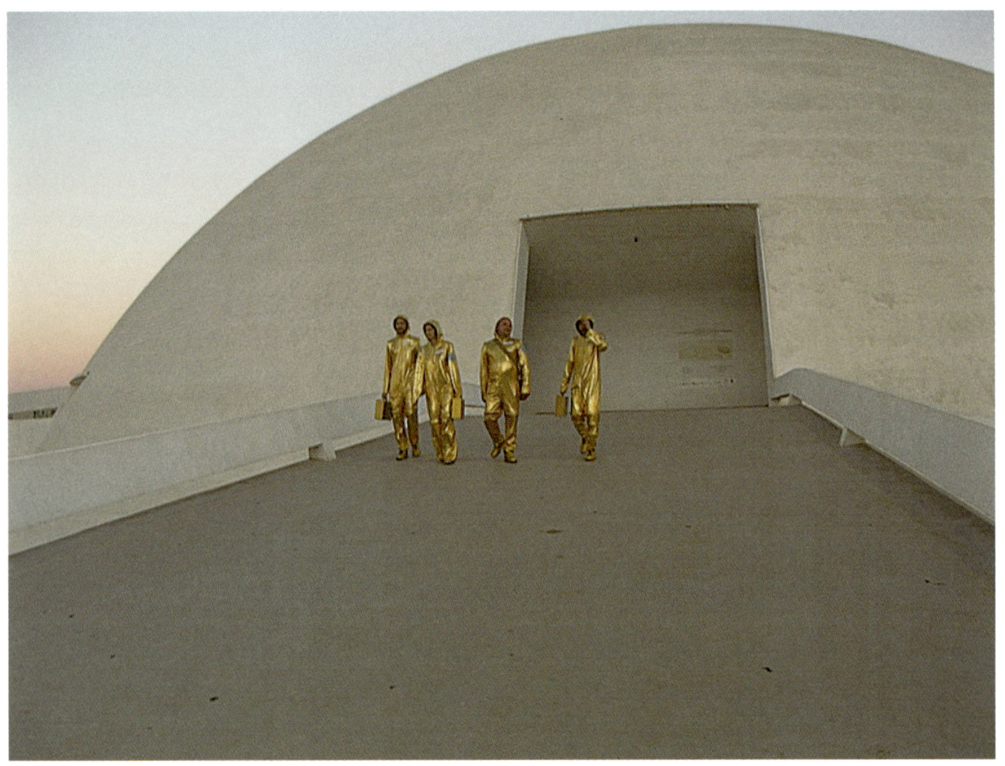

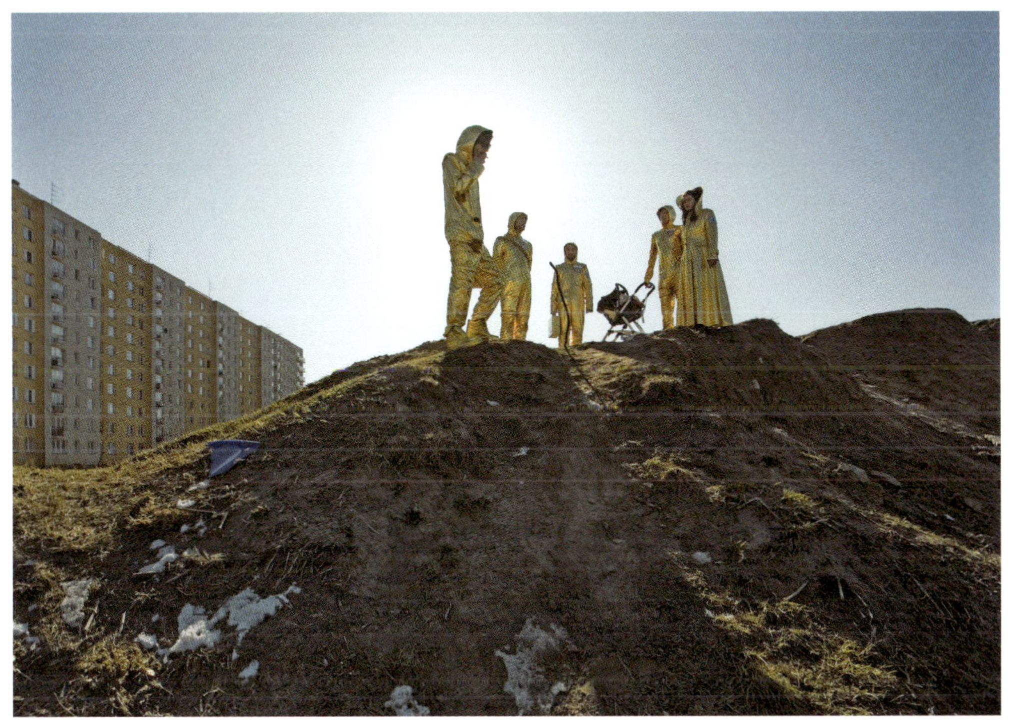

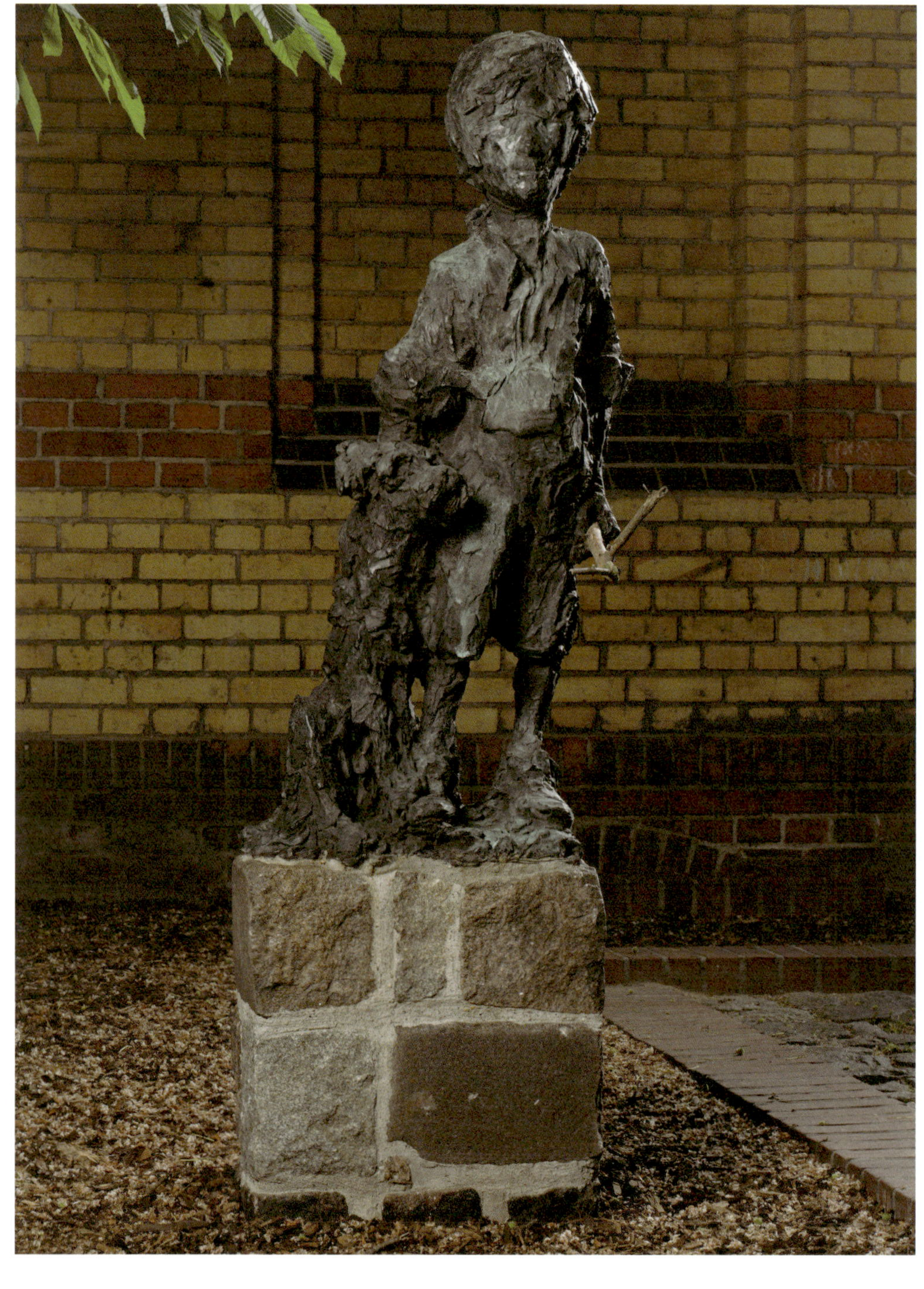

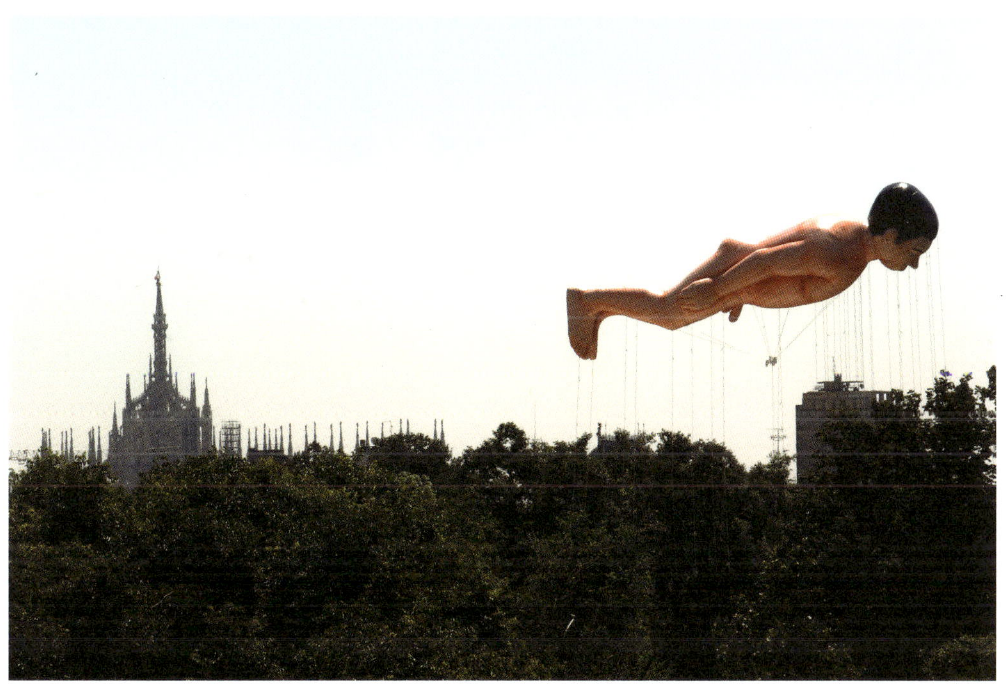

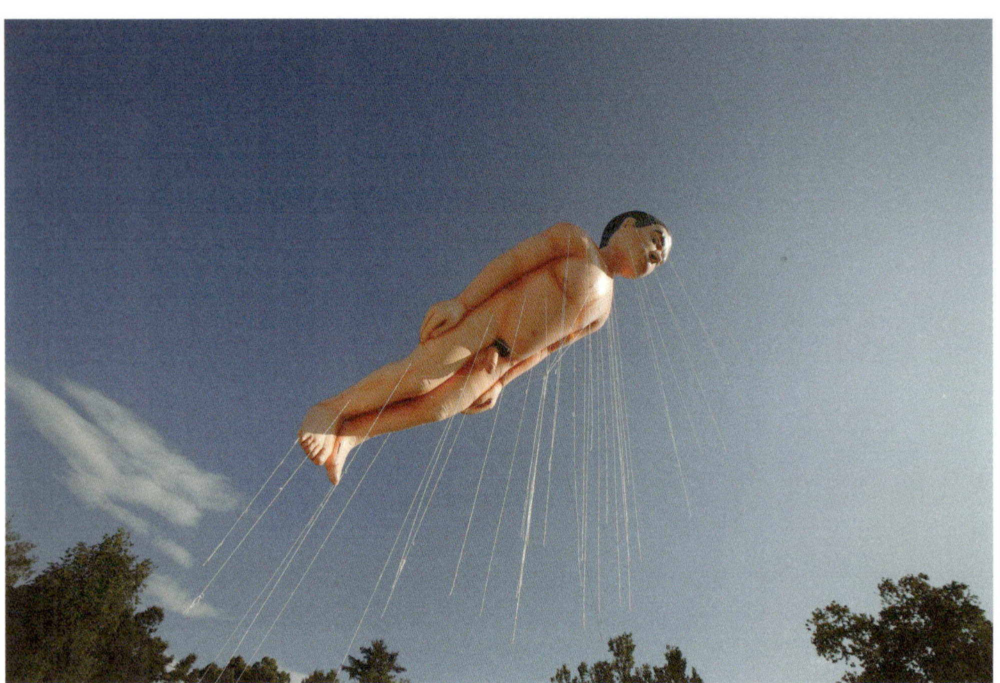

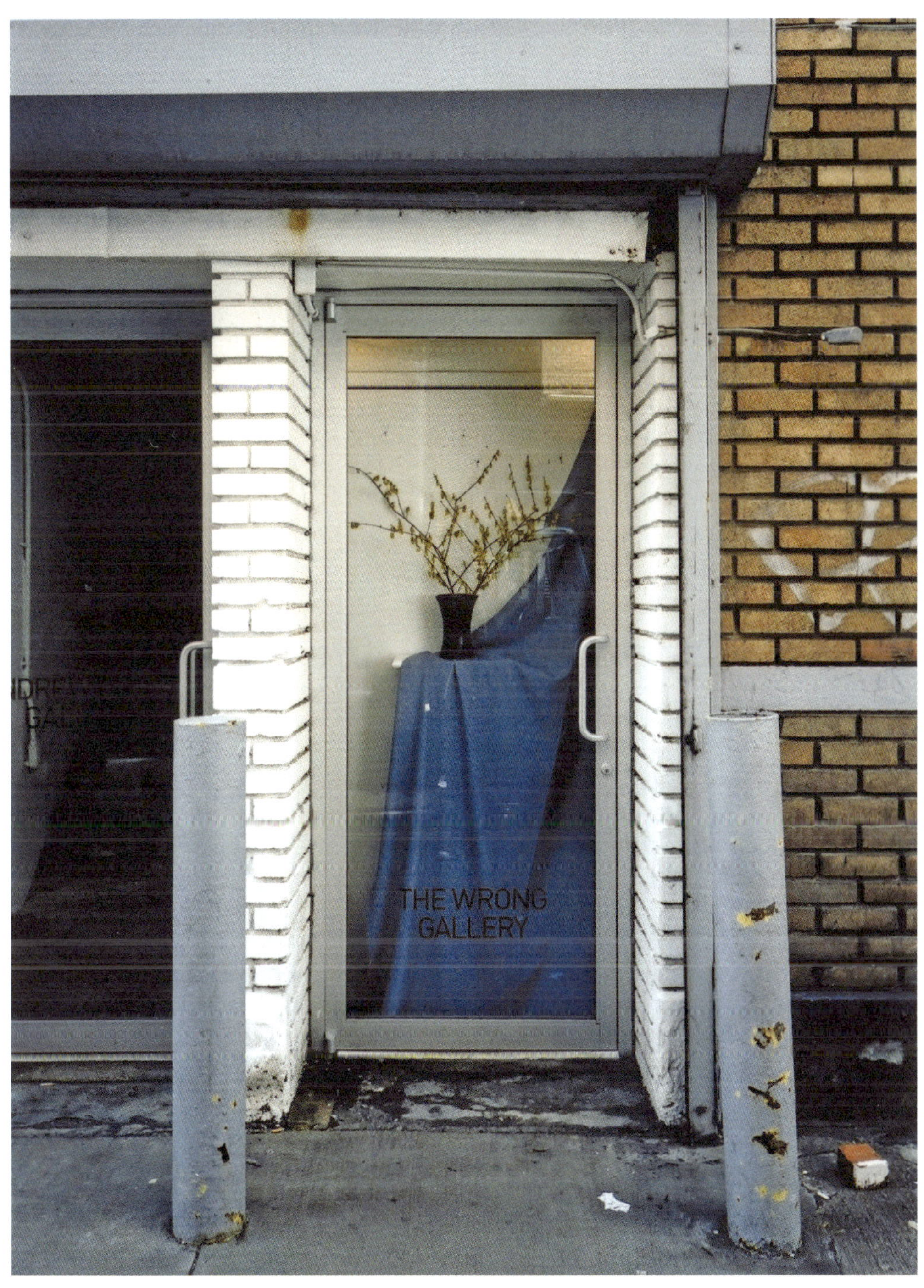
THE WRONG
GALLERY

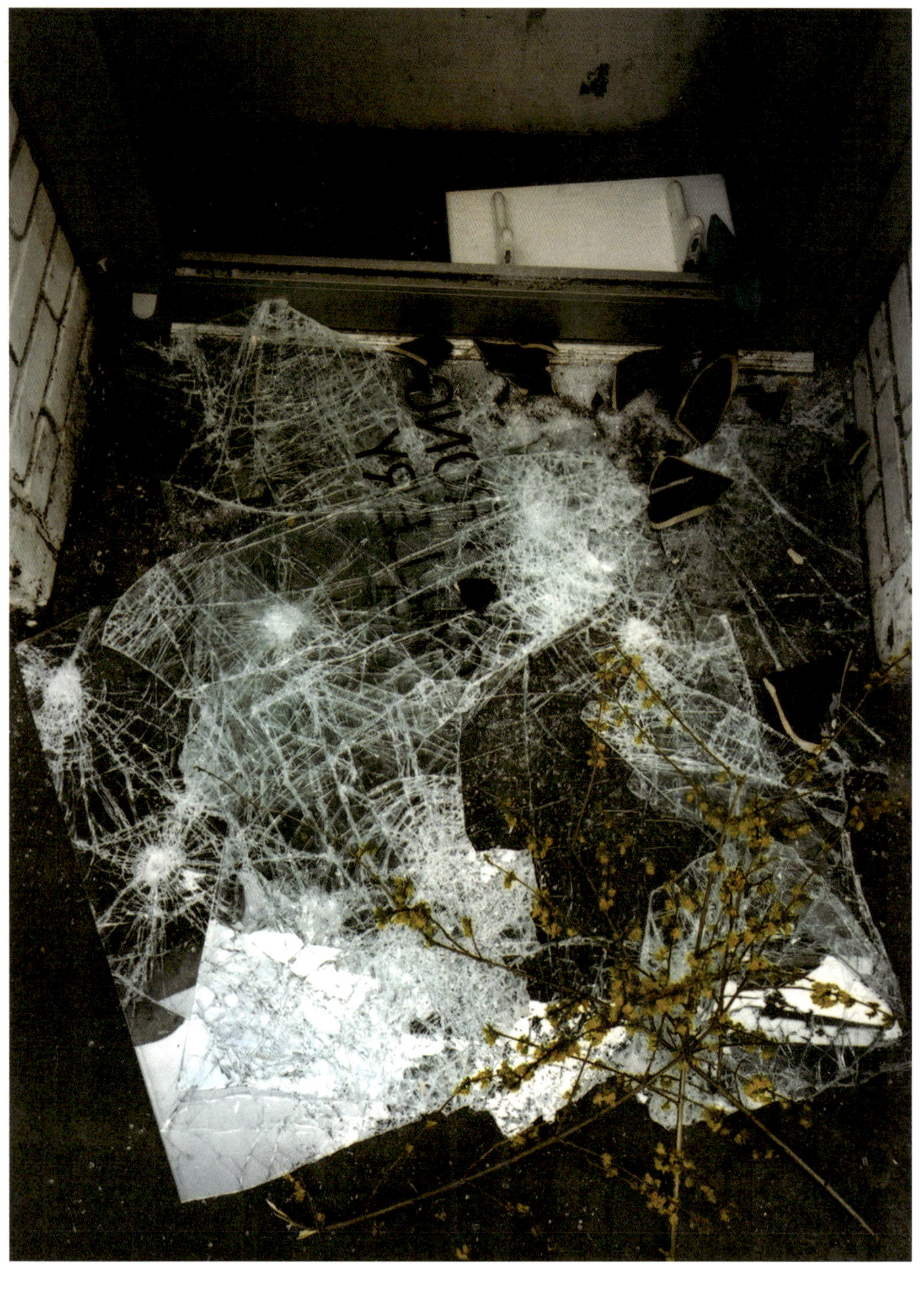

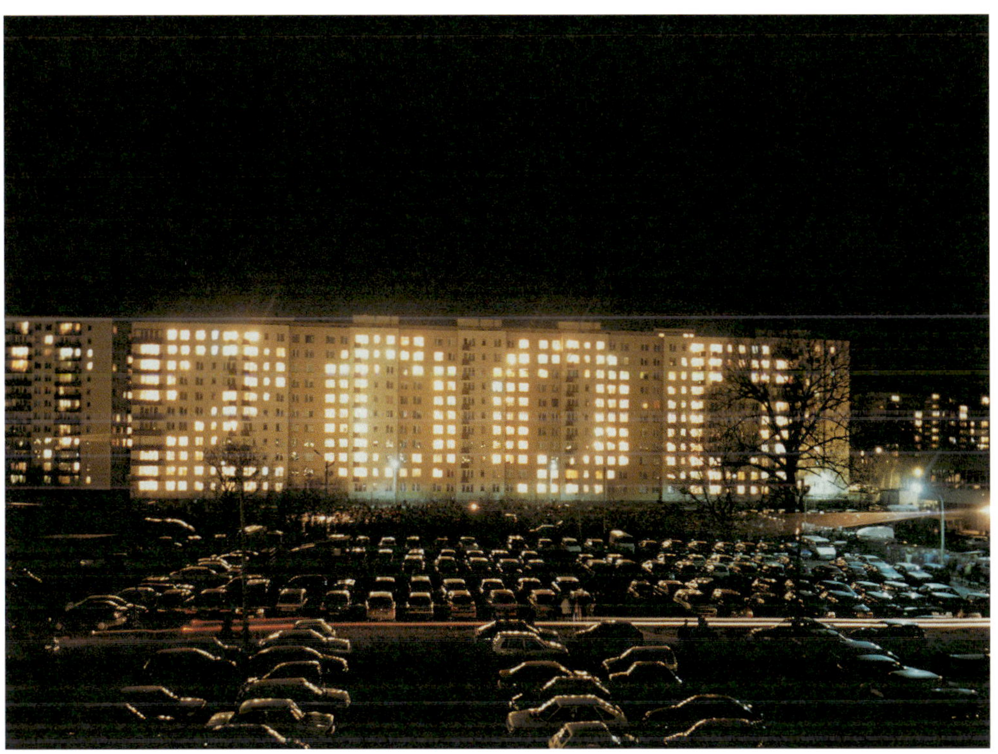

Marc Bijl

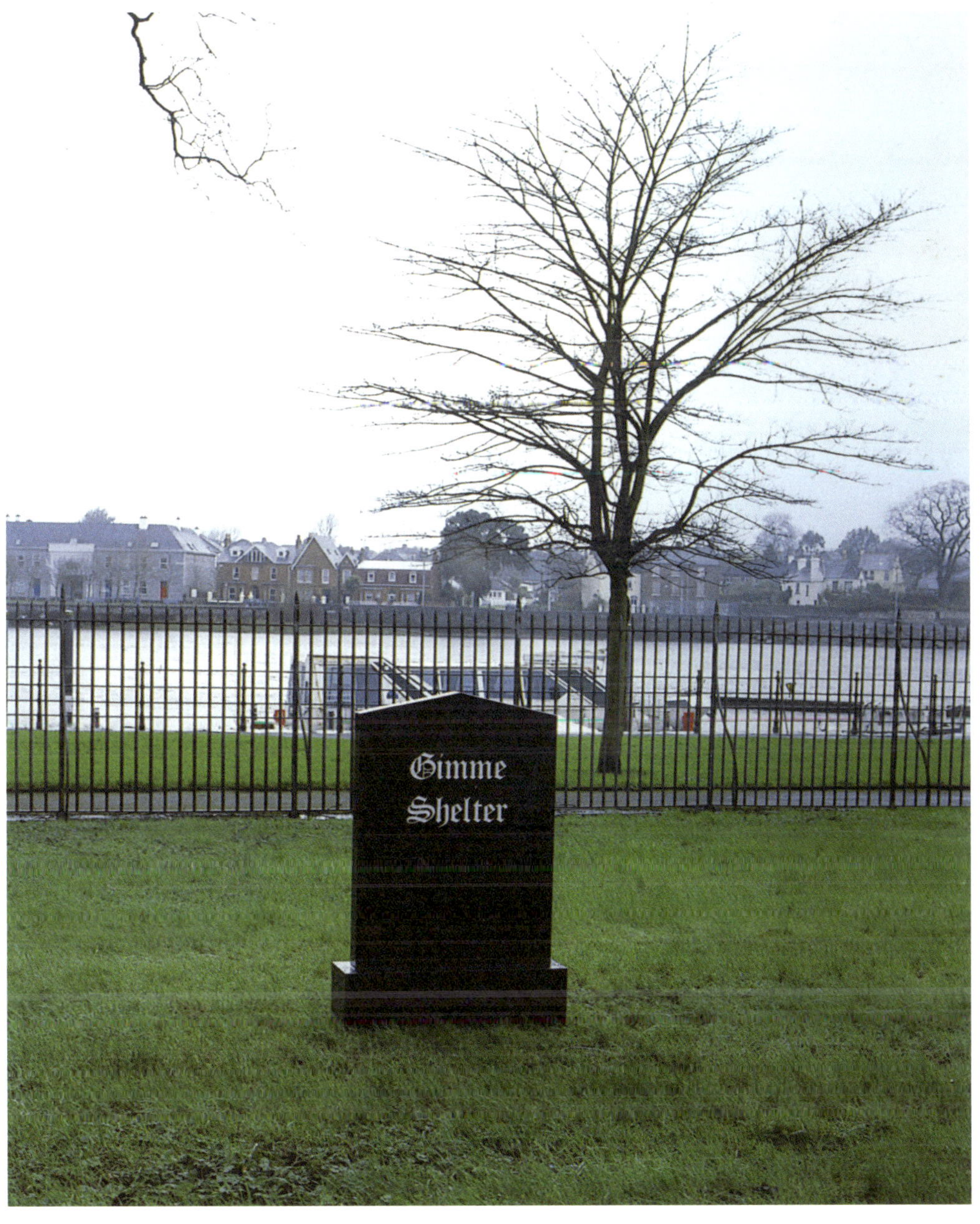

Gimme
Shelter

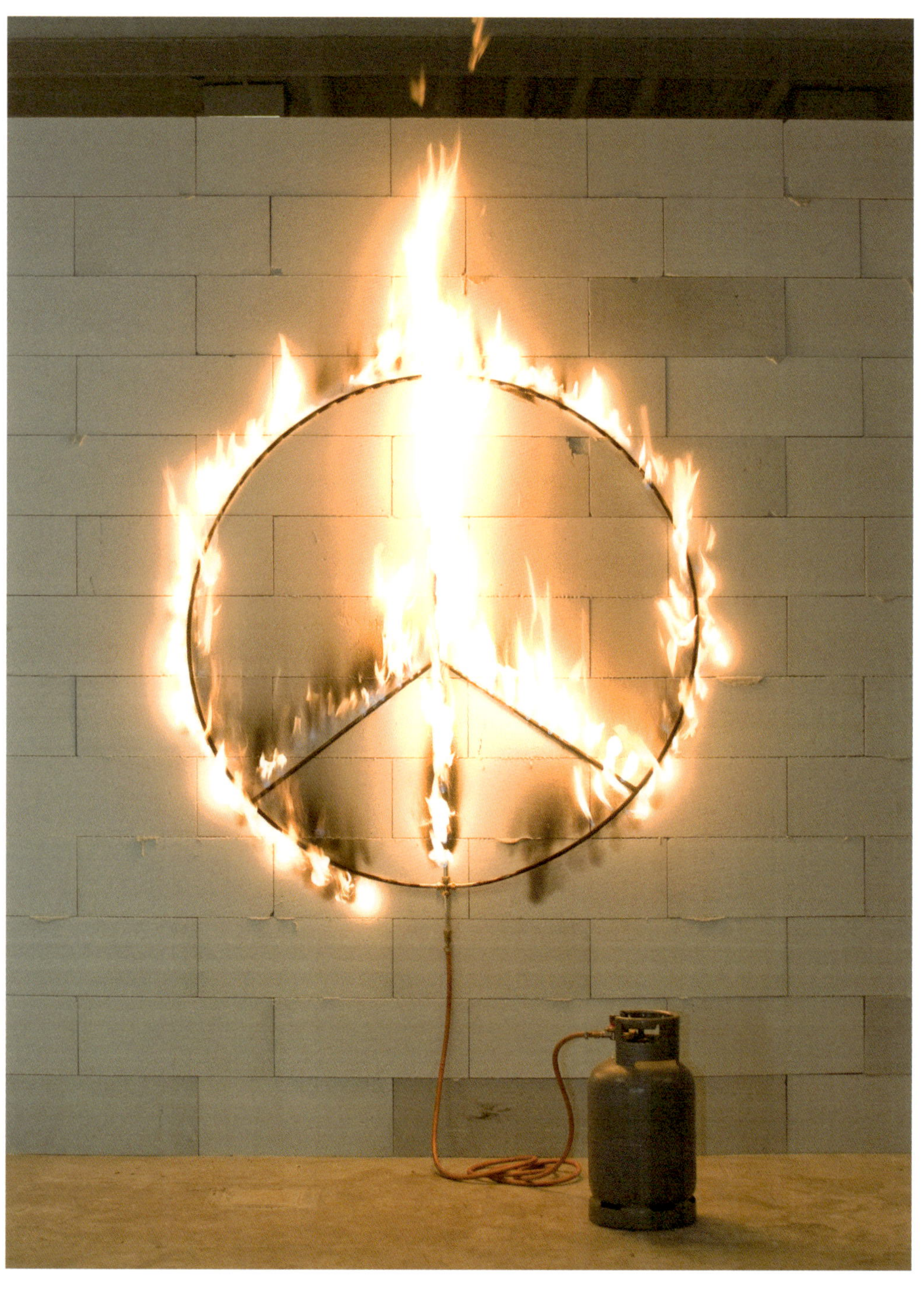

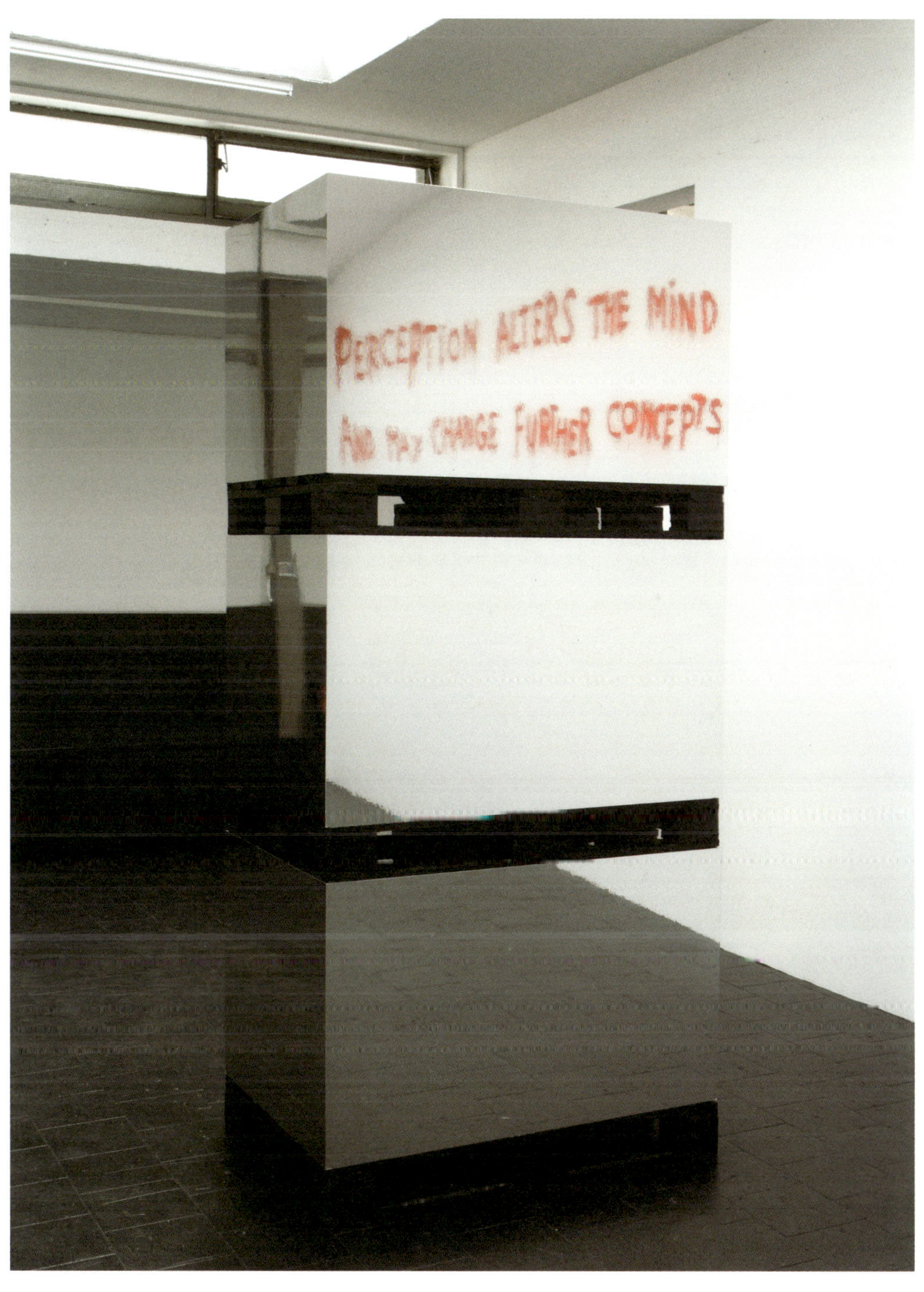
PERCEPTION ALTERS THE MIND
AND MAY CHANGE FURTHER CONCEPTS

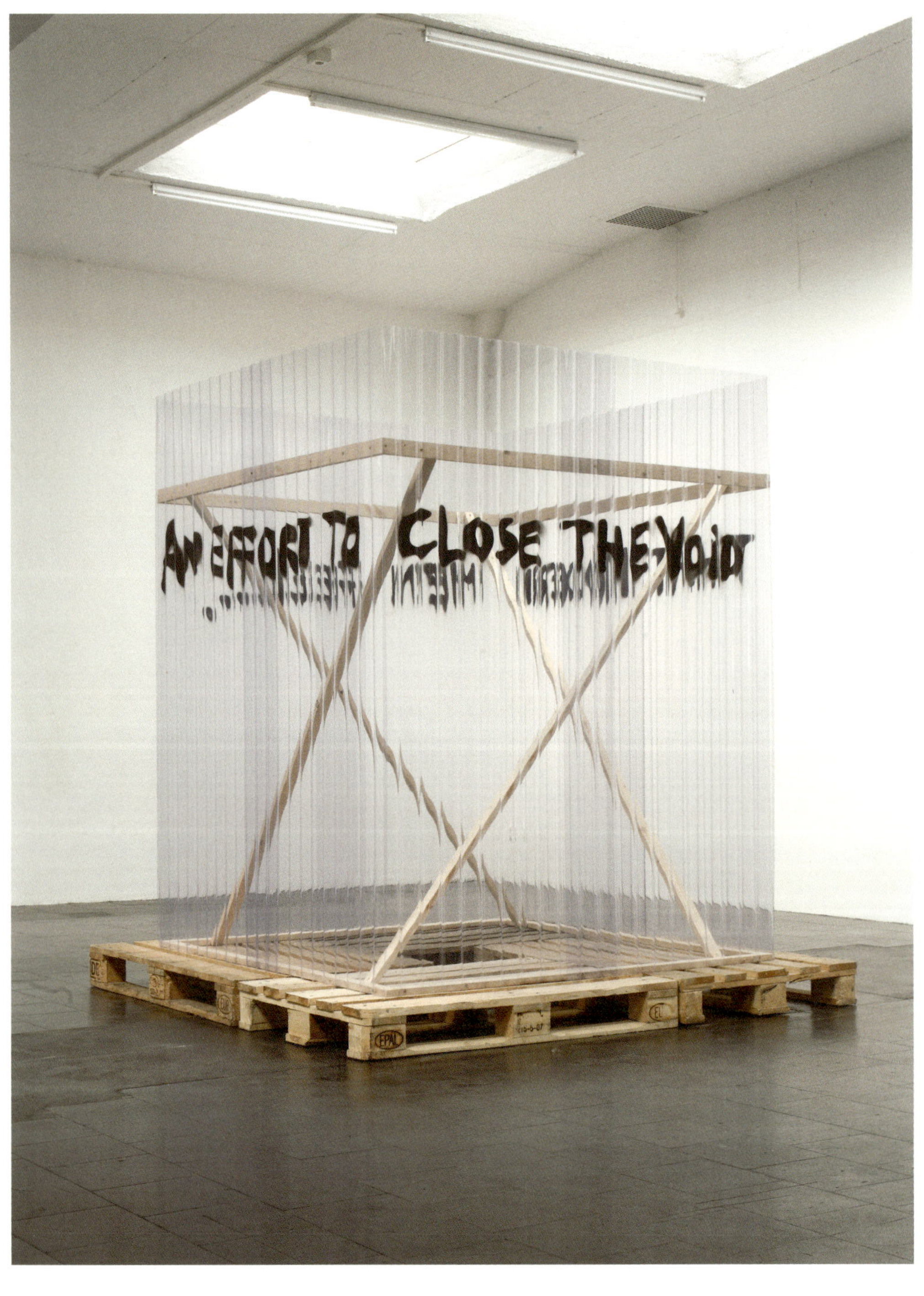
AN EFFORT TO CLOSE THE VOID

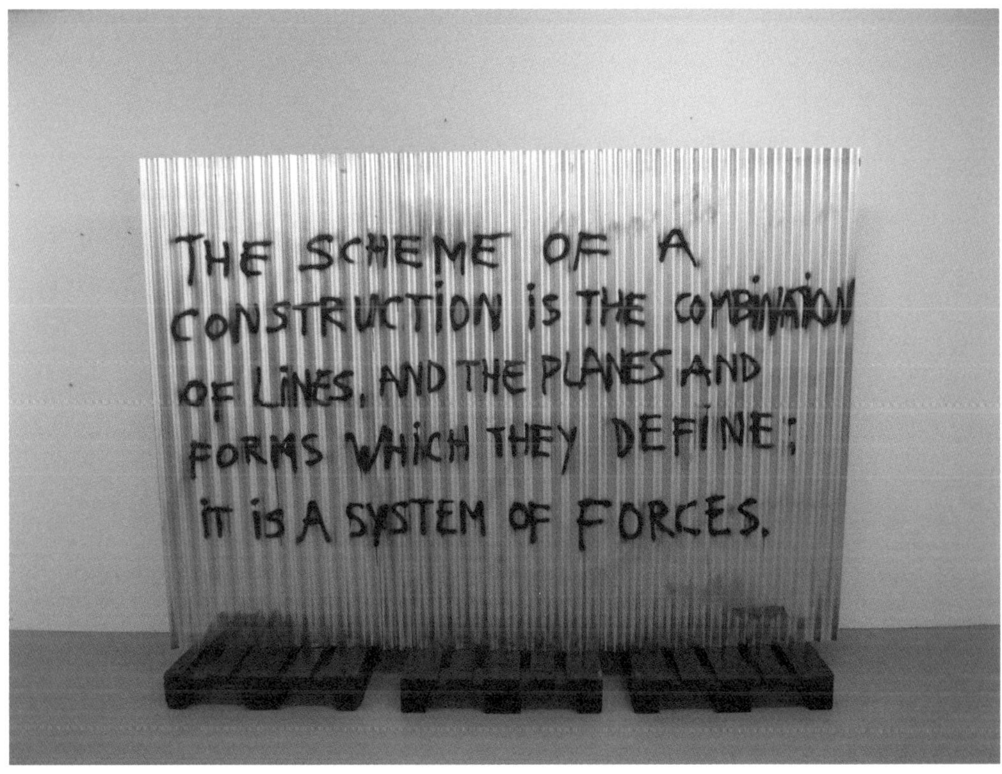
THE SCHEME OF A
CONSTRUCTION IS THE COMBINATION
OF LINES, AND THE PLANES AND
FORMS WHICH THEY DEFINE;
IT IS A SYSTEM OF FORCES.

Lara Favaretto

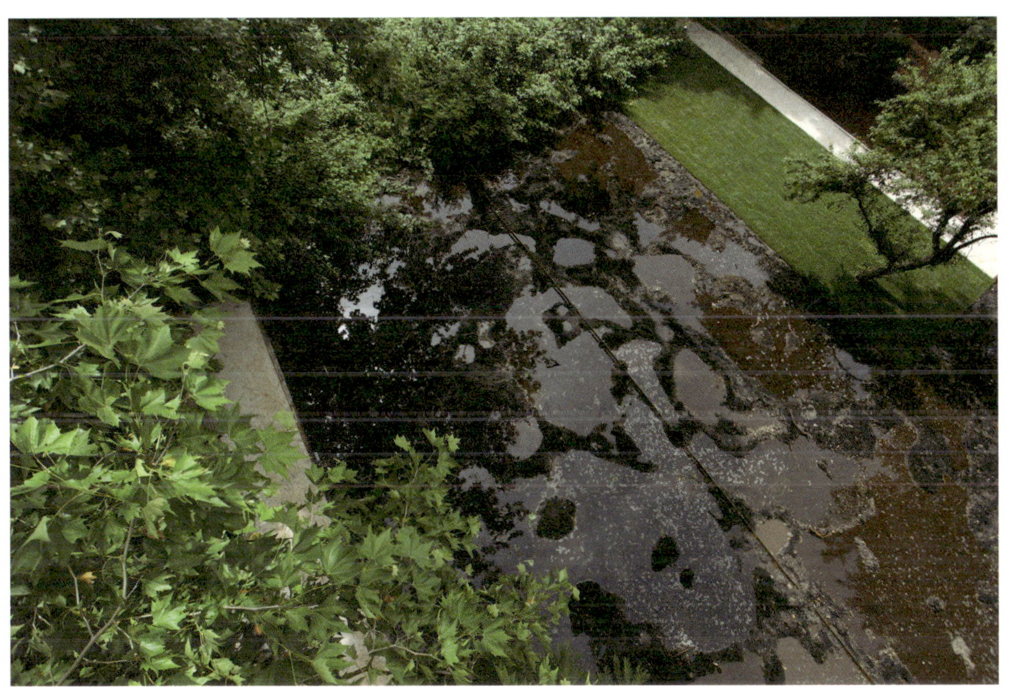

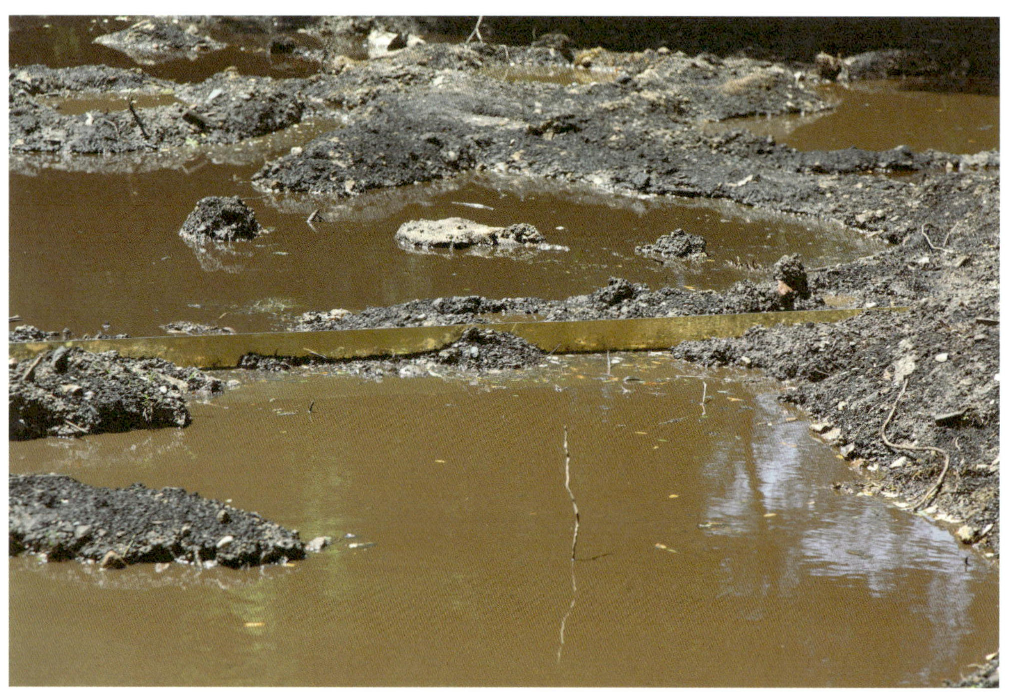

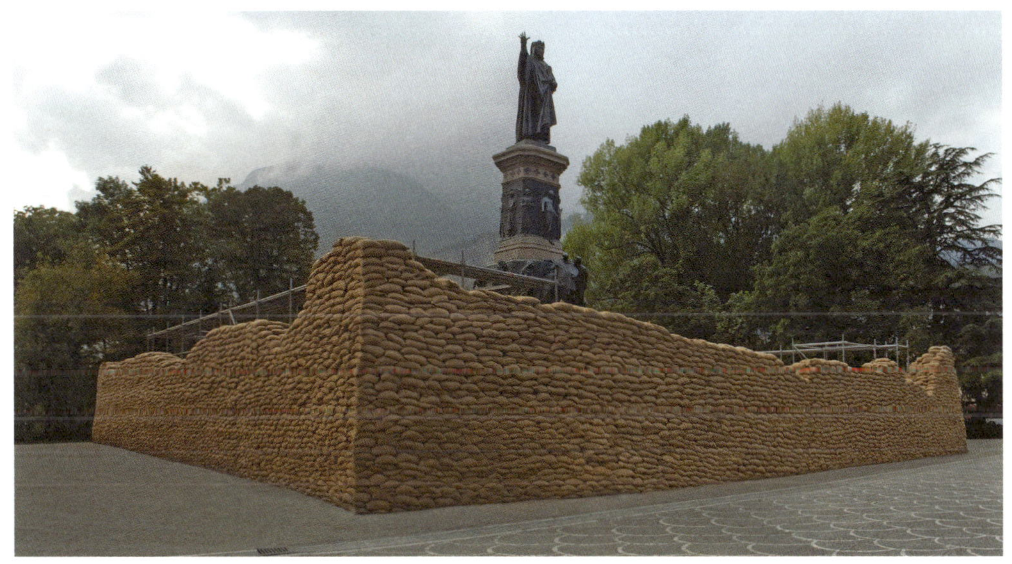

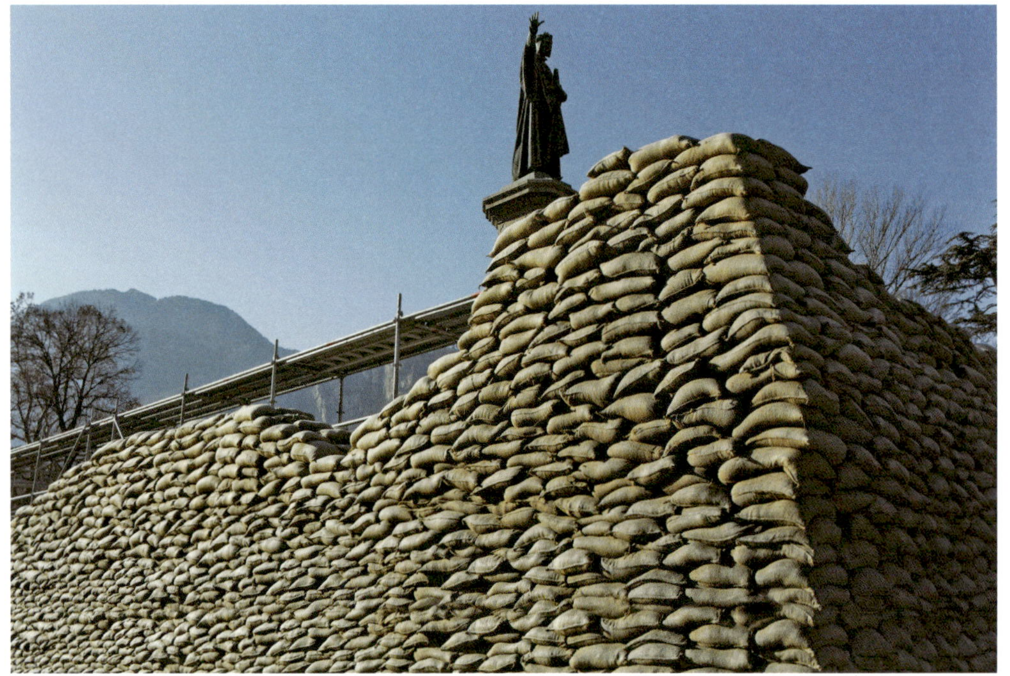

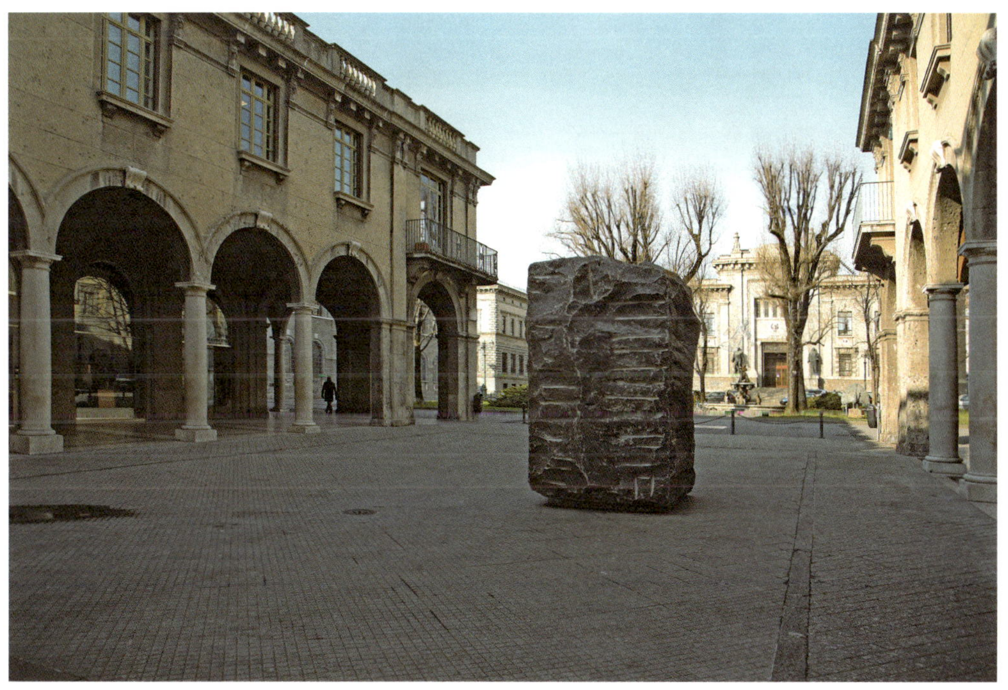

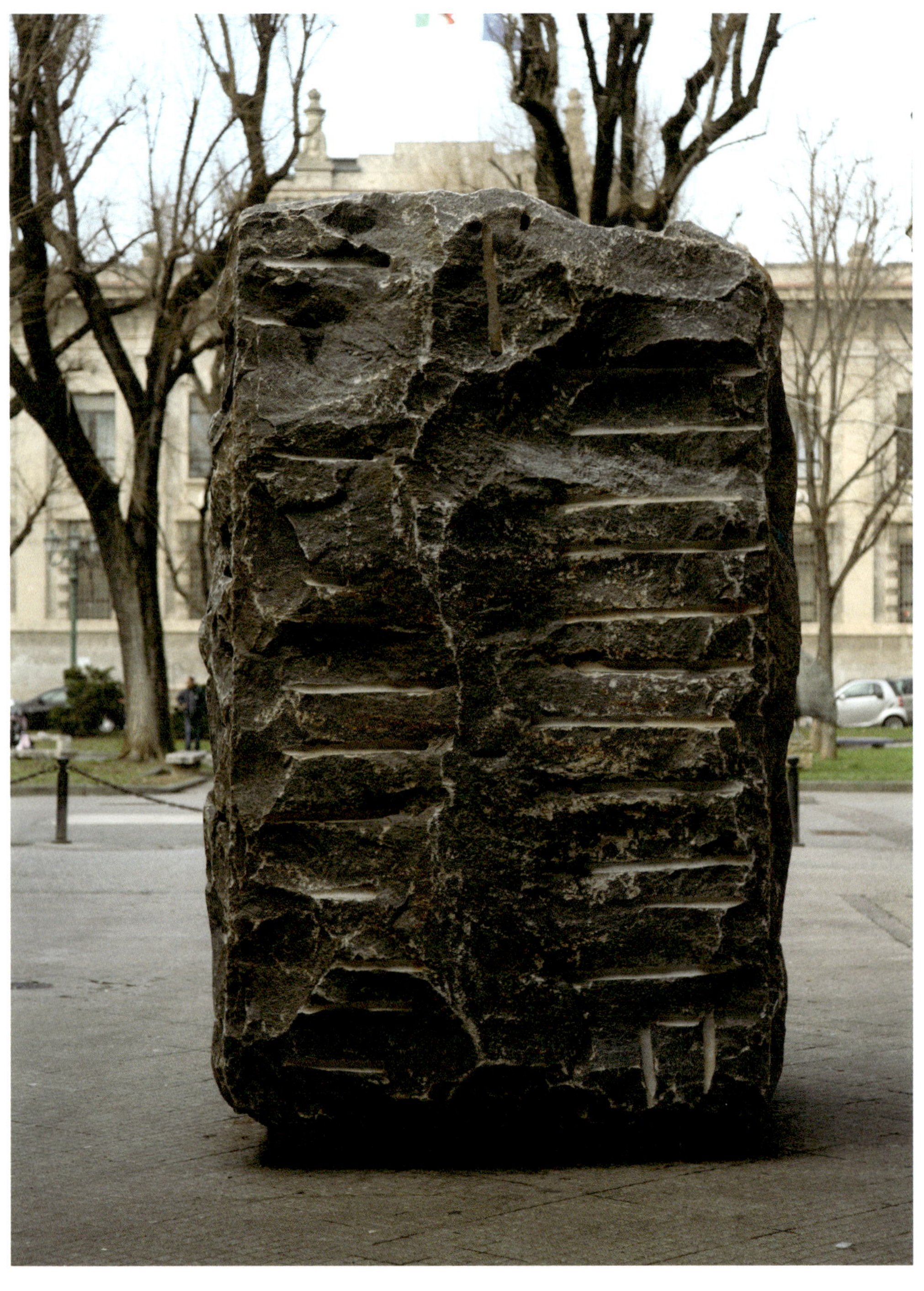

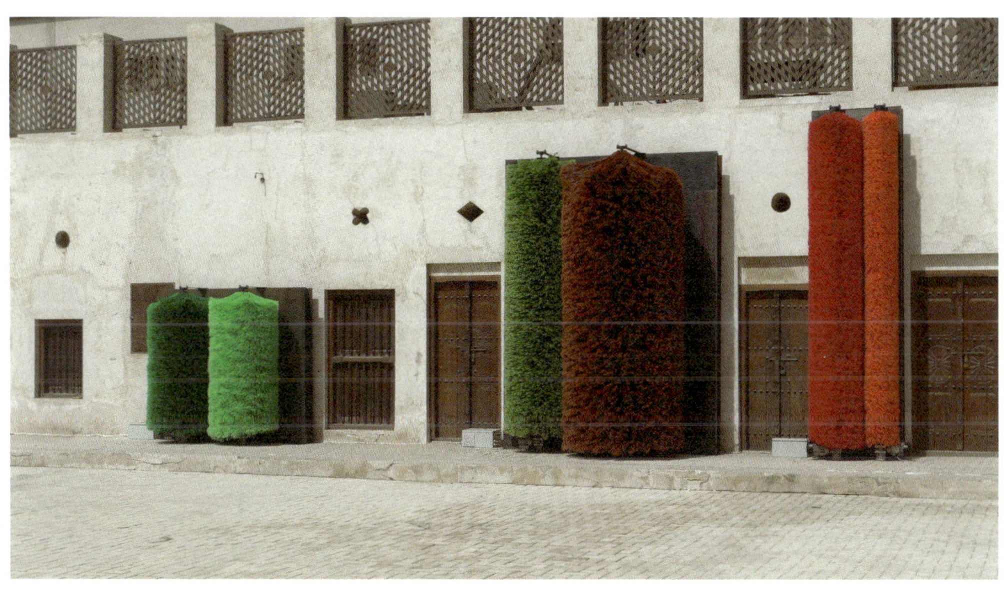

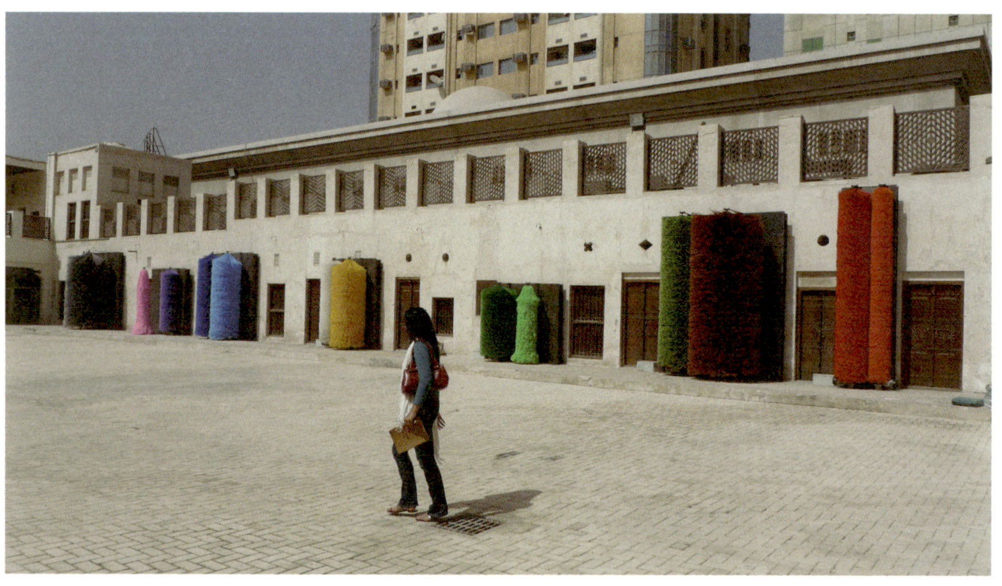

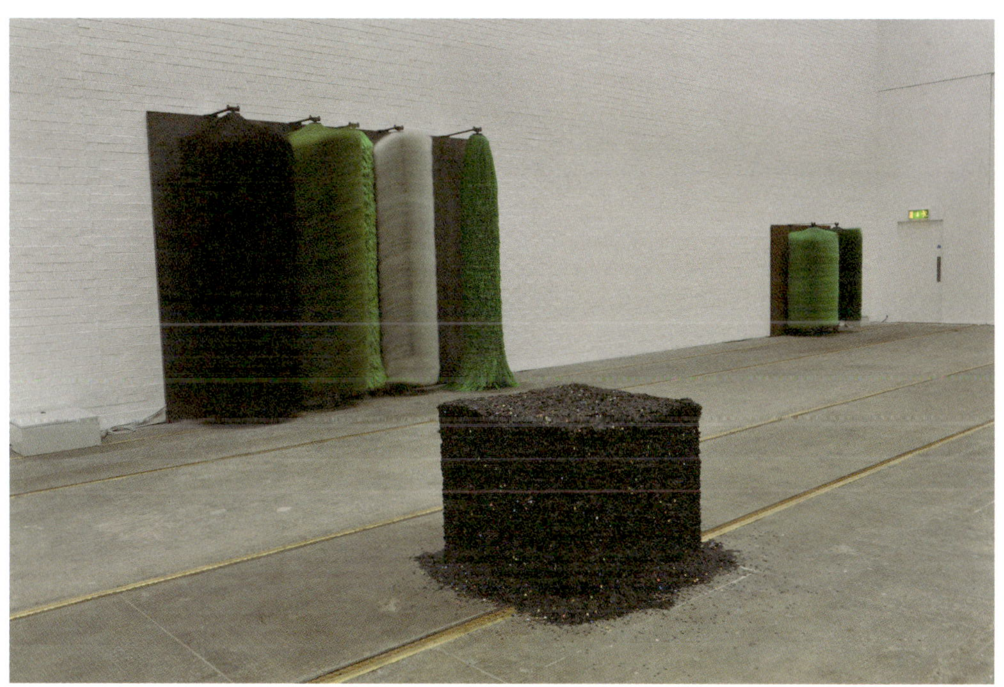

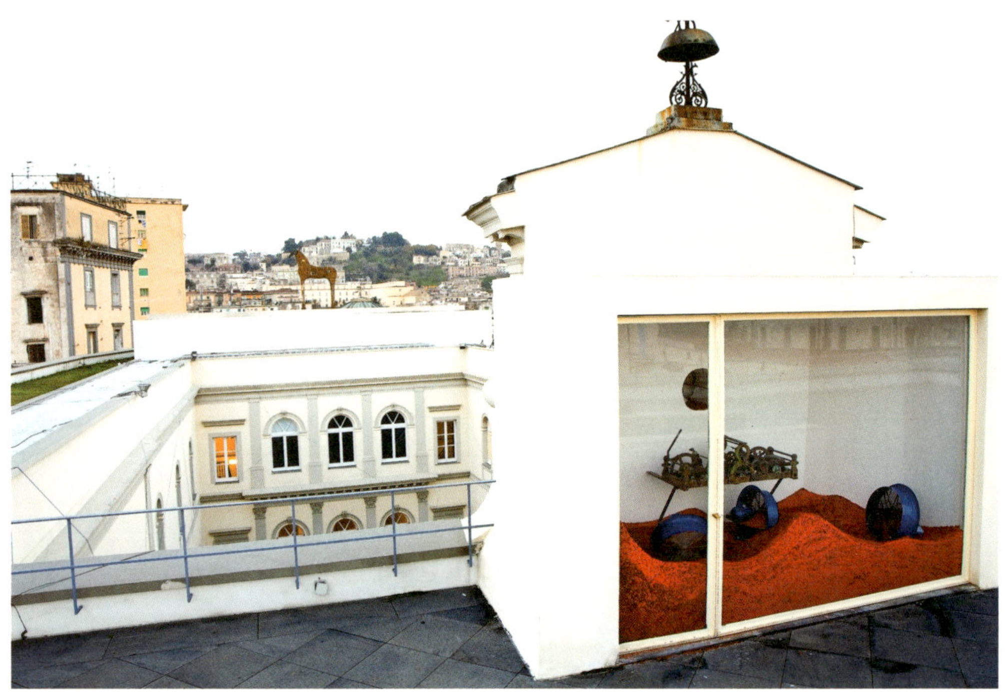

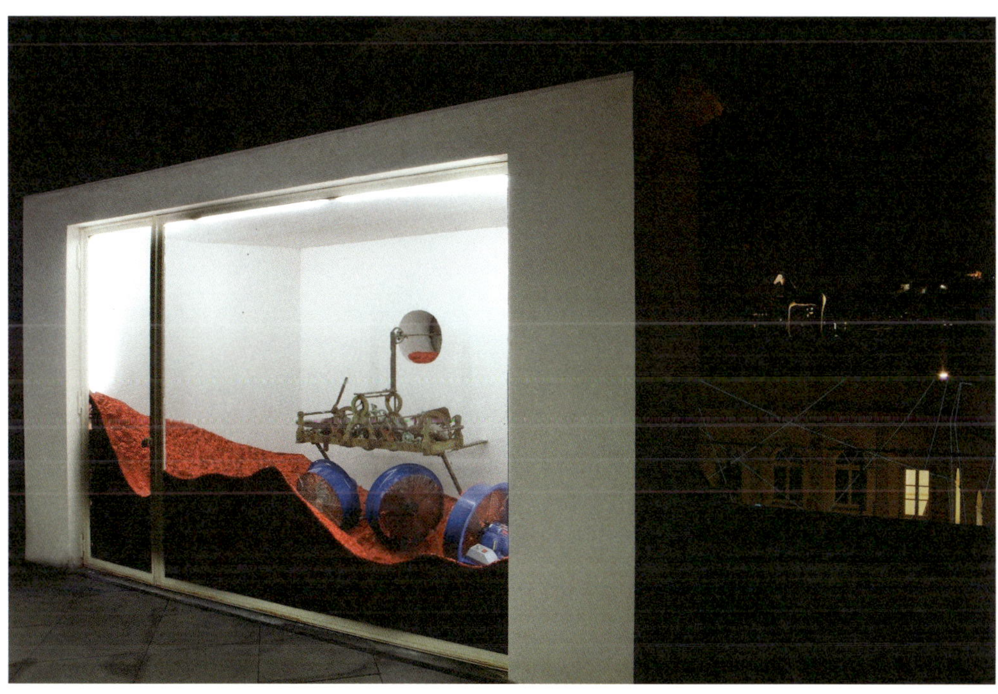

Geof Oppenheimer

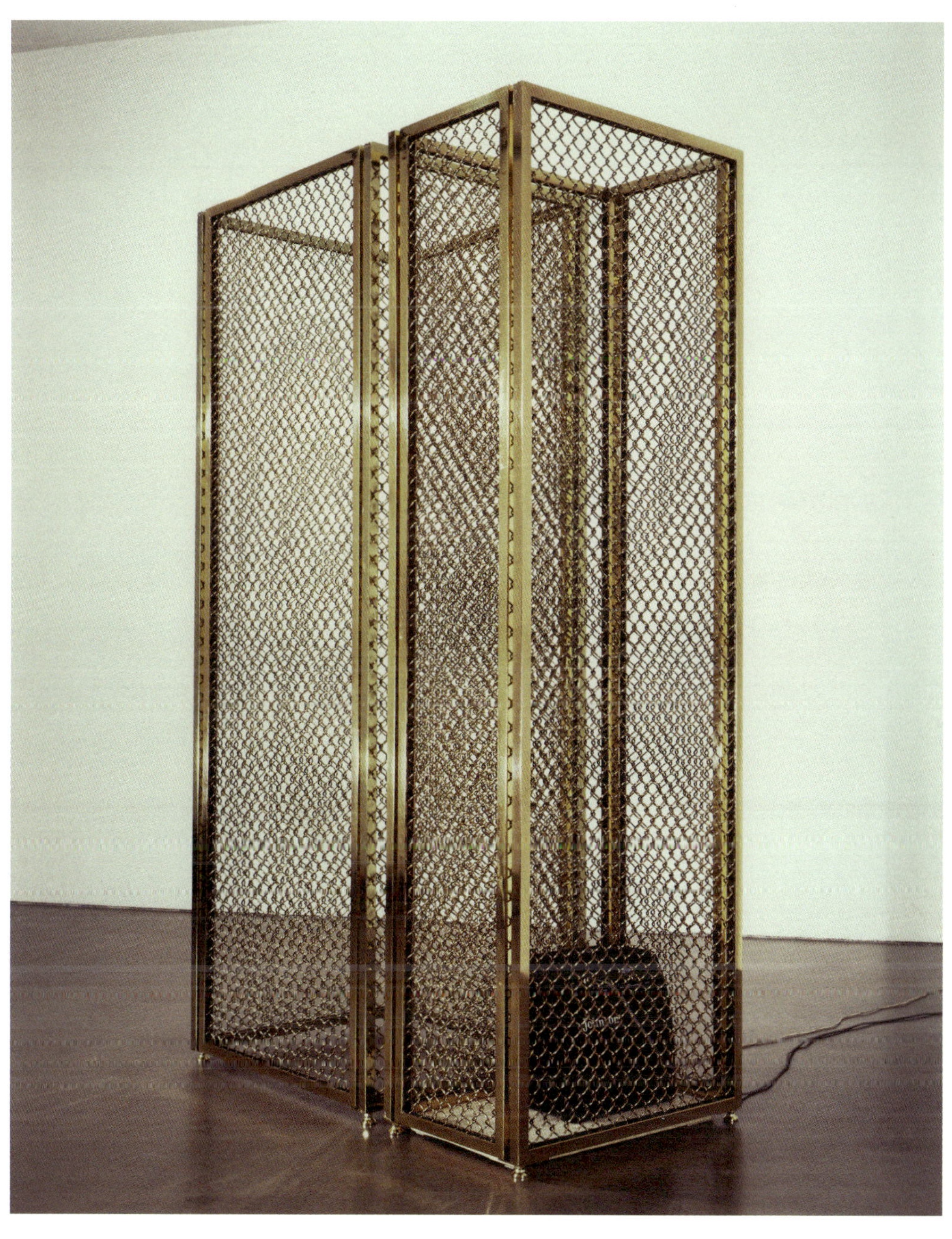

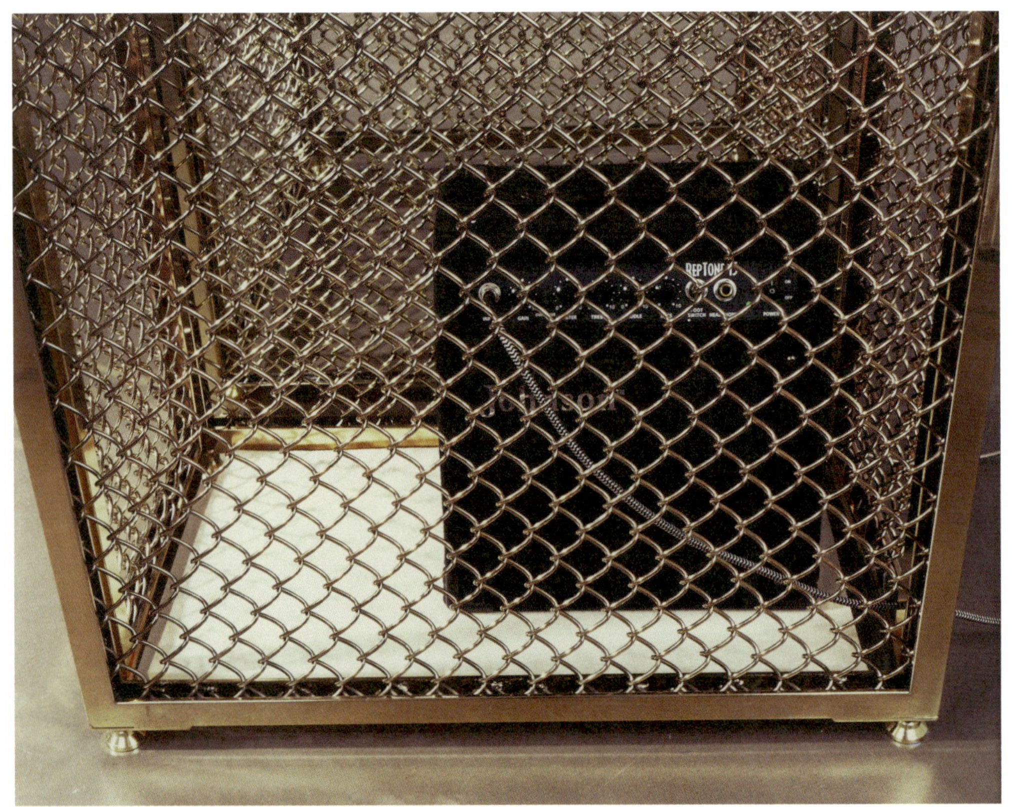

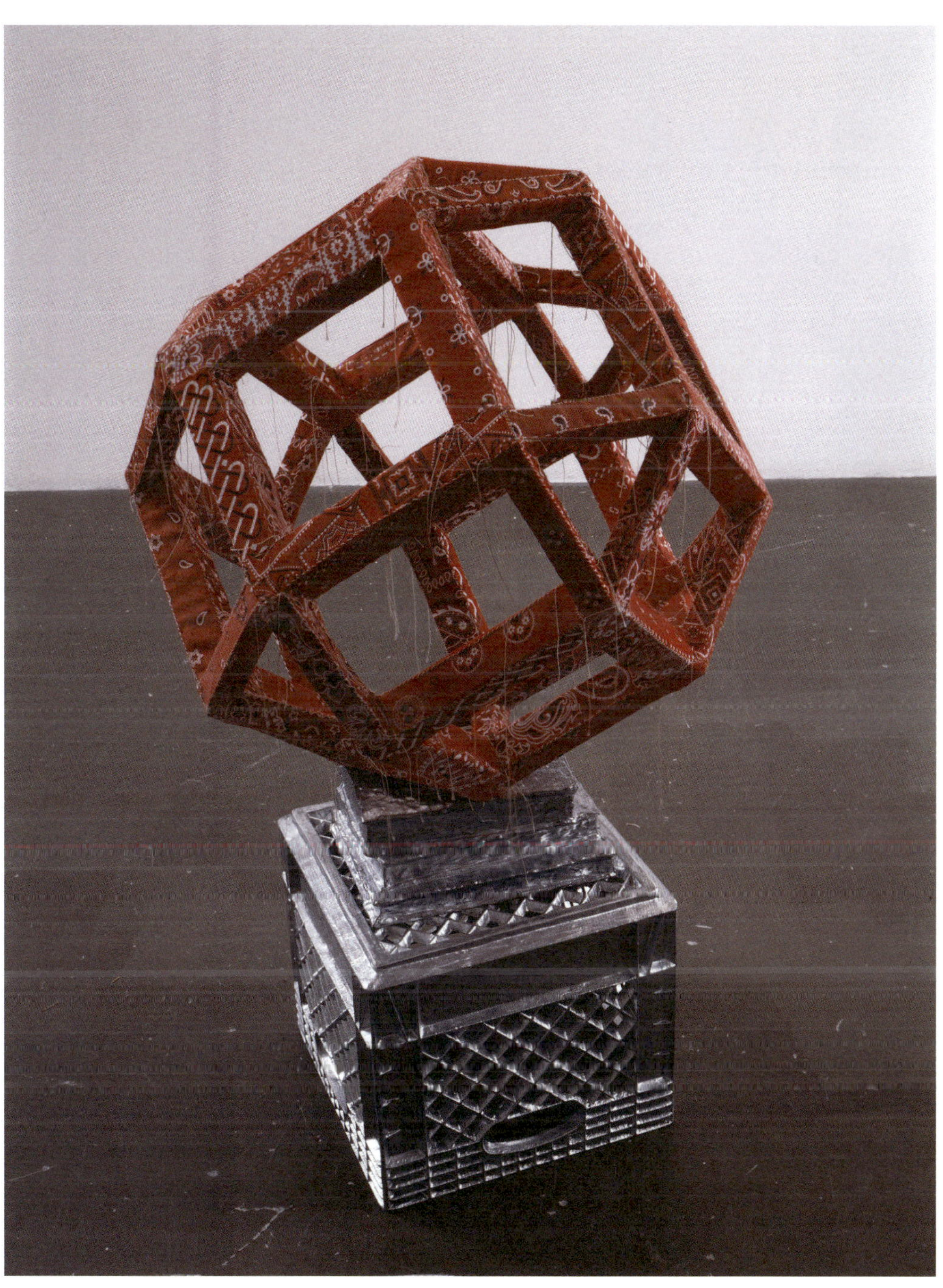

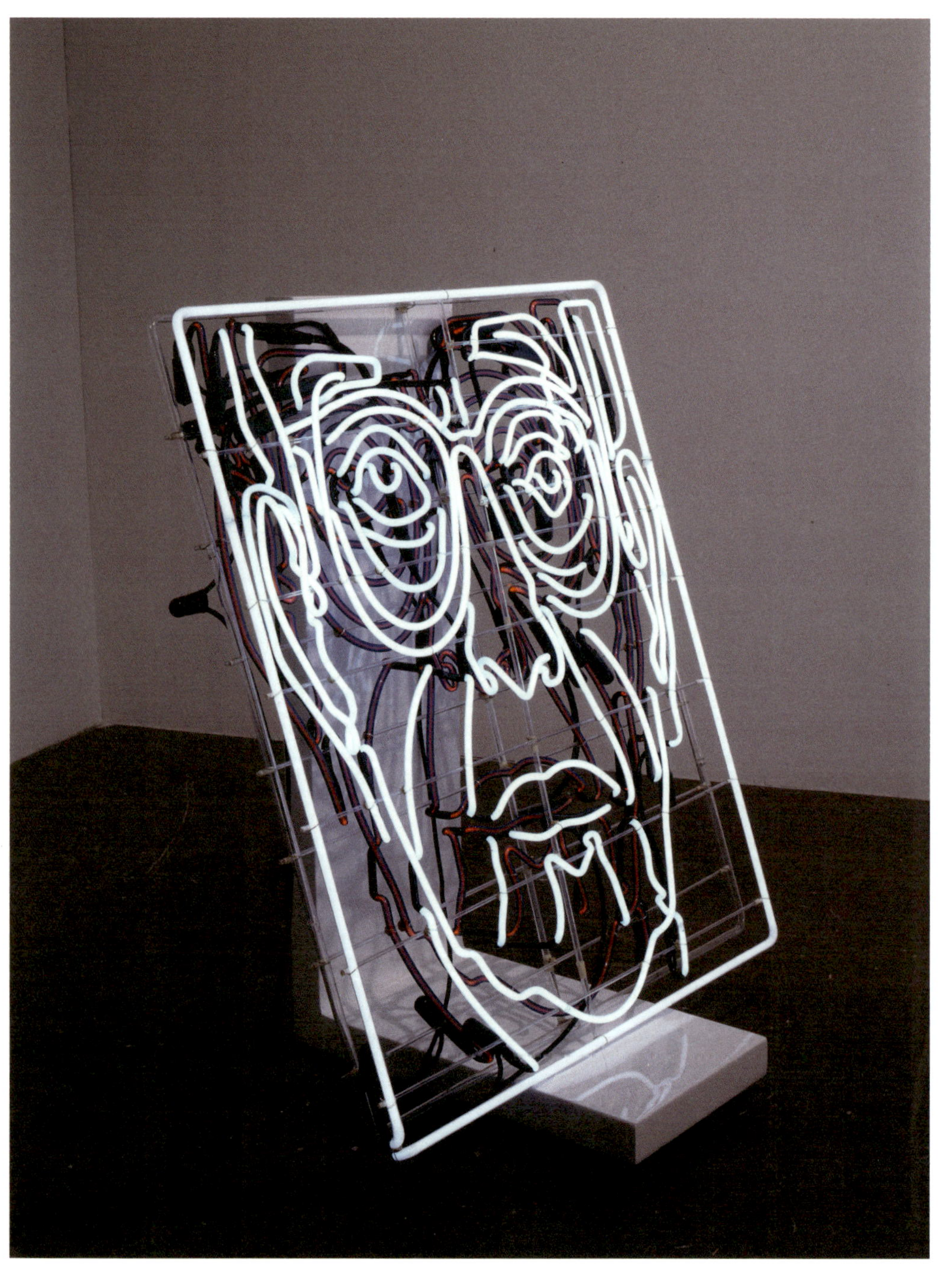

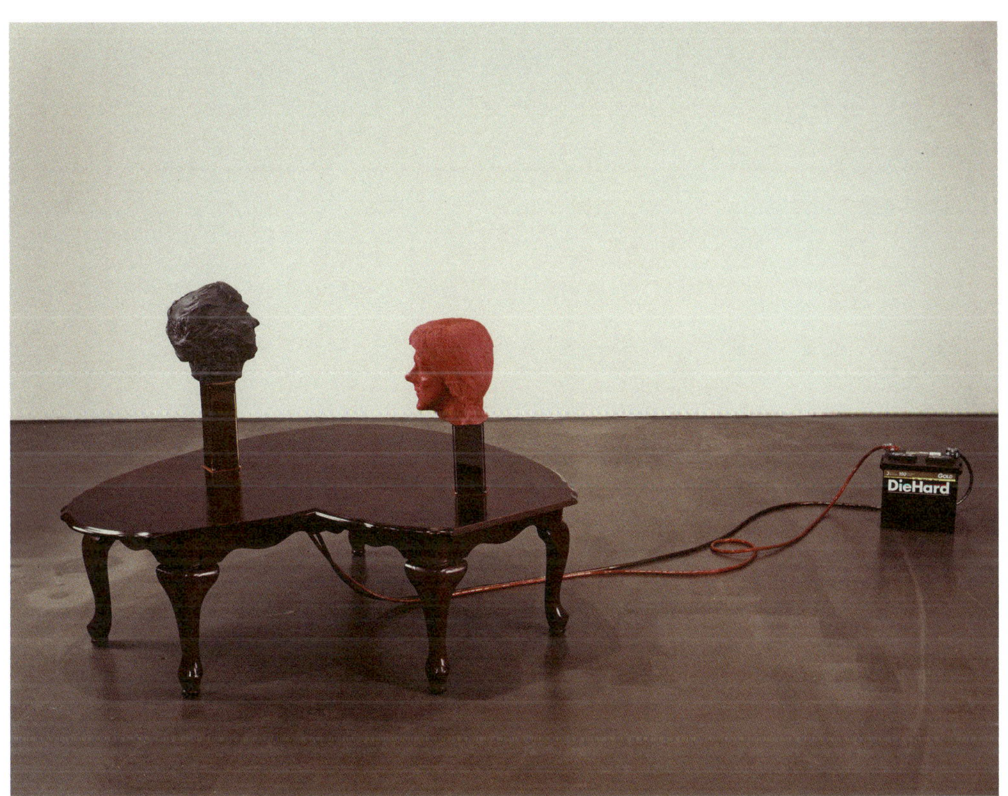

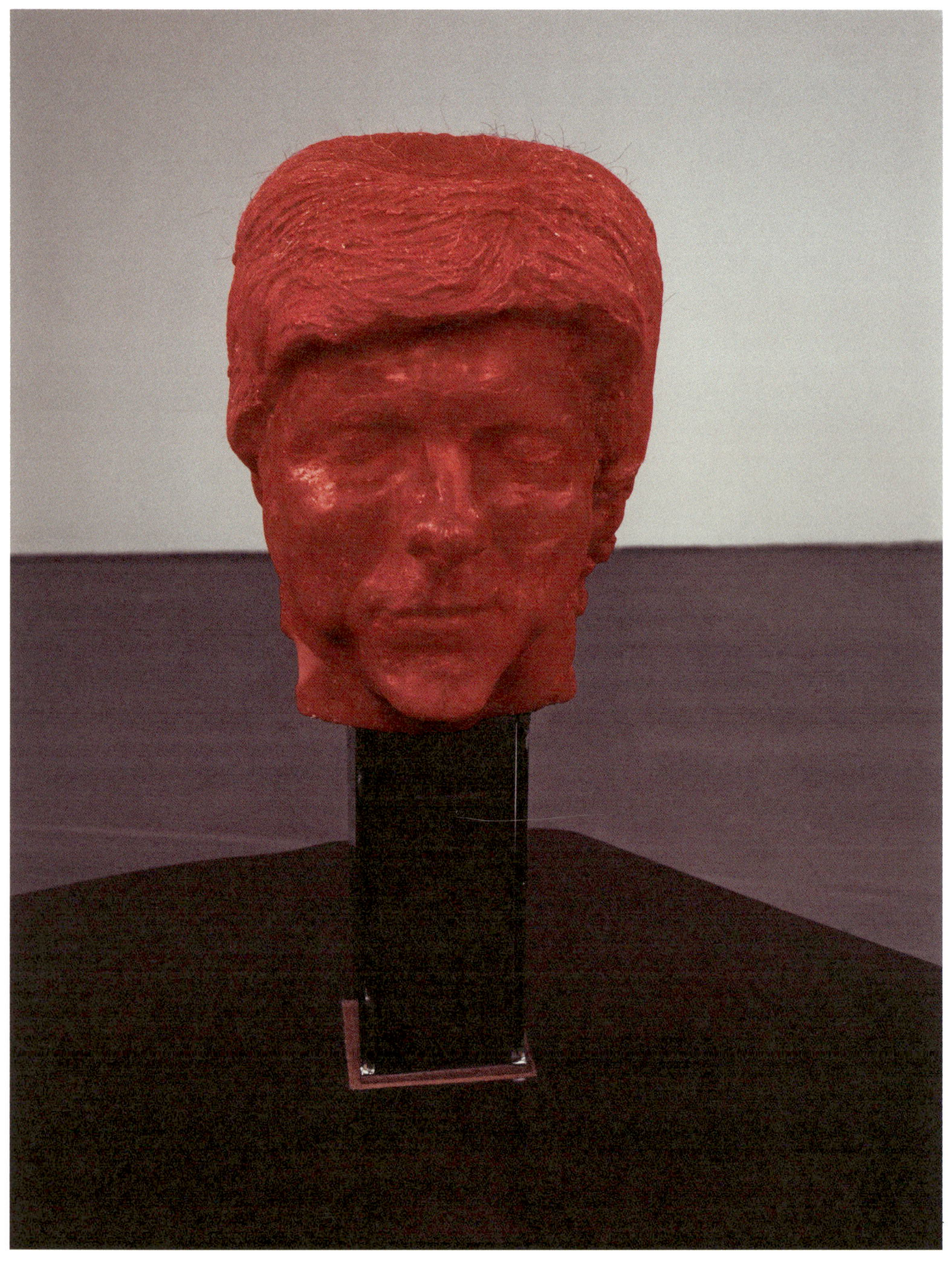

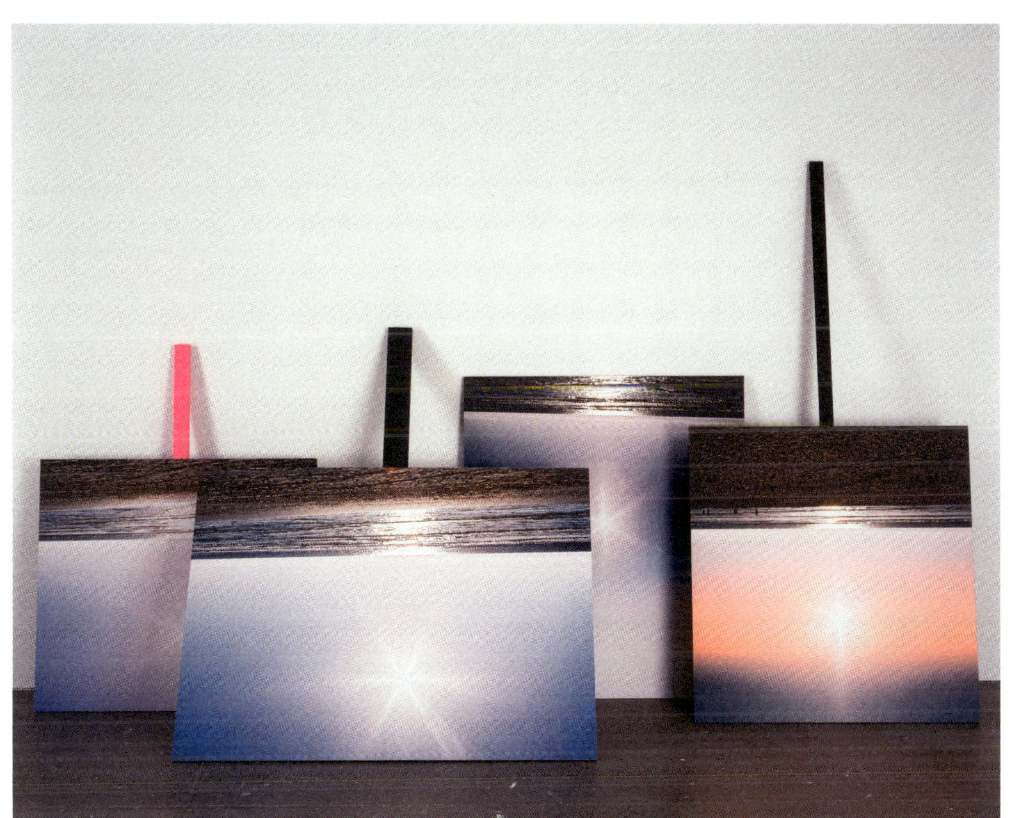

Lars Ø. Ramberg

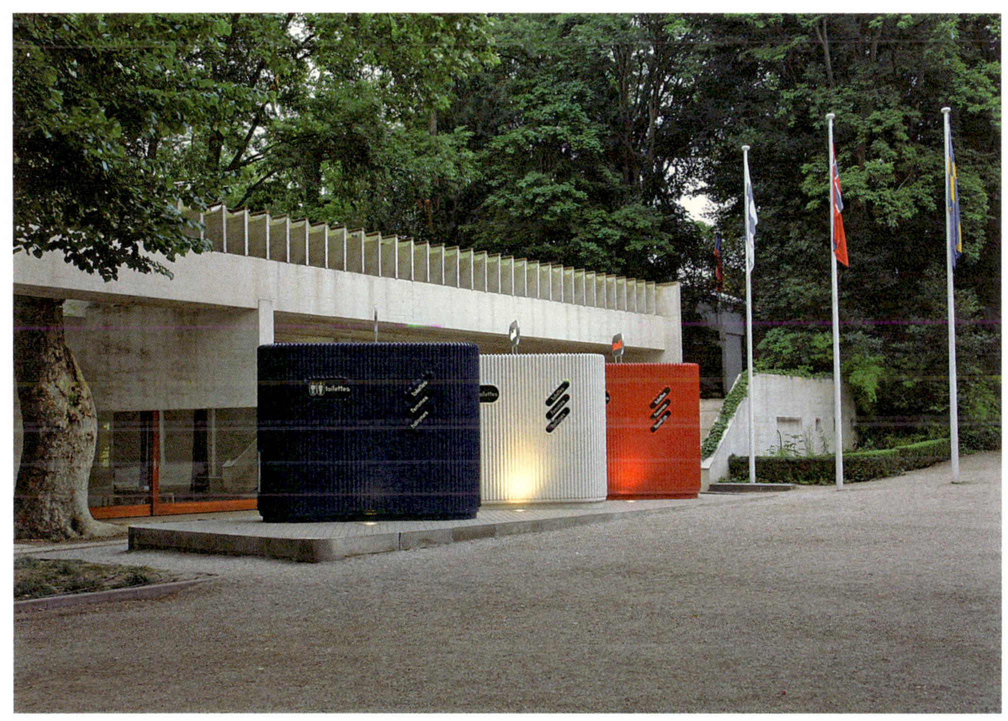

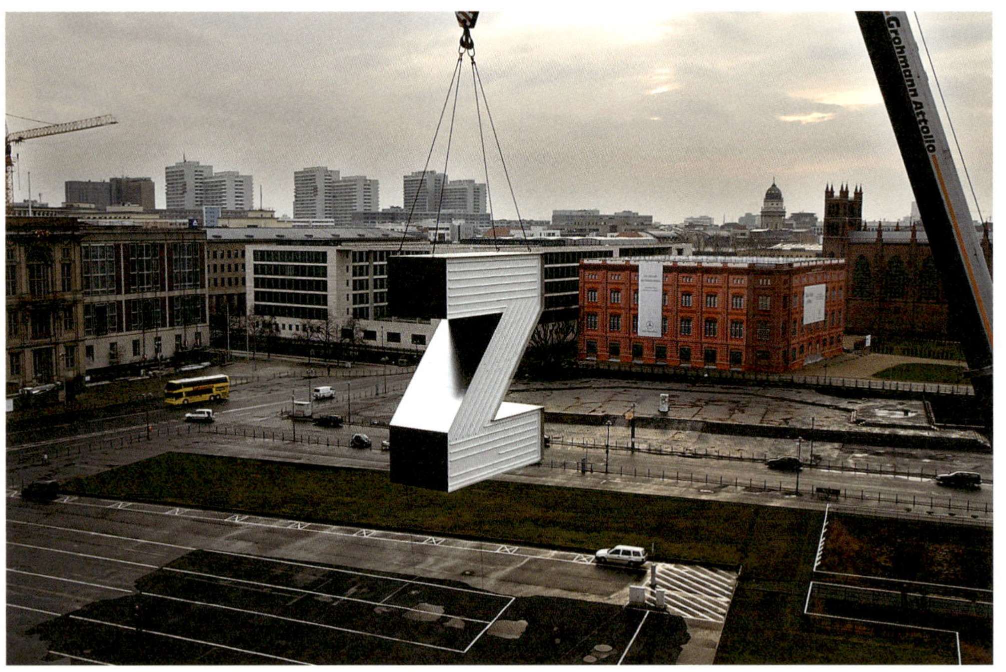

Grohmann Attollo

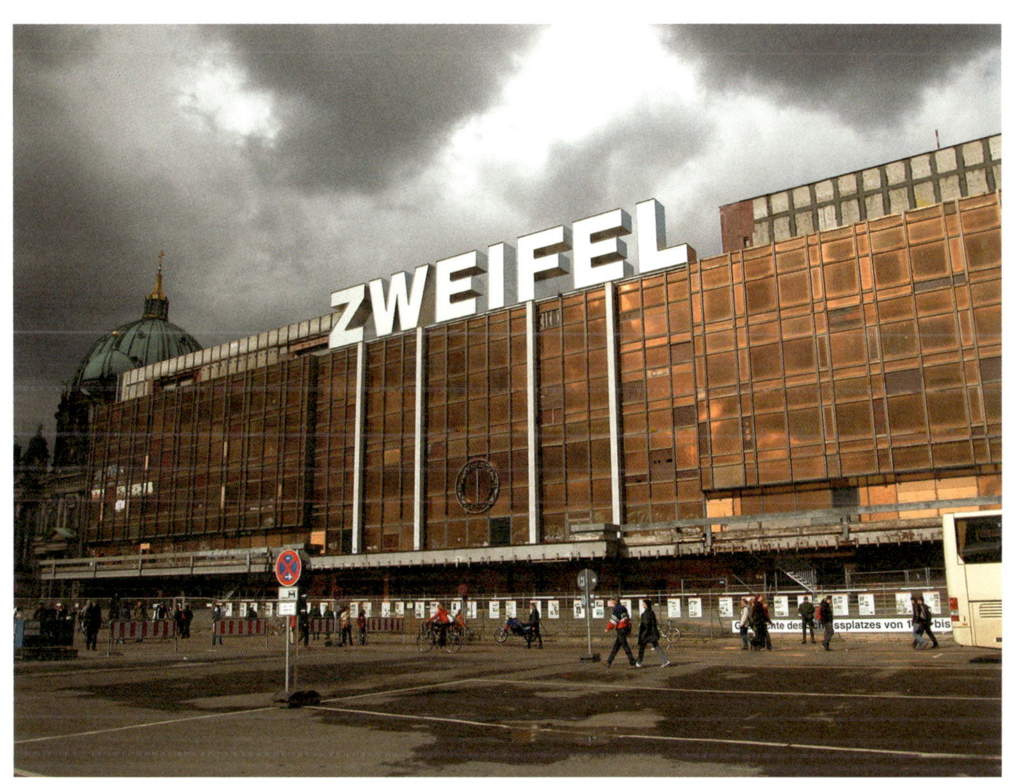

ZWEIFEL

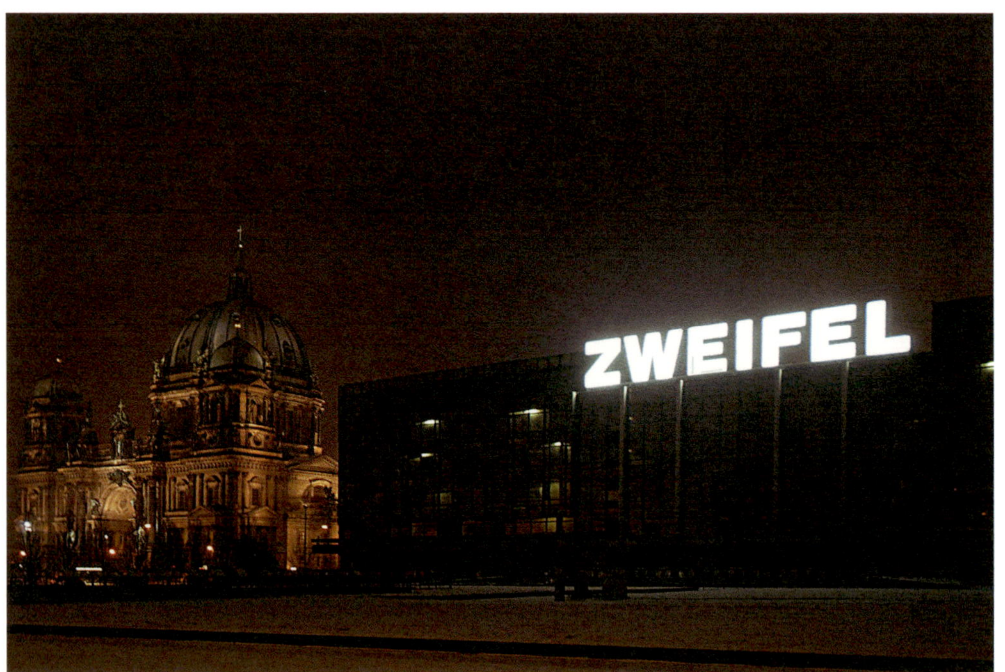

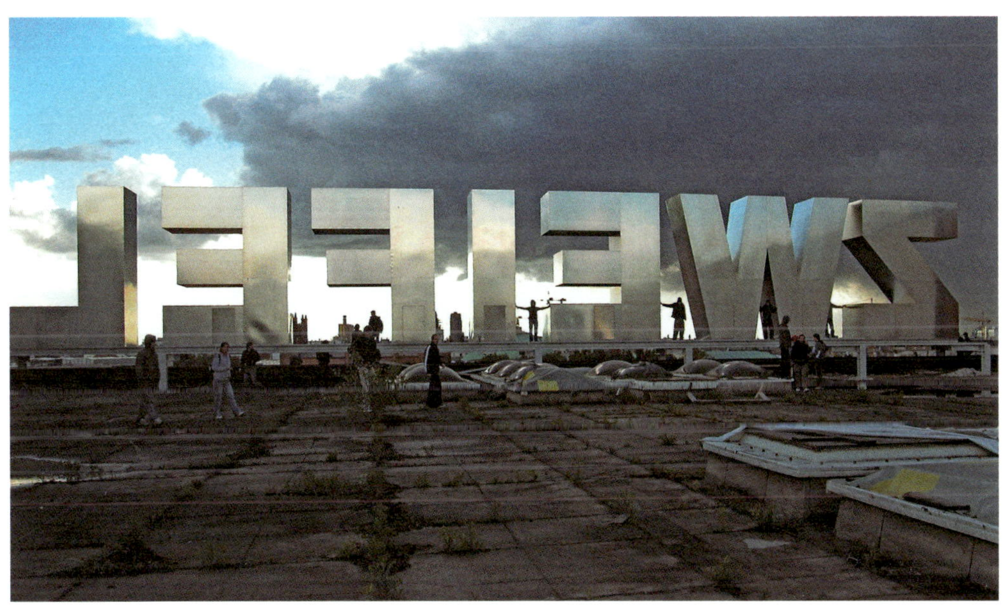

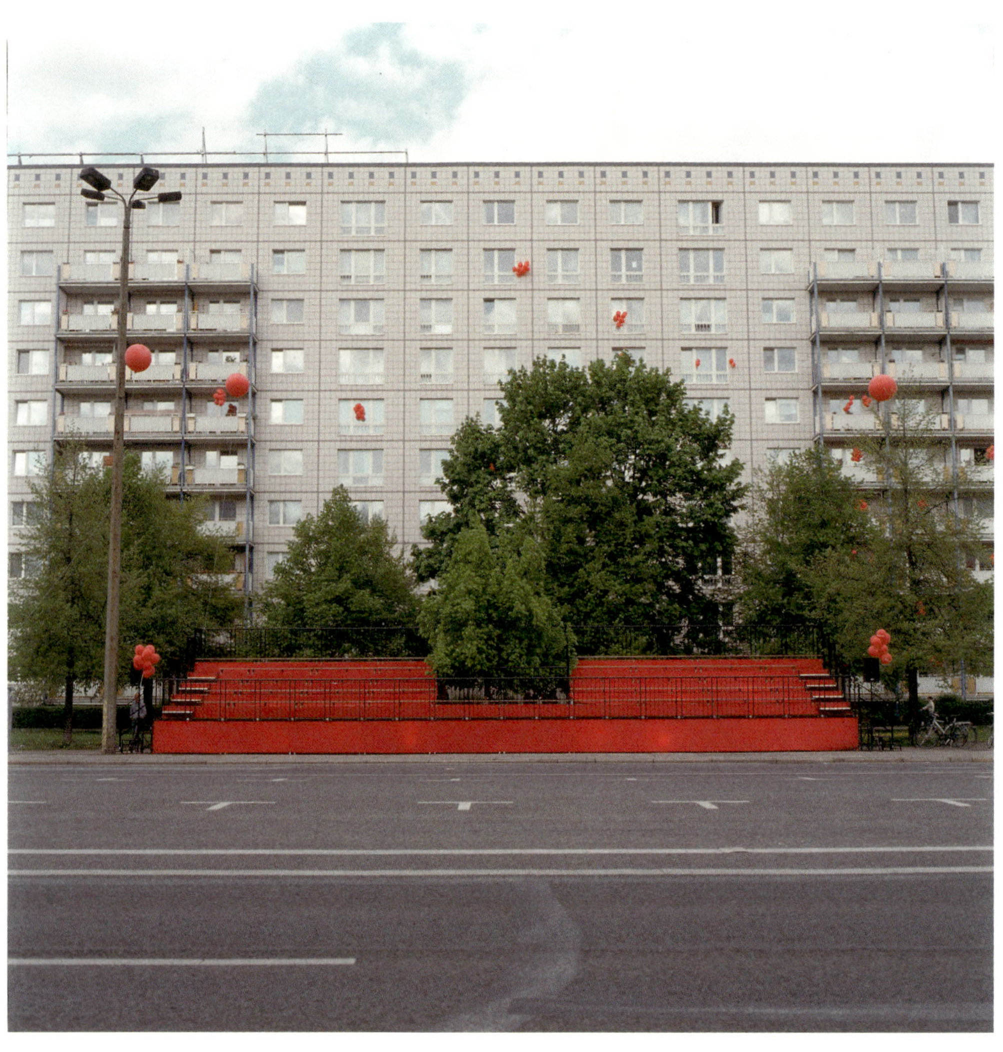

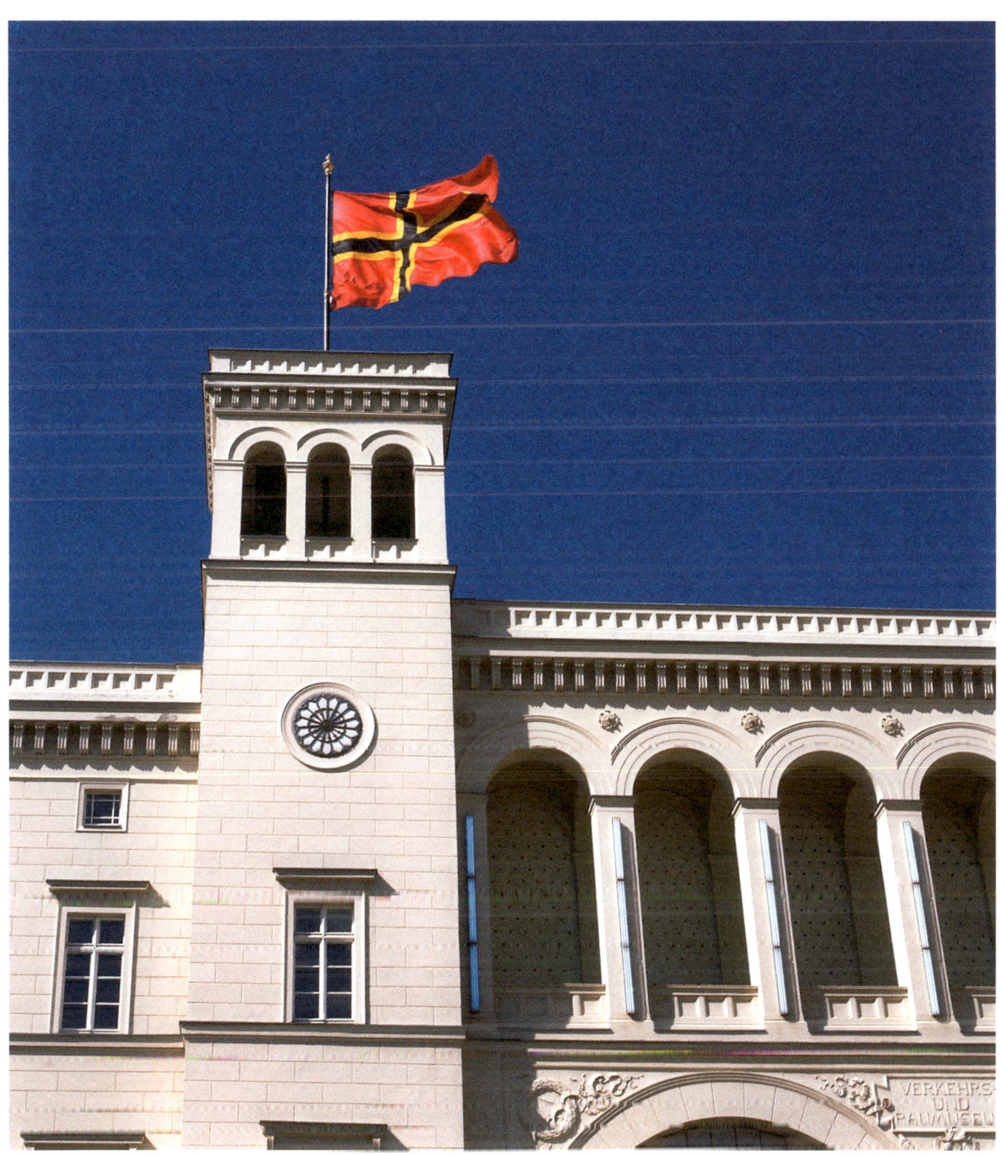

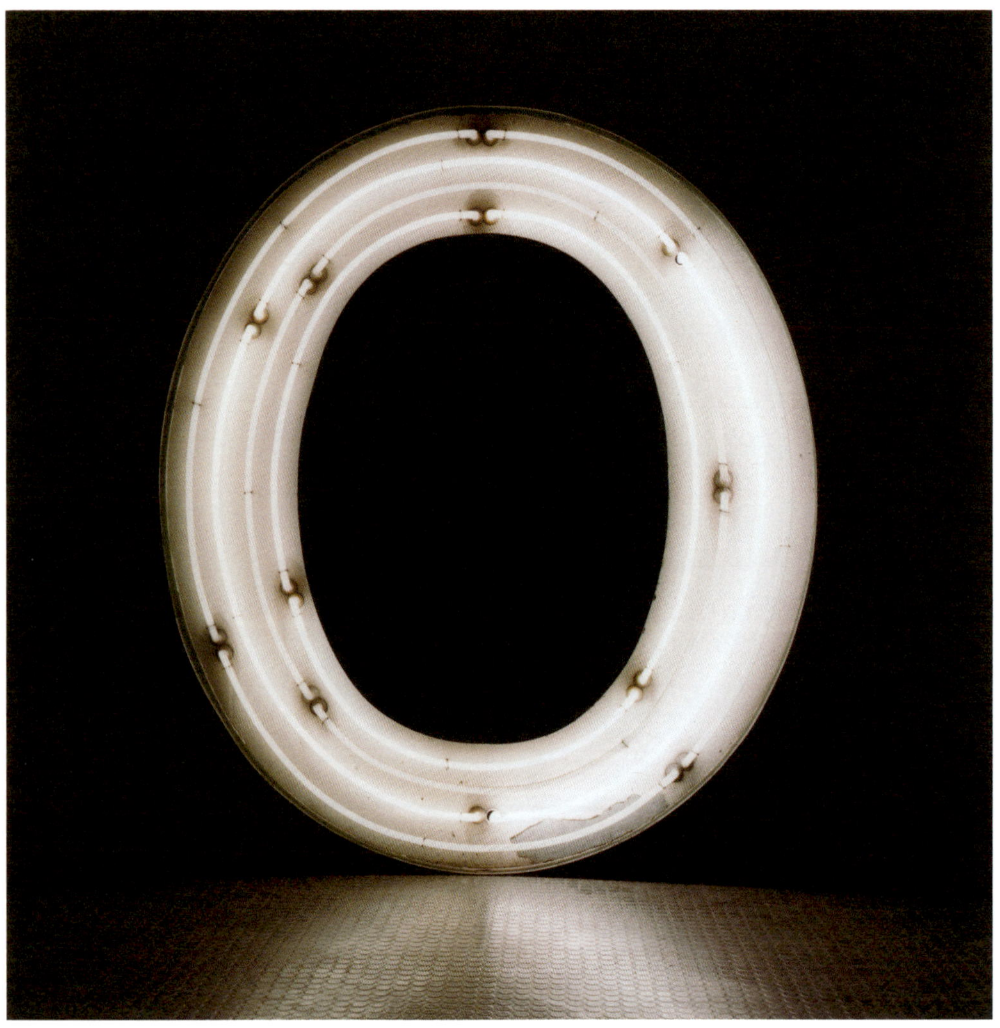

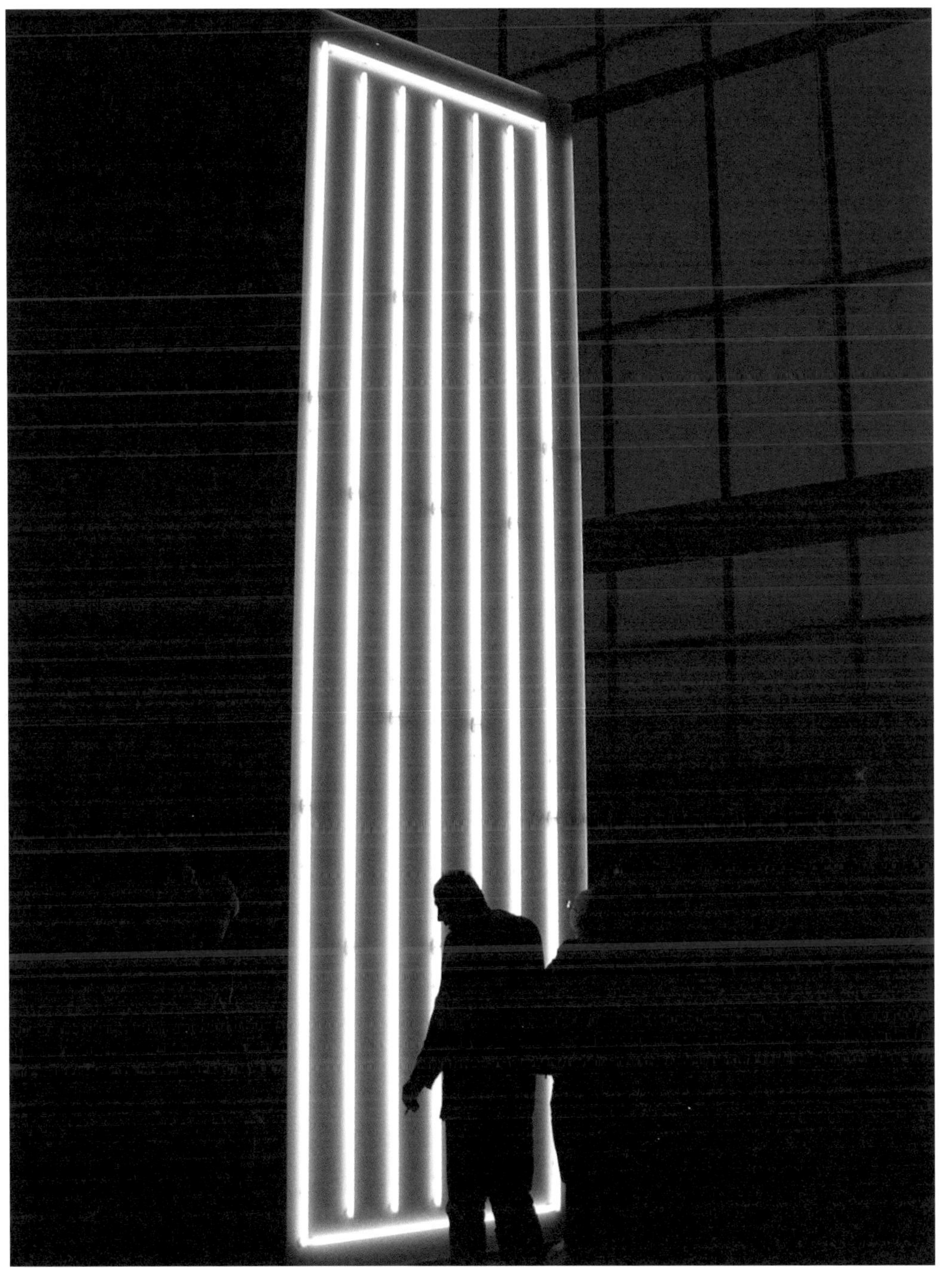

Frances Stark

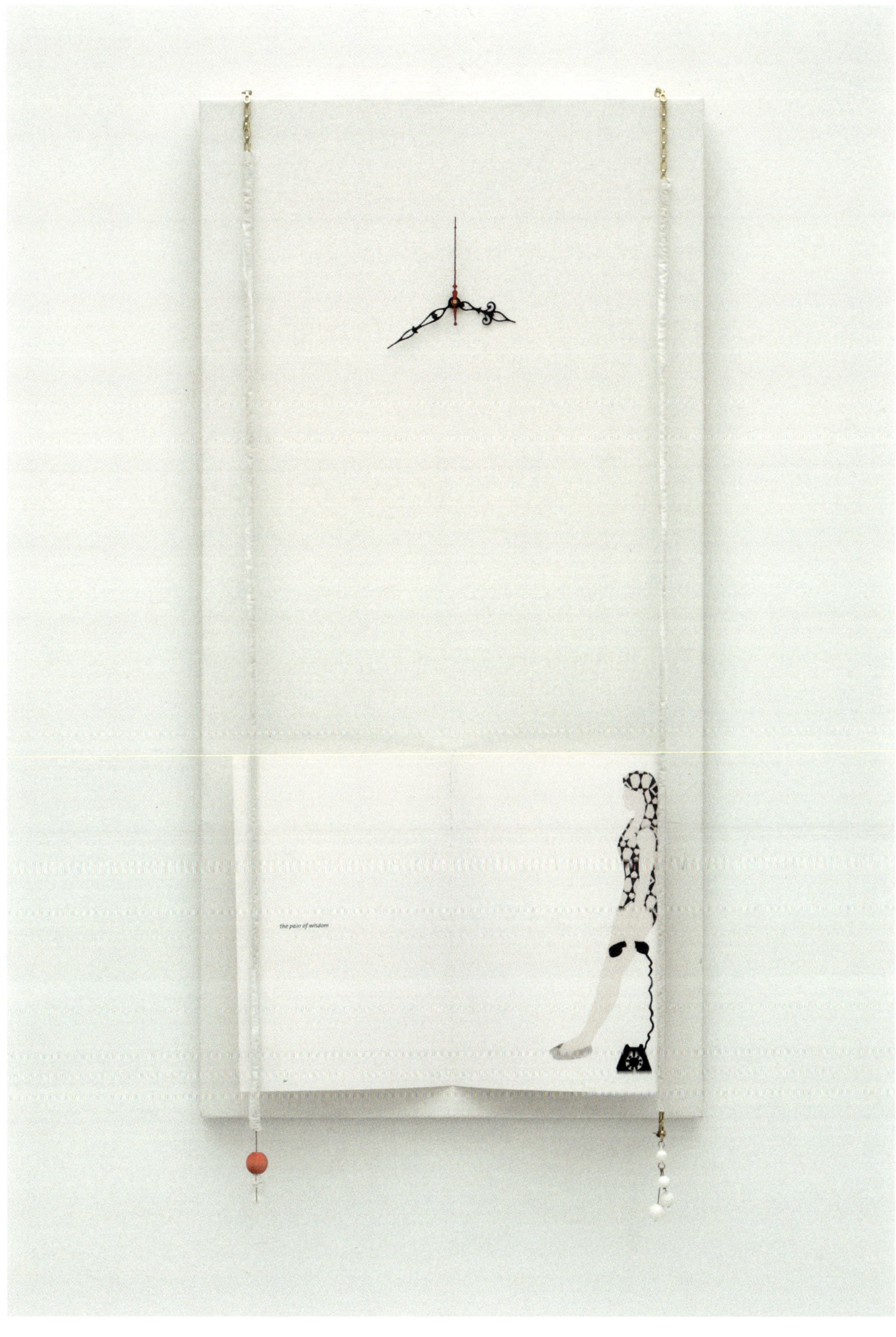

the pain of wisdom

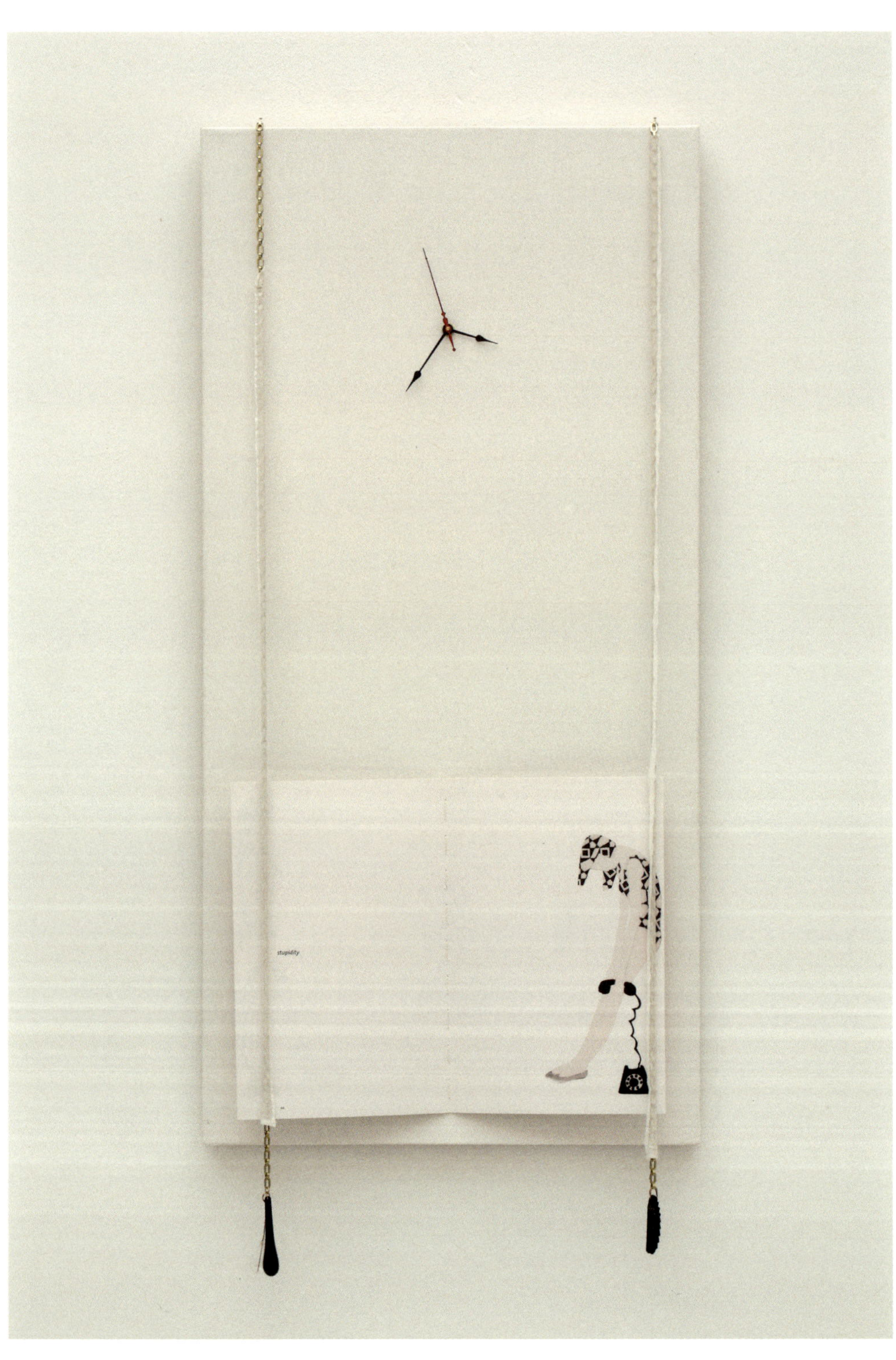
stupidity

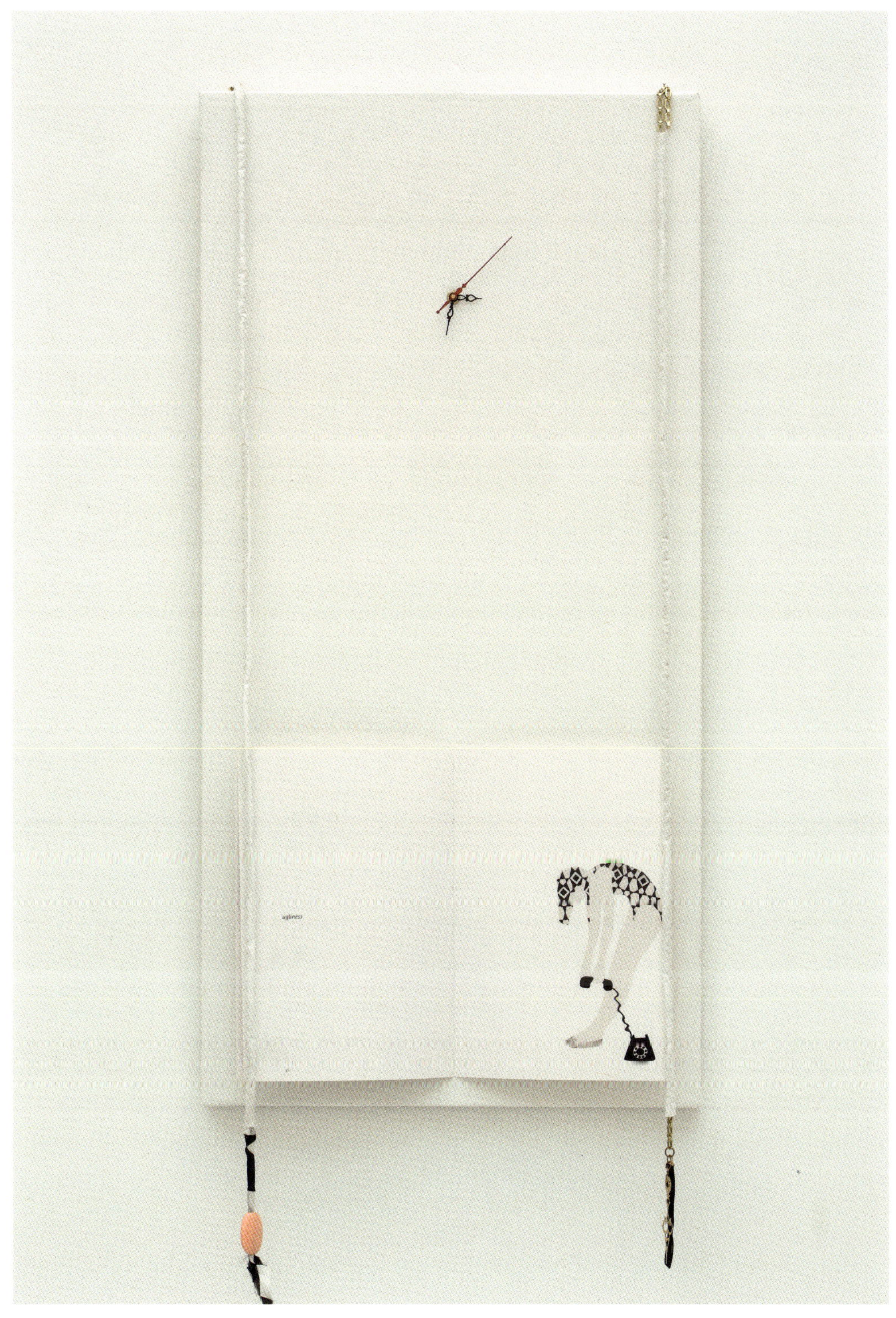
ugliness

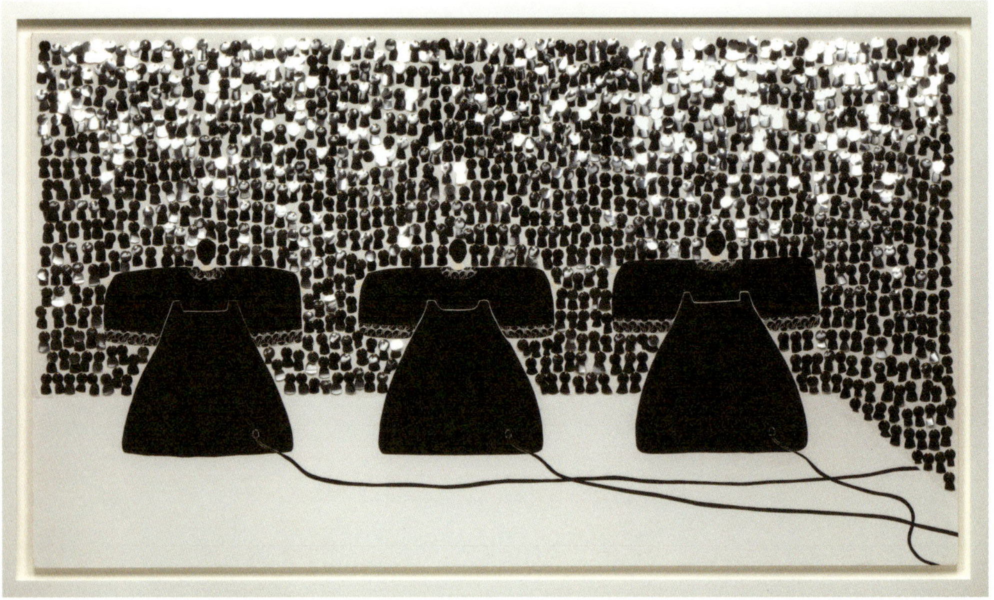

The desolation of acting a part ,

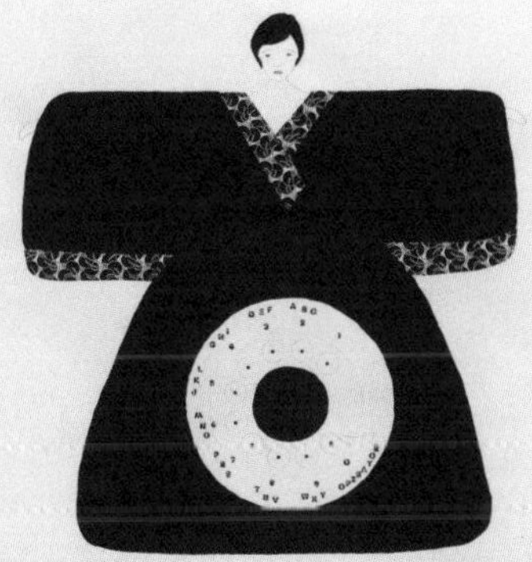

the desperation of imitation , the brutalizing

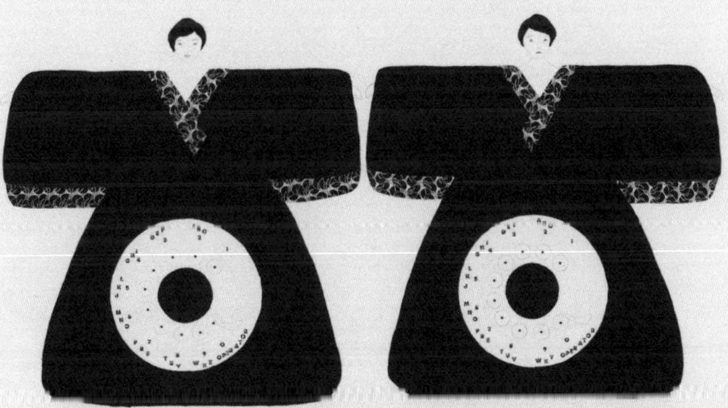

torment of brutalization and of saying the same thing over and over again .

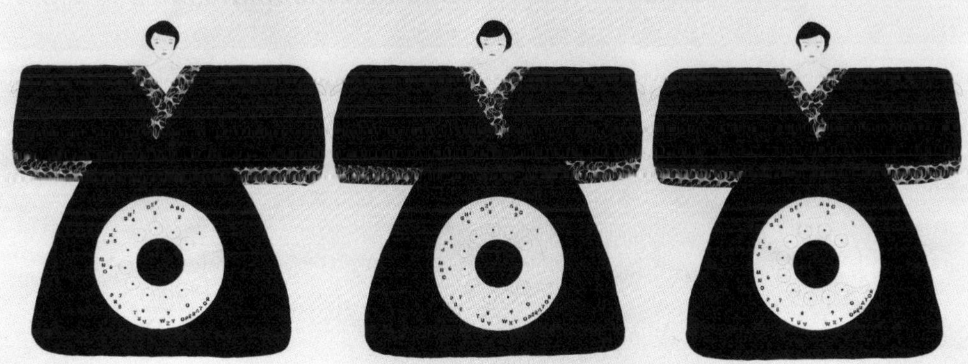

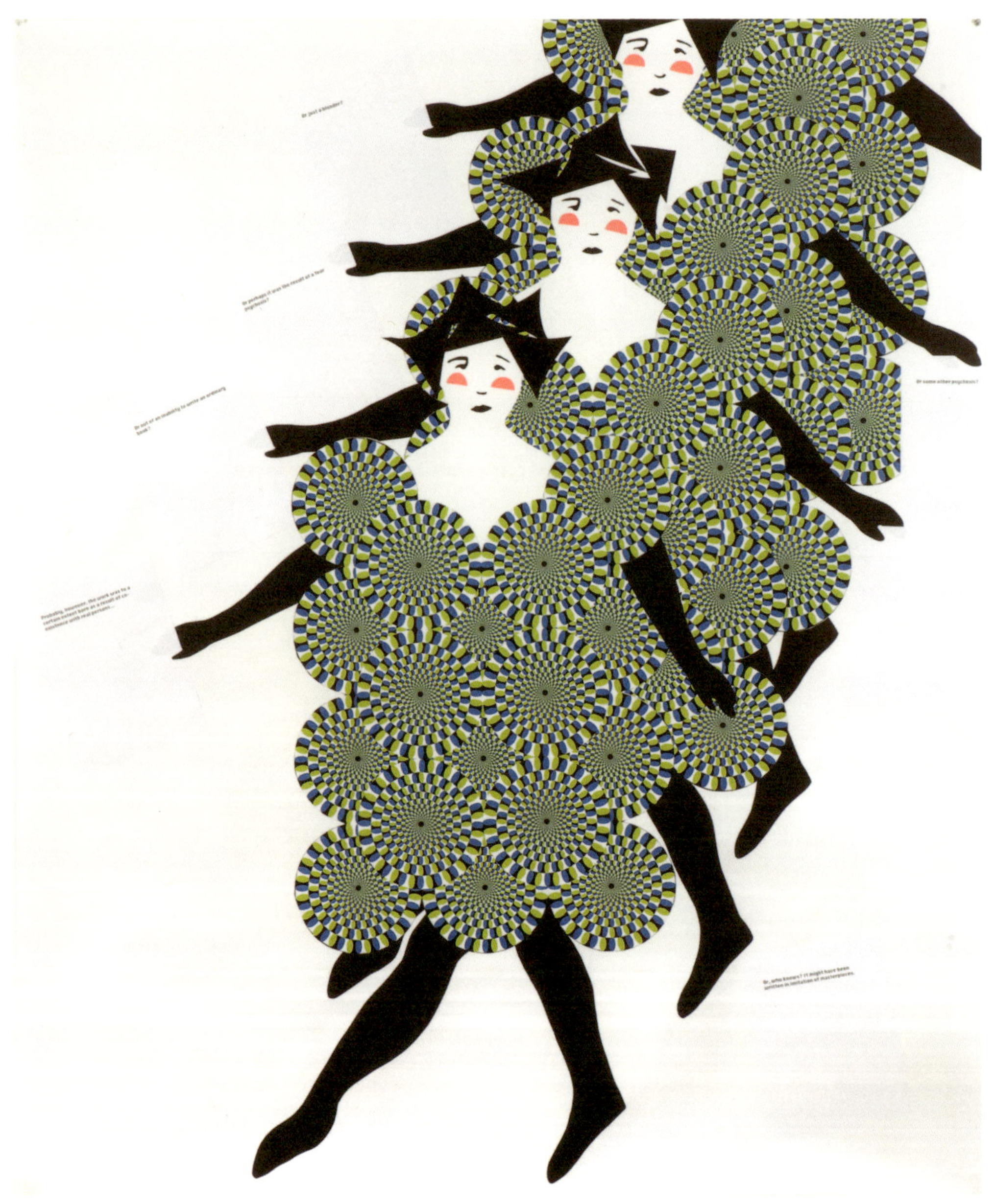

Or just a blunder?
Or perhaps it was the result of a fear psychosis?
Or of an inability to write an ordinary book?
Or some other psychosis?
Probably, however, the work was to a certain extent born as a result of coincidence with real persons...
Or, who knows? It might have been written in imitation of masterpieces.

Mark Wallinger

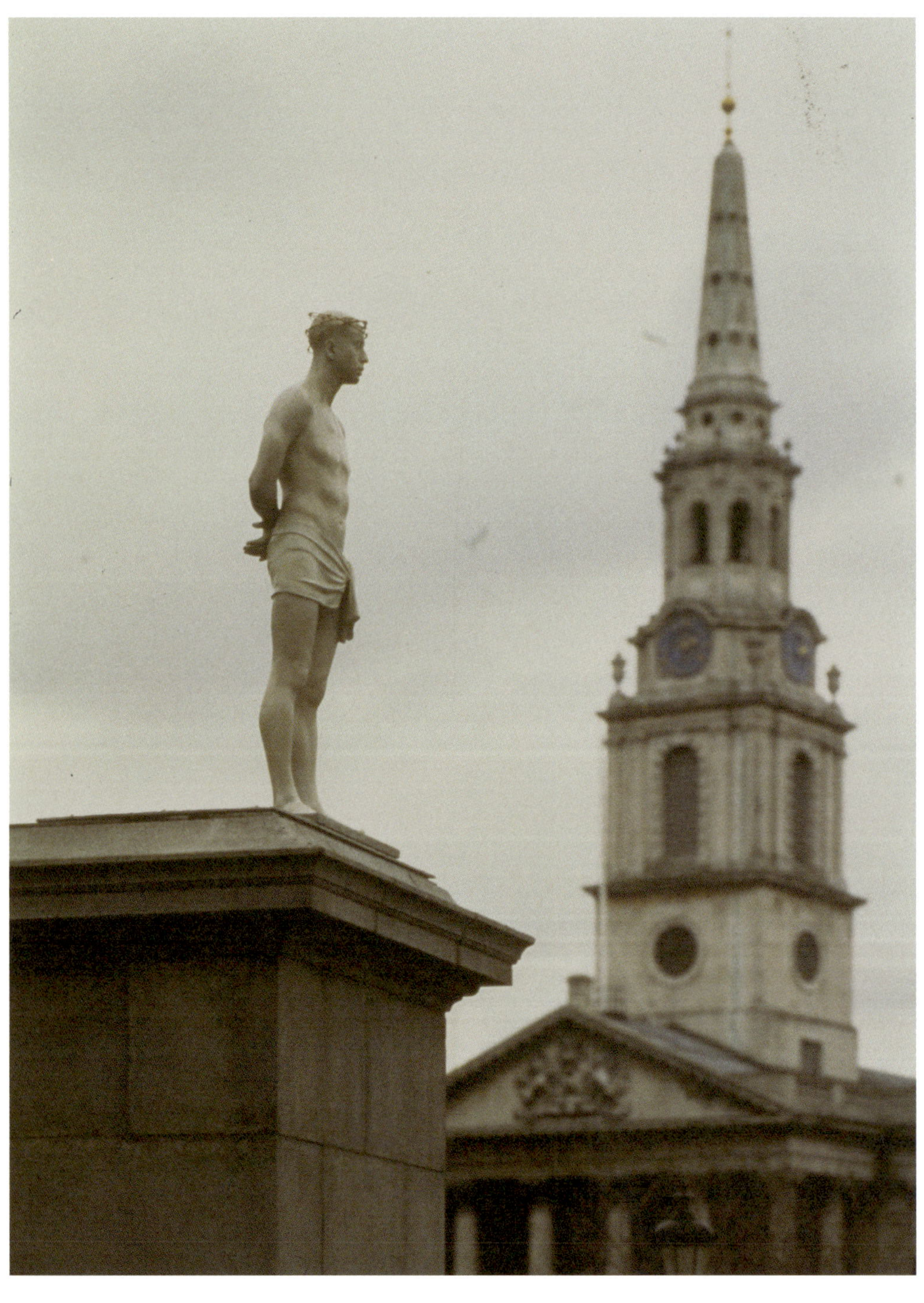

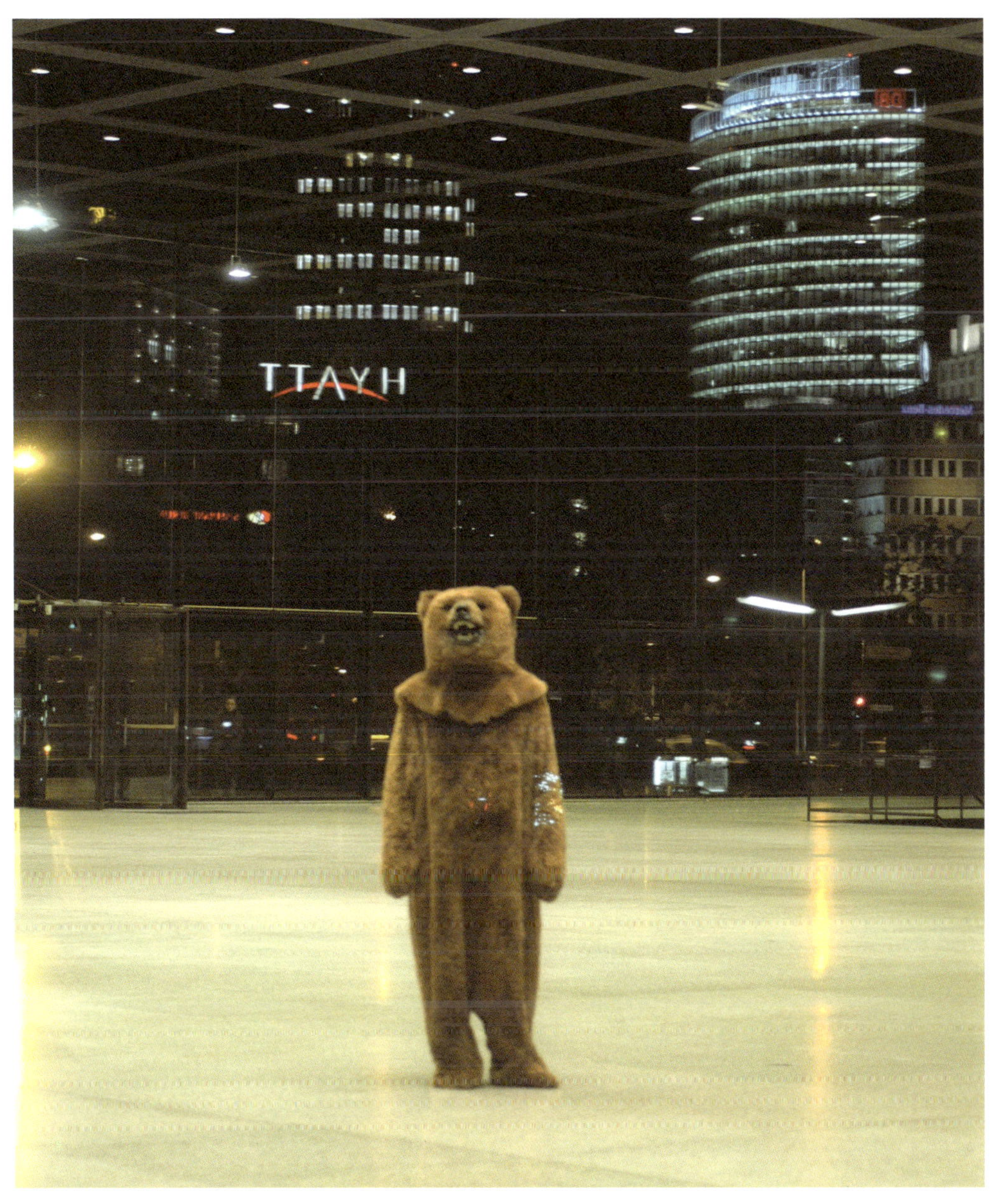

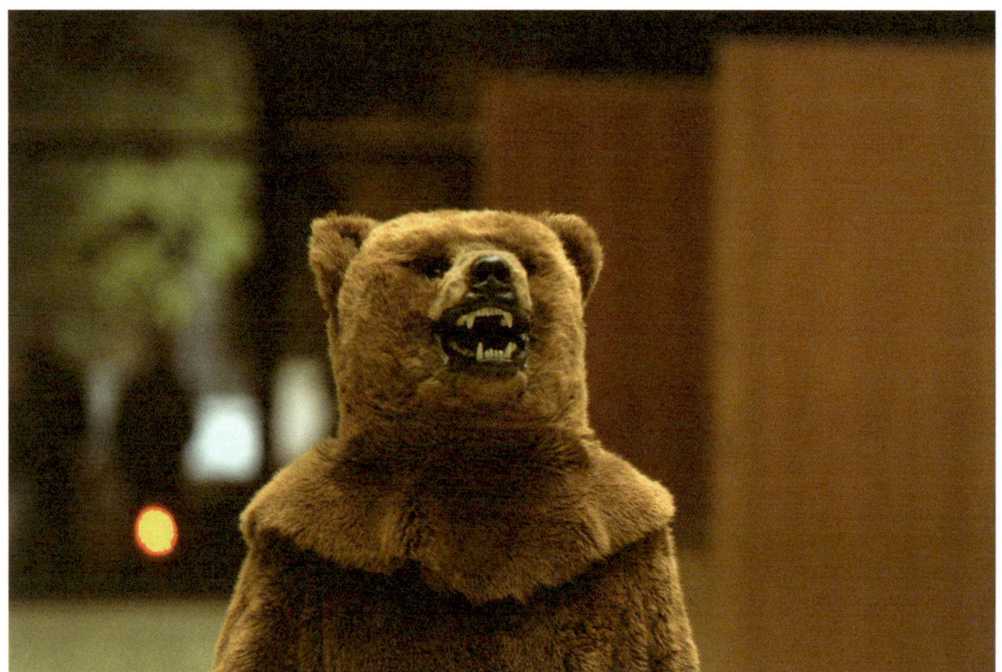

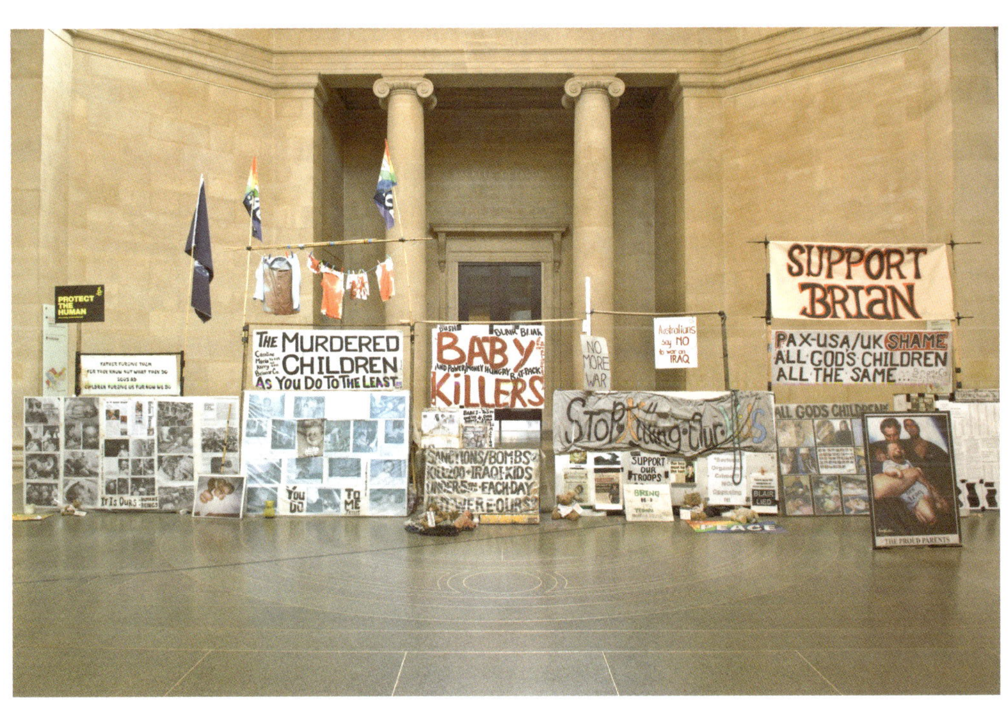
PROTECT THE HUMAN
THE MURDERED CHILDREN
AS YOU DO TO THE LEAST
YOU DO TO ME
BUSH
BABY KILLERS
AND POWER/MONEY HUNGRY RAT-PACK
SANCTIONS/BOMBS KILL 200+ IRAQI KIDS UNDER 5 EACH DAY
NO MORE WAR
Australians say NO to war on IRAQ
STOP
SUPPORT OUR TROOPS
PEACE
ALL GOD'S CHILDREN
SUPPORT BRIAN
PAX-USA/UK SHAME ALL GOD'S CHILDREN ALL THE SAME...
ALL GODS CHILDREN
THE PROUD PARENTS

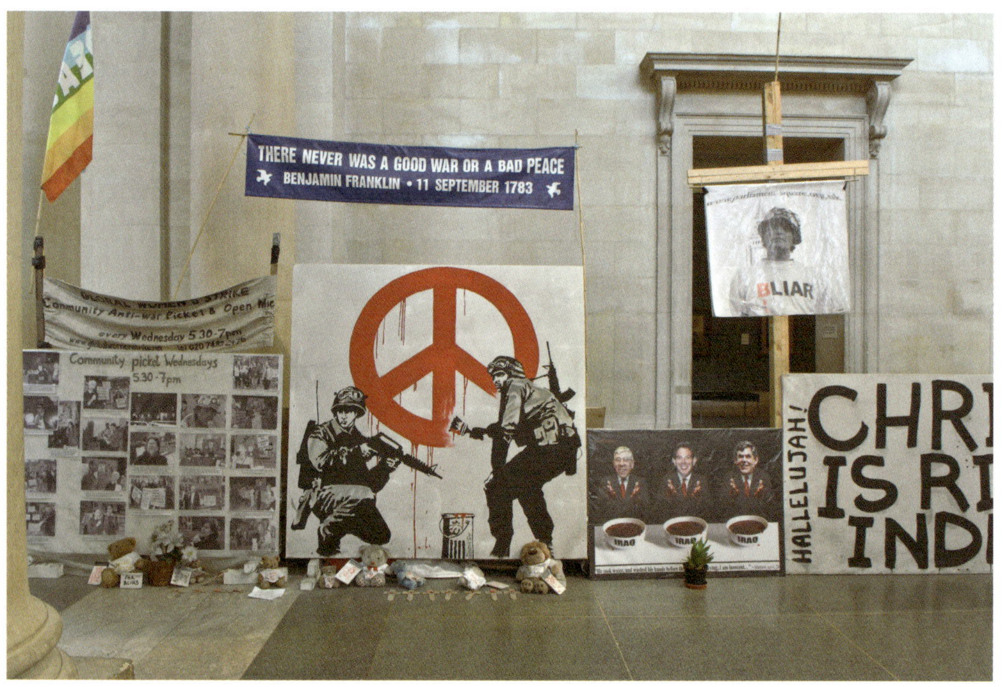
THERE NEVER WAS A GOOD WAR OR A BAD PEACE
BENJAMIN FRANKLIN • 11 SEPTEMBER 1783
Community Anti-War Picket & Open Mic
every Wednesday 5.30-7pm
Community picket Wednesdays
5.30-7pm
BLIAR
HALLELUJAH!
CHR
IS RI
IND
IRAQ
IRAQ
IRAQ

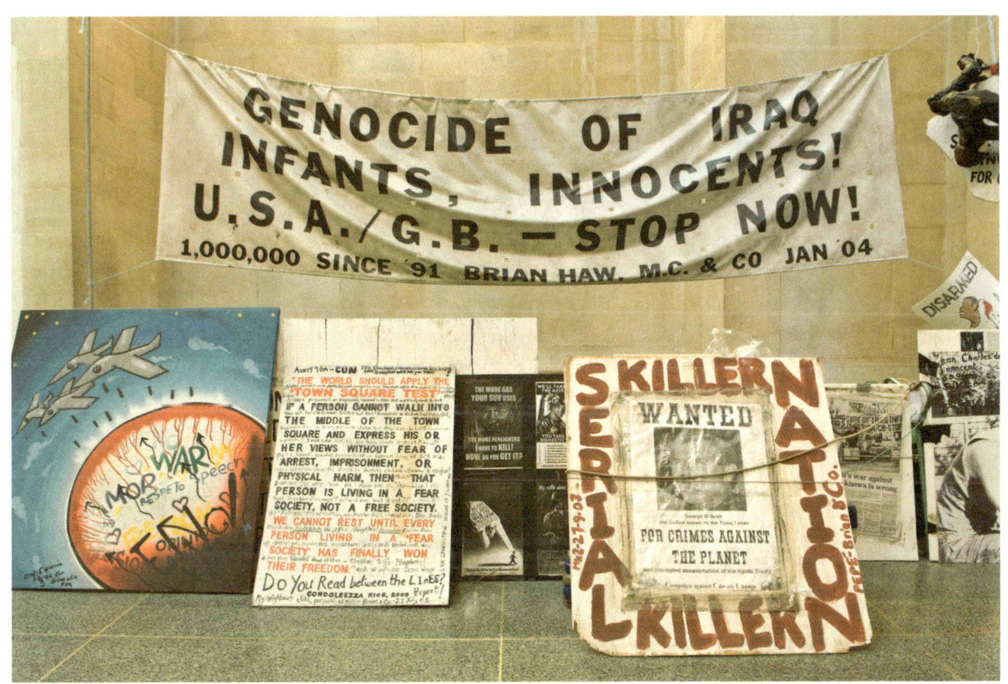
GENOCIDE OF IRAQ
INFANTS, INNOCENTS!
U.S.A./G.B. – STOP NOW!
1,000,000 SINCE '91 BRIAN HAW, M.C. & CO JAN '04
WANTED
FOR CRIMES AGAINST
THE PLANET
SERIAL KILLERN
NATION
SKILLERN
KILLERN

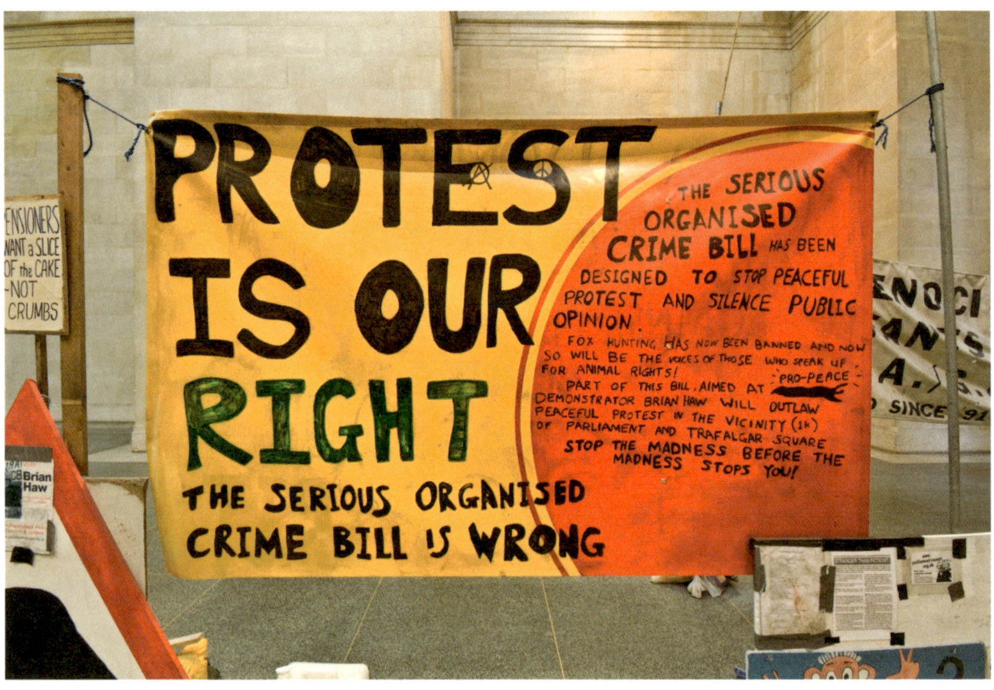
PROTEST
IS OUR
RIGHT
THE SERIOUS ORGANISED
CRIME BILL IS WRONG
THE SERIOUS ORGANISED CRIME BILL HAS BEEN DESIGNED TO STOP PEACEFUL PROTEST AND SILENCE PUBLIC OPINION.
FOX HUNTING HAS NOW BEEN BANNED AND NOW SO WILL BE THE VOICES OF THOSE WHO SPEAK UP FOR ANIMAL RIGHTS!
PART OF THIS BILL, AIMED AT PRO-PEACE DEMONSTRATOR BRIAN HAW WILL OUTLAW PEACEFUL PROTEST IN THE VICINITY (1k) OF PARLIAMENT AND TRAFALGAR SQUARE
STOP THE MADNESS BEFORE THE MADNESS STOPS YOU!
PENSIONERS WANT a SLICE OF the CAKE -NOT CRUMBS
Brian Haw

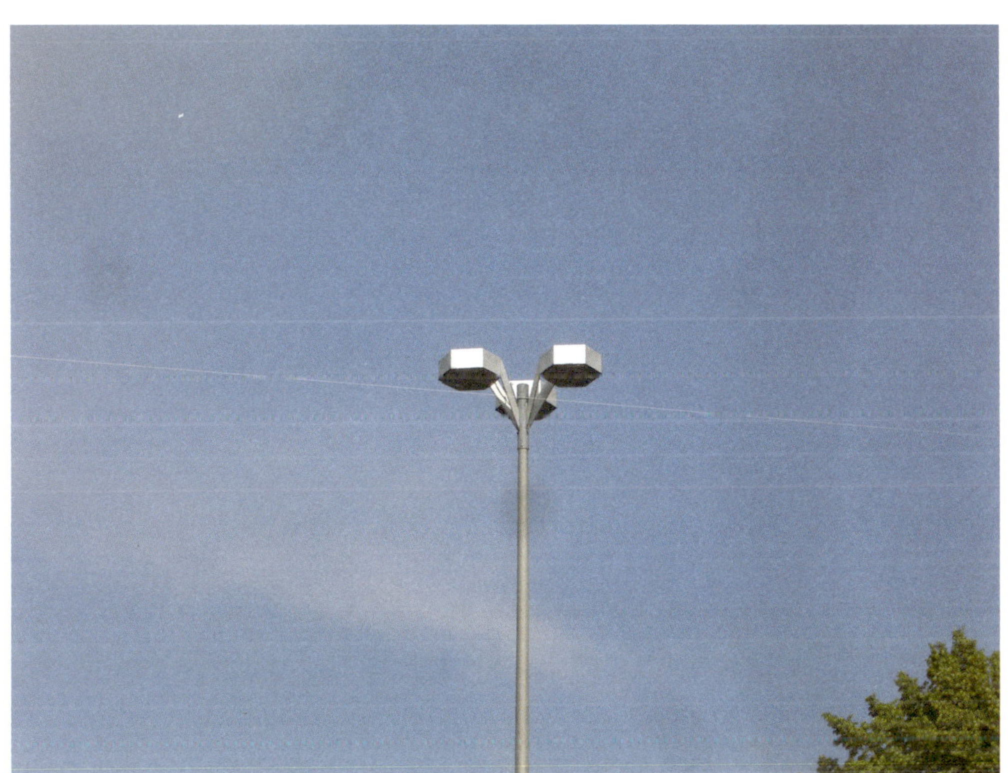

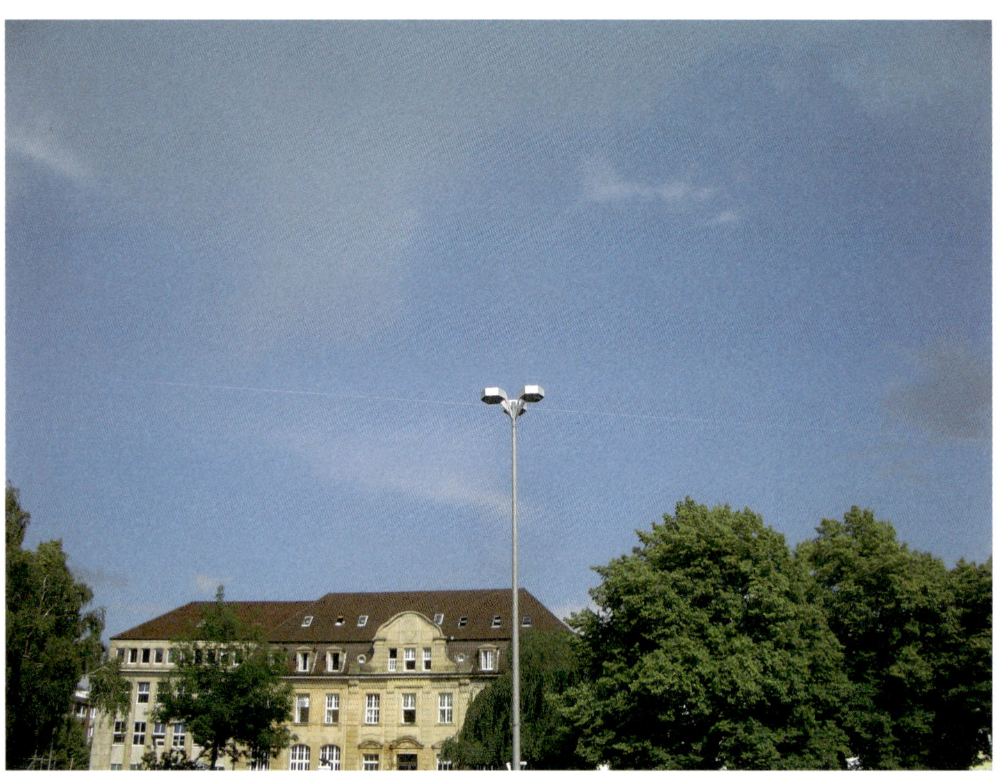

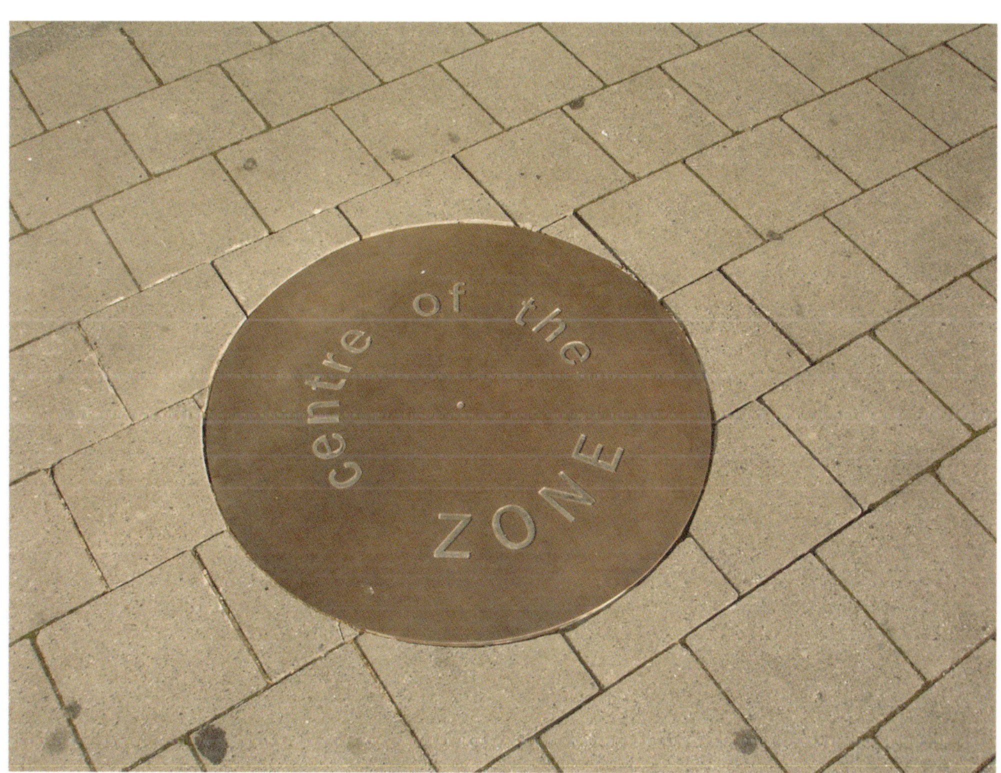

centre of the
ZONE

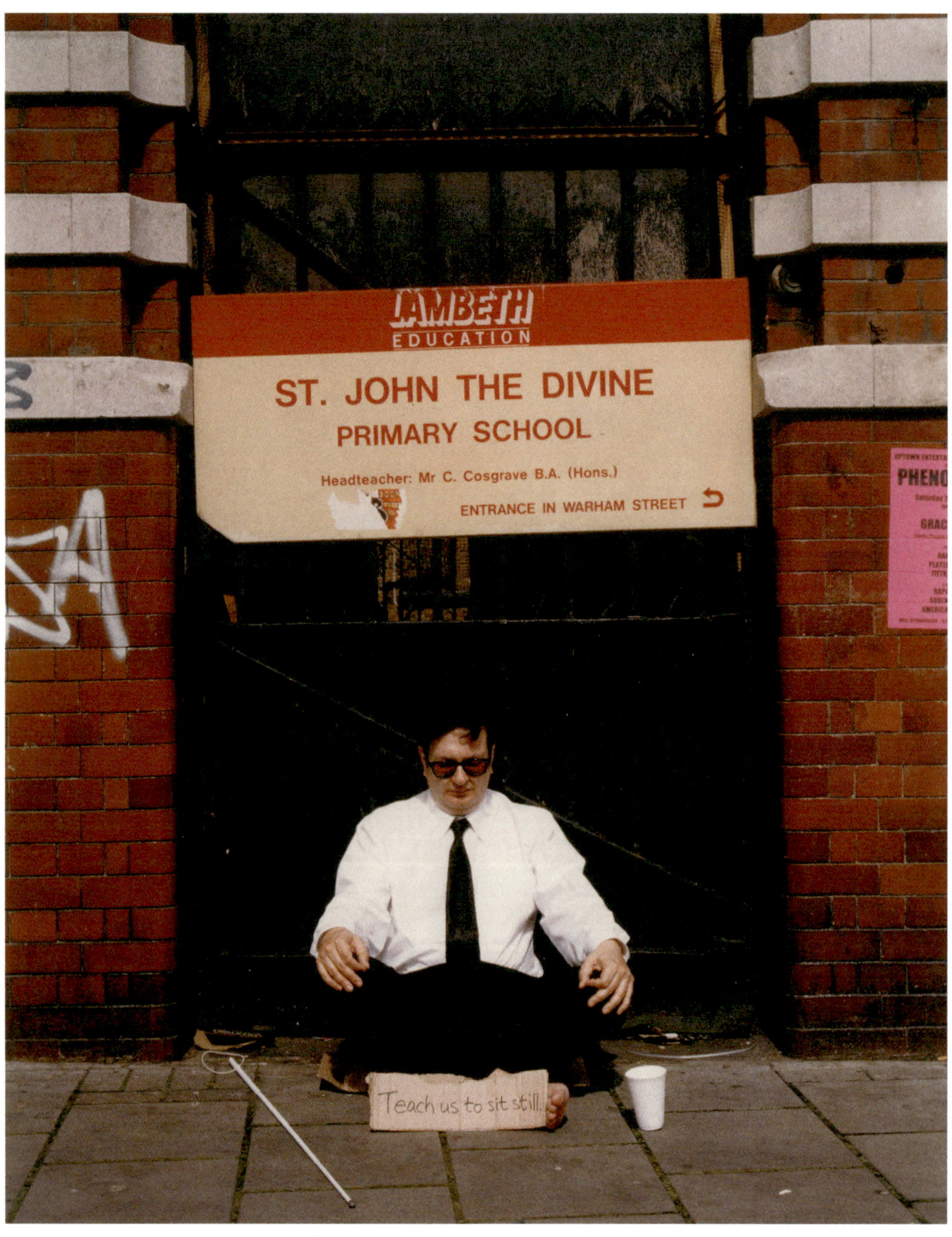
LAMBETH
EDUCATION
ST. JOHN THE DIVINE
PRIMARY SCHOOL
Headteacher: Mr C. Cosgrave B.A. (Hons.)
ENTRANCE IN WARHAM STREET
PHENO
GRAC
Teach us to sit still.

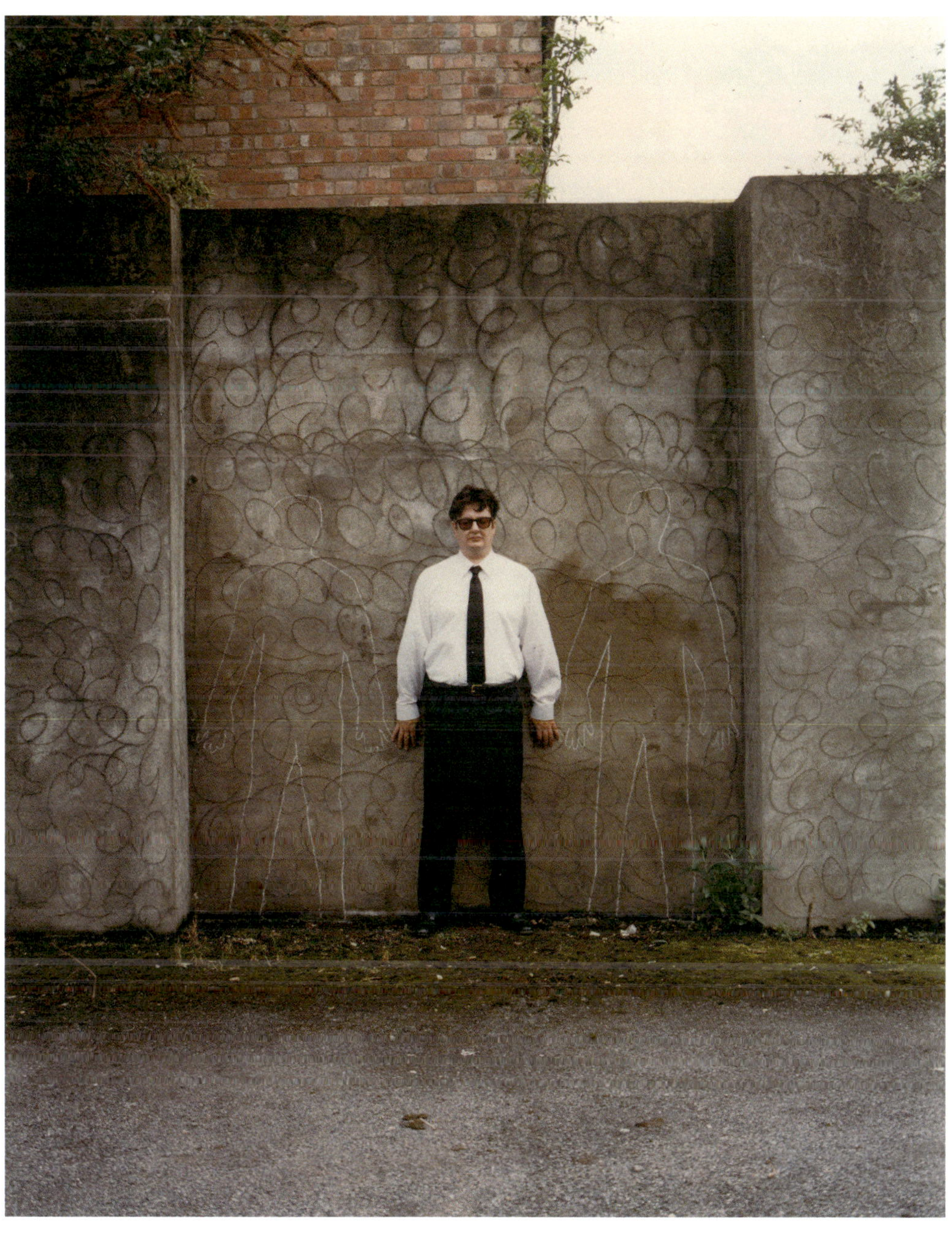

Artist Biographies

Allora & Calzadilla, who have collaborated since 1995, combine sculpture, photography, performance, sound, and video to examine the coherence of ideas such as nationality and democracy. With a playful sense of humor and a sharp sense of the power of everyday materials and processes, they draw on history, culture, and politics to frame our increasingly globalized world. Allora & Calzadilla live and work in Puerto Rico. Jennifer Allora was born in 1974 in Philadelphia, and Guillermo Calzadilla was born in 1971 in Havana, Cuba. Allora & Calzadilla have had solo exhibitions at the National Museum of Art, Architecture and Design, Oslo, Norway; San Francisco Art Institute; Renaissance Society at the University of Chicago; Center for Contemporary Art, Kitakyushu, Japan; Dallas Museum of Art; and Museum of Contemporary Art, Los Angeles.

Pawel Althamer invites a range of different people, including children, the homeless, and residents of Warsaw housing estates, to participate in his projects. Through his sculptures, installations, and performances, Althamer employs humor and compassion to engage individual experience in the face of sweeping social change. Althamer was born in 1967 in Warsaw, Poland, where he currently lives and works. He has had solo exhibitions at the Centre Pompidou, Paris, and Museum of Contemporary Art Chicago. His work has been included in numerous group exhibitions, among them *Mimétisme, Extra City*, Center for Contemporary Art, Antwerp, 2008; *Double Agent*, Institute of Contemporary Arts, London, 2008; *After Nature*, New Museum, New York, 2008; *The World as a Stage*, Tate Modern, London, 2007; *Skulptur Projekt Münster*, 2007; 27th Biennial of Graphic Arts, Ljubljana, 2007; *Strange Powers*, Creative Time, New York, 2006; Istanbul Biennial, 2005; and *54th Carnegie International*, Carnegie Museum of Art, Pittsburgh, 2004.

Marc Bijl incorporates personal and political references into his sculptures and installations to interrogate social structures and their use of symbols and slogans. Bijl's work uncovers the complex dangers of essentialist positions while at the same time revealing deep romantic desires and an unflagging seriousness about the possibility for finding truth in art as well as in life. Bijl was born in 1970 in Leerdam, the Netherlands, and currently lives and works in Berlin. He has had solo exhibitions at Kunsthalle Fridericianum, Kassel, Germany; Domus Artium, Salamanca, Spain; and Museum Het Valkhof, Nijmegen, the Netherlands. Bijl's work has been included in numerous group exhibitions, among them *Double Dutch*, Hudson Valley Center for Contemporary Art, New York, 2009; *Memorial to the Iraq War*, Institute of Contemporary Arts, London, 2007; Moscow Biennale, 2007; *Ruby Satellite*, UCR/California Museum of Photography, Riverside, 2006; *Superstars*, Kunsthalle Vienna, 2005; and *Afterhours*, GEM Museum for Contemporary Art, The Hague, the Netherlands, 2005; and The Hague Museum of Photography, the Netherlands, 2005.

Lara Favaretto's work expresses the will to believe in the face of impossibility or the absurd. Her complex, often mechanized sculptures and installations are at once playful and melancholic, providing moments of surprise for the viewer while at the same time highlighting the contradictions involved in relating the personal to a larger social group. Favaretto was born in 1973 in Treviso, Italy, and currently lives and works in Turin. Her work has been included in numerous group exhibitions, among them *Making Worlds*, 53rd Venice Biennale, 2009; *Revolution—Forms That Turn*, 16th Sydney Biennale, 2009; and *Ecstasy: In and About Altered States*, Museum of Contemporary Art, Los Angeles, 2005.

Through his diverse artistic practice, Geof Oppenheimer addresses the problems of rigid binaries in society and art, frequently examining the place of individual agency within larger systems. Oppenheimer was born in 1973 in Washington, D.C., and currently lives and works in Chicago. His work has been included in numerous group exhibitions, among them *The Gold Standard*, P.S.1 Contemporary Art Center, New York, 2006; *Five Star*, University of California, Berkeley Art Museum and Pacific Film Archive, 2001; and *Snapshot*, Contemporary Museum, Baltimore, Maryland, 2000.

Lars Ø. Ramberg's sculptural interventions in public space are intended as a platform to change the viewers' relationships with one another and their surroundings. With an incisive wit, his works examine the often unquestioned routines, customs, and perspectives of a given place, thereby revealing rich meaning in apparently insignificant situations. Ramberg was born in 1964 in Oslo, Norway, and currently lives and works in Berlin. His work has been included in numerous group exhibitions, among them the 52nd Venice Biennale, 2007; Dreamworks, Rotterdam Film Festival, the Netherlands, 2004; *Where am I now?* Museum of Contemporary Art, Oslo, Norway, 2002; and *Gluck & Casino*, Kunsthalle Dresden, Germany, 2000.

Frances Stark's hybrid practice is a complex oscillation between art and writing. Taking formal cues from writing and the activities that often accompany it, Stark's work becomes a layered self-portrait that freely mixes literary references with popular culture and openly expresses personal doubt and anxiety. Stark was born in 1967 in Newport Beach, California, and currently lives and works in Los Angeles. She has had solo exhibitions at Portikus, Frankfurt am Main, Germany; Nottingham Contemporary, United Kingdom; Museum of Fine Arts, Houston; Van Abbemuseum, Eindhoven, the Netherlands; Kunstverein Munich, Germany; ArtPace San Antonio; and Hammer Museum, Los Angeles.

Mark Wallinger's works examine how the individual situates himself within society. His conceptual gestures combine humor with a penetrating insight into the ways that the symbols of a culture seep into the conscious of a people. Wallinger was born in 1959 in Chigwell, United Kingdom, and currently lives and works in London. He has had solo exhibitions at the the Aargauer Kunsthaus, Aarau, Switzerland; Portikus, Frankfurt am Main, Germany; Kunstverein Braunschweig, Germany; Neue Nationalgalerie, Berlin; Tate Britain, London; and Museo de Arte Carrillo Gil, Mexico City. He represented Britain in the 49th Venice Biennale, and in 2007 he participated in Skulptur Projekt Münster and was awarded the Turner Prize.

Exhibition Checklist

Allora & Calzadilla
Hope Hippo, 2005
Mud, whistle, daily newspaper, live person
60 x 192 x 72 inches
Courtesy of the artists and Lisson Gallery, London

Pawel Althamer
Guma, 2008
Polyurethane elastomer, polyurethane foam, steel, steel springs,
plastic
60 1/4 x 29 1/8 x 18 1/2 inches
Courtesy of Nancy and Bob Magoon

Marc Bijl
deconstruction-site # 1, 2010
Galvanized corrugated steel and spray paint
78 x 78 x 78 inches
Courtesy of the artist

Marc Bijl
deconstruction-site # 2, 2010
Galvanized corrugated steel and spray paint
78 x 78 x 78 inches
Courtesy of the artist

Lara Favaretto
Cominciò ch'era finita (It began while it was already over), 2006
Wood, steel, canvas, motor, wooden chair, costume, neon letters
149 5/8 x 139 3/8 inches
Courtesy of Klosterfelde, Berlin

Geof Oppenheimer
*The Morally Ambiguous Precedent of Abstraction, Police Press
Conference, Chicago, Illinois, 2008*, 2009
UltraChrome photograph
50 1/2 x 66 inches
Courtesy of the artist

Geof Oppenheimer
Public Sculpture (Edits), 2009–2010
Ceramic, steel, artificial hair, plastics
Installation dimensions variable
Courtesy of the artist

Lars Ø. Ramberg
Benchmark (Memorial to Hunter S. Thompson), 2010
Eight spruce benches with gold leaf inlay
Approximately 36 x 70 x 30 inches each
Courtesy of the artist

Frances Stark
The Inchoate Incarnate: After a Drawing, Toward an Opera, but before a Libretto Even Exists, 2009
Wearable fabric costume (astrachan cloth)
58 x 70 x 32 inches
Courtesy of the artist and Marc Foxx, Los Angeles

Frances Stark
I've Had It! and I've Also Had It!, 2010
Performance at the Wheeler Opera House
June 30, 2010

Frances Stark
Promotional Material for I've Had It! and I've Also Had It! (Spoiler Alert!), 2010
Diptych, 87 1/2 x 60 inches each
Paint, paillettes, paper on paper
Courtesy of the artist and Marc Foxx, Los Angeles

Mark Wallinger
Amerika, 2010
Vinyl billboard
128 x 192 inches
Courtesy of the artist and
Anthony Reynolds Gallery, London

National Council
2009 - 2010

Eleanore and Domenico De Sole, *Chairs*
Pamela Alexander, *Vice Chair*
Toby Devan Lewis, *Vice Chair*
Carol Heckman Balbach and Charles E. Balbach
Anne H. Bass
Maria and William Bell
Barbara and Bruce Berger
Marie and Robert Bergman
Jill and Jay Bernstein
Barbara and William Broeder
Melva Bucksbaum and Raymond Learsy
Simona and Jerome A. Chazen
Dathel and Tommy Coleman
Bunni and Paul Copaken
Isabella and Theodor Dalenson
Frances Dittmer
Holly and David Dreman
Stefan T. Edlis and Gael Neeson
Richard Edwards
Suzanne Farver
Christy Ferer
Marilyn and Larry Fields
Merrill Ford
Barbara and Michael Gamson
Ramiro and Gabriela Garza
Linda and Bob Gersh
Jan and Ronald K. Greenberg
Diane and Bruce T. Halle
Sharon and John Hoffman
Phyllis S. Hojel
Toni and Daniel Holtz
Ann and Edward R. Hudson Jr.
Holly Hunt
Pam Hurst
Soledad and Robert Hurst
Allison and Warren Kanders

Sylvia and Richard Kaufman
Barbara Bluhm-Kaul and Don Kaul
Sally and Jonathan Kovler
Evelyn and Leonard Lauder
Barbara and Jonathan Lee
Vicki and Kent Logan
Karen and Courtney Lord
Marianne and Sheldon Lubar
Nancy and Robert Magoon
Marlene and Fred V. Malek
Susan and Larry Marx
Nancy and Peter C. Meinig
Meryl and Robert Meltzer
Gail and J. Alec Merriam
Lisa and Will Mesdag
Jane and Marc Nathanson
Judith Neisser
John and Amy Phelan
Carolyn and William Powers
Allen and Kelli Questrom
Jeanne Greenberg-Rohatyn and Nicolas Rohatyn
Michelle and Jason Rubell
Lisa and John Runyon
Pamela and Arthur Sanders
Mary and Patrick Scanlan
Danner and Arno D. Schefler
Barbara and F. Eugene Schmitt
Debra and Dennis Scholl
June and Paul Schorr
Vicki and Ronald Simms
Shirley and Albert Small
Sandy and Art Soares
Sarah Dodd-Spickelmier and Keith Spickelmier
Jennifer and David Stockman
Gayle and Paul Stoffel
Ellen and Steve Susman
Mary and Harold Zlot

List of Illustrations

Pages 116-117
Pawel Althamer, *Matea*, 2006/2008. Courtesy of the artist, neugerriemschneider, Berlin, and Foksal Gallery Foundation, Warsaw. Photographed by Jens Ziehe, Berlin.

Page 118
Pawel Althamer, *Common Task*, 2009. Image taken in Brazil. Courtesy of the artist, neugerriemschneider, Berlin, Foksal Gallery Foundation, Warsaw.

Page 119
Pawel Althamer, *Common Task*, 2009. Image taken in Warsaw. Courtesy of the artist, neugerriemschneider, Berlin, Foksal Gallery Foundation, Warsaw. Photograph by Krzysztof Kozanowski.

Page 120
Pawel Althamer, *Abram and Burus*, 2007. Courtesy of the artist, neugerriemschneider, Berlin, and Foksal Gallery Foundation, Warsaw. Photographed by Jens Ziehe, Berlin.

Pages 121-122
Pawel Althamer, *Balloon*, 1999/2007. Courtesy of the artist, neugerriemschneider, Berlin, and Foksal Gallery Foundation, Warsaw. Photography by Marco de Scalzi.

Page 123-124
Pawel Althamer, *Untitled*, 2003. Courtesy The Wrong Gallery, New York.

Page 125
Pawel Althamer, *Brodno*, 2000. Courtesy of the artist, neugerriemschneider, Berlin, and Foksal Gallery Foundation, Warsaw.

Page 127
Marc Bijl, *Gimme Shelter*, 2006. Private Collection, Istanbul. Courtesy Upstream Gallery, Amsterdam.

Page 128
Marc Bijl, *Burning Peace*, 2004. Courtesy Upstream Gallery, Amsterdam.

Page 129
Marc Bijl, *Fundamentality VII (open system altering the mind)*, 2009. Courtesy the Breeder, Athens.

Page 130
Marc Bijl, *An effort to close the void*, 2009. Courtesy the Breeder, Athens.

Page 131
Marc Bijl, *Constructed Composition II*, 2008. Courtesy Upstream Gallery, Amsterdam.

Page 133-134
Lara Favaretto, *Momentary Monument*, 2009. Installation view 53rd Venice Biennial, Italy. Courtesy the artist and Galleria Franco Noero, Torino.

Page 135-136
Lara Favaretto, *Momentary Monument*, 2009. Installation view Fondazione Galleria Civica di Trento. Courtesy the artist and Galleria Franco Noero, Torino.

Pages 137-138
Lara Favaretto, *Momentary Monument*, 2009. Installazione Piazzetta Piave, Bergamo 'Twister', GAMeC, Bergamo – Rete musei Lombardia per l'arte contemporanea.

Pages 139-140
Lara Favaretto, *Coppi Semplici /Simple Couples*, 2009. Installation views at 'Provisions for the Future', 9th Sharjah Biennial, curated by Jack Persekian and Isabel Carlos, United Arab Emirates, 2009 Courtesy the artist and Galleria Franco Noero, Torino Rennie Collection, Vancouver BC.

Pags 141
Lara Favaretto, *Absolutely No Donations*, 2009. Installation view at the solo exhibition, *Tramway*, Glasgow, 2009. Courtesy the artist and Galleria Franco Noero, Torino.

Pages 142-143
Lara Favaretto, *Tutti giù per terra*, 2004. Installation views at "Barock – Arte, Scienza, Fede e Tecnologia nell'Età Contemporanea", MADRE – Museo d'Arte Contemporanea Donna Regina – Napoli, December 2009 – April 2010 Courtesy the artist and Galleria Franco Noero, Torino Collezione Renato Alpegiani, Torino.

Page 145
Geof Oppenheimer, *Goldchains Headspace Freedom*, 2005-2006. Courtesy of the artist and the Project, New York.

Page 146
Geof Oppenheimer, *Goldchains Headspace Freedom*, 2005-2006 (detail). Courtesy of the artist and the Project, New York.

Pages 147-148
Geof Oppenheimer, *Mason Dixon Lines*, 2005-2007. Courtesy of the artist and the Project, New York.

Page 149
Geof Oppenheimer, *Republic Mashup*, 2005-2006. Courtesy of the artist.

Page 150
Geof Oppenheimer, *Republic Mashup*, 2005-2006 (detail). Courtesy of the artist.

Page 151
Geof Oppenheimer, *Fucking Up With the Sun*, 2006-2007. Courtesy of the artist.

Page 153
Lars Ø. Ramberg, *Liberté*, 2007. Installation view Venice Biennial Nordic Pavillion. Copyright Studio Ramberg.

Pages 154-157
Lars Ø. Ramberg, *Palast des Zweifels*, 2005. Installation view Berlin. Copyright Studio Ramberg.

Page 158
Lars Ø. Ramberg, *NOCHMAL*, 2008. Installation view on Karl Marz Allé Berlin. Copyright Studio Ramberg.

Page 159
Lars Ø. Ramberg, *FREMDGEHEN*, 2004. Installation view Hamburger Bahnhof - National Museum Contemporary Art, Berlin. Copyright Studio Ramberg.

Page 160
Lars Ø. Ramberg, *OSTBAHNHOF*, 2000. Installation view Künstlerhaus Bethanien Berlin. Copyright Studio Ramberg.

Page 161
Lars Ø. Ramberg, *Palast des Zweifels*, 2005 (detail). Installation view Berlin. Copyright Studio Ramberg.

Page 163
Frances Stark, *Wisdom, Stupidity, Ugliness: 2 in an ongoing series*, 2008. Courtesy of the artist.

Page 164
Frances Stark, *Wisdom, Stupidity, Ugliness: 3 in an ongoing series*, 2008. Courtesy of the artist.

Page 165
Frances Stark, *Wisdom, Stupidity, Ugliness: 4 in an ongoing series*, 2008. Courtesy of the artist.

Page 166
Frances Stark, *Back Side of the Performance*, 2007. Courtesy of the artist. Photographed by Robert Wedemeyer.

Page 167
Frances Stark, *Called upon (Same thing over and over)*, 2007. Courtesy of the artist. Photographed by Robert Wedemeyer.

Page 168
Frances Stark, *Chorus Line*, 2008. Courtesy of the artist. Photographed by Robert Wedemeyer.

Page 170
Mark Wallinger, *Ecce Homo*, 1999. Photographed by John Riddy. Copyright of the artist. Courtesy Anthony Reynolds Gallery, London.

Pages 171-172
Mark Wallinger, *Sleeper*, 2004. Photographed by Stefan Maria Rother. Copyright of the artist. Courtesy Anthony Reynolds Gallery, London.

Pages 173-176
Mark Wallinger, *State Britain*, 2007. Photographed by Dave Morgan. Copyright of the artist. Courtesy Anthony Reynolds Gallery, London.

Pages 177-178
Mark Wallinger, *Zone*, 2007. Installation view Skulptur Projekt Münster. Copyright of the artist. Courtesy Anthony Reynolds Gallery, London.

Page 179
Mark Wallinger, *The Word in the Desert III*, 2000. Copyright of the artist. Courtesy Anthony Reynolds Gallery, London.

Pages 180-181
Mark Wallinger, *The Word in the Desert IV*, 2000. Copyright of the artist. Courtesy Anthony Reynolds Gallery, London.

Restless Empathy
May 20 – July 18, 2010
Aspen Art Museum

Copyright © 2010 Aspen Art Museum
590 North Mill Street, Aspen, CO 81611
www.aspenartmuseum.org

Library of Congress Control Number 2010926080
ISBN 978-0-934324-49-6

Texts by Heidi Zuckerman Jacobson, Christian Rattemeyer,
and Matthew Thompson

Edited by Richard Slovak

Catalogue design by Jared Rippy

Published by Aspen Art Press

Printed by Perry/Granger & Associates San Francisco

Restless Empathy is organized by the Aspen Art Museum,
funded in part by the AAM National Council with major support
provided by Stefan Edlis and Gael Neeson. General exhibition
support provided by The Andy Warhol Foundation for the Visual
Arts. Generous publication support provided by Toby Devan
Lewis. Exhibition lectures are presented by the Questrom
Lecture Series.

Available through D.A.P./Distributed Art Publishers
155 Sixth Avenue, 2nd Floor, New York, N.Y. 10013
Tel: (212) 627-1999 Fax: (212) 627-9484